"*Growing a Farmer* is kind of like a Walden for the twenty-first century, a book that both takes us back to the essence of something real (in this case, food) while at the same time problematizing the cultural constructs we've built around the whole endeavor. . . . In this day and age we're way too jaded for the pastoral idealism of days gone by, but Timmermeister is forging a new ideal in this book." —Tami Parr, *Pacific Northwest Cheese Project* blog

"Kurt exudes respect for everything he does. . . . Through his experiences, we come to reconsider where our food comes from and the importance of eating locally." —Jenn Risko, *Shelf Awareness*

"A finely observed education in ethics and animals, crops and cheesemaking, an up-and-down journey that transformed land into a farm and a man into a farmer." —Rebekah Denn, *Christian Science Monitor*

"Fans of that small genre of live-off-the-land stories . . . will find much to appreciate in Timmermeister's ability to take a concept back to its root and parse it until the simplest, most elemental truths remain." —Paul Constant, *The Stranger*

"A wonderful and inspiring story of transformation. . . . Timmermeister invites us all to the table to share what he has learned. He shows that it was more his passion and sweat than his knowledge of food or farming that opened the door for his success as a farmer." —*Edible Louisville*

"Anyone interested in where real food comes from will love this book. I was charmed by Kurt Timmermeister's story of becoming a farmer and found myself fascinated as he describes how he learned to install bees in a hive, establish an orchard, milk cows, make cheese, and that slaughtering chickens is no party."

—Jerry Traunfeld, chef/owner of Poppy
and author of *The Herbfarm Cookbook*

"All farmers will nod knowingly at Timmermeister's exploits, and soon-to-be farmers should take notes as they read this satisfying memoir." —Novella Carpenter, author of
Farm City: The Education of an Urban Farmer

"Kurt Timmermeister created his life as a farmer from scratch—a grand improvisation. *Growing a Farmer* journals his struggles with the uncertain forces of nature, his happy discoveries in food production, and his quest to improve the land to which he has committed himself."

—Paul Bertolli, founder, Fra' Mani Handcrafted
Salumi, Berkeley, California

"Candid, charming, and remarkably informative—an inspiring must-read for any city dwellers who have ever dreamed of ditching their condo for the countryside."

—Kathleen Flinn, author of
The Sharper Your Knife, the Less You Cry

"An entertaining and revealing account of how a successful urbanite becomes a farmer. Kurt's personal and farm-related stories, setbacks, and celebrations will give you pause and laughter. This is a delicious story." —David Gremmels,
chairman, American Cheese Society

Growing a Farmer

Growing a Farmer

How I Learned to Live Off the Land

Kurt Timmermeister

W. W. Norton & Company
New York • London

*To my long-deceased father, August "Bud" Timmermeister,
a man I only know through photographs
but whose continued presence has shaped my life
in ways that only slowly reveal themselves.*

Copyright © 2011 by Kurt Timmermeister

Printed in the United States of America
First published as a Norton paperback 2012

Frontispiece: © Clare Barboza

For information about permission to reproduce selections from this book,
write to Permissions, W. W. Norton & Company, Inc.,
500 Fifth Avenue, New York, NY 10110

For information about special discounts for bulk purchases, please contact
W. W. Norton Special Sales at specialsales@wwnorton.com or 800-233-4830

Manufacturing by Courier Westford
Book design by M. Kristen Bearse
Production manager: Anna Oler

Library of Congress Cataloging-in-Publication Data

Timmermeister, Kurt.
Growing a farmer : how I learned to live off the land /
Kurt Timmermeister. — 1st ed.
p. cm.
Includes bibliographical references and index.
ISBN 978-0-393-07085-9 (hardcover)
1. Farm life—Washington (State)—Vashon Island.
2. Country life—Washington (State)—Vashon Island. I. Title.
S521.5.W5T56 2011
630.92—dc22
[B]
2010034825

ISBN 978-0-393-34129-4 pbk.

W. W. Norton & Company, Inc.
500 Fifth Avenue, New York, N.Y. 10110
www.wwnorton.com

W. W. Norton & Company Ltd.
Castle House, 75/76 Wells Street, London W1T 3QT

1 2 3 4 5 6 7 8 9 0

Contents

Introduction

I live in a lovely place. It is a small farm, just a few acres, but it is beautiful. I created this farm over many years, and it is still evolving, and will continue to for many years hence. I never intended to be a farmer and yet it feels right. I enjoy a connection to the land, to the animals here, and I am endlessly thrilled to make food; to feed people.

The primary product of this farm is cheese. A small herd of Jersey cows also call this bit of ground home. Twice a day they head down from the upper pastures to the barn. There I will meet them, milk them and in the hours and days to come transform that milk into cheese.

When I say that I live in a lovely place, I also mean *place* in the abstract sense. I work for myself; I have no boss. This is not to say that it is a perfect job, or one without challenges. Each day brings new setbacks and new rewards. This farm, this business, changes every year, sprawls in every direction seemingly without a plan. I pretend to control it, but often it controls me.

This is the story of a farm. It is the story of my journey from the city life of a restaurateur to my present life as a farmer. It is not a cookbook, although the preparation of food is discussed. It is not a how-to guide to farming, although much can be learned about farming from these pages. It is not a treatise on agriculture in America, although I certainly have opinions on the health and viability of small farms.

My wish for this book is to add a perspective on the food we eat: where our food comes from, what goes into producing it and how it was traditionally prepared. I would be thrilled if some who read this book quit their day jobs, moved out of the city and built small farms. I doubt, however, that this will happen, and I wouldn't necessarily recommend it. I would be content if the reader, while at the supermarket the next week, picks up a small round of cheese from a local farm, pauses and contemplates how it was made. If that reader looks at carrots at the farmers' market next weekend and marvels at their existence, picks them up and smells the earth that they had come from hours before, that would bring a smile to my face.

One

Before the Farm

When I was twenty-four years old I opened my first restaurant. It was a small, actually very small, ten-foot by twenty-foot, café. With just four tables squeezed together and a minuscule kitchen on the side, this humble space represented the start of my career. I had worked as a waiter and a pastry cook around town and felt that I could run a restaurant better than my much more experienced bosses and coworkers. Despite this confidence, I really had no clue what I was up against and was immediately overwhelmed by the difficulties of owning and managing a business.

Every morning at four I would walk the two blocks from my small studio apartment in downtown Seattle to the café and bake pastries in the manner of a home cook. The kitchen was tiny, the equipment of small scale and my volume of baked goods originally very limited; one pound cake, a couple of coffee cakes, four dozen biscuits. At seven in the morning the café would open and I would sell the fresh pastries and coffee to the receptive locals who would line up daily. They could see into the small kitchen, see the mixer, watch the rolls come out of the oven and onto the counter in front of them. What was significant to me about this entire process was there was integrity; I bought butter and flour and baked it into pastries and handed it to people to eat right there. Yes, this is the description of every bakery the world over, but I thought, perhaps arrogantly, that no one was doing it so directly. I reached into the oven, pulled out a biscuit and placed it on a plate. I had made that biscuit, I had served it and the customer ate it. There were no cake mixes, no canned fillings, no waiters, no corporate offices. I sold goods for cash and then walked across the street to the bank and put the money in the bank. It was real and it was good. This influenced the way I would look at my world henceforth, though this simple and satisfying arrangement couldn't last.

As the café grew to be more popular and therefore more profitable, I realized I could afford to buy a house and settle down, move out of my small studio in the city. If I could have afforded a home in the city, I most likely would have stayed in Seattle. Even then, twenty years ago, the price of real estate in the city was quite high and well out of my reach.

My universe at the time was the café and my apartment, both in downtown Seattle. I began to look for less expensive places to live that had the luxury of space. Seattle is located on Puget Sound, an expansive protected body of water dotted with islands that extend northward to Canada. The island closest to downtown Seattle, and accessed by ferryboats that docked a few blocks from my apartment, is Bainbridge Island. Originally I checked out homes there, but found them to be too costly. South of Bainbridge Island is Vashon Island, accessed by state ferryboats as well, but much less conveniently; the dock is located in West Seattle, a long trek from downtown Seattle.

In addition to simply finding a home on Vashon Island cheaper than I could in Seattle, there was also the pull of nature. My impression at that time was that life would be easier in a small town, that life outside of the turmoil of a large city would be serene, orderly and tranquil. I confess that all these many years later I continue to fall into this flawed thinking. And so I began my search for a new home: I wanted more space than my humble apartment offered, situated far enough from the city to be affordable. I wasn't looking to become a farmer; the thought hadn't even crossed my mind. I just wanted a place where I could unwind after my grueling days at the café.

I had never learned to drive and did not have a driver's license. I never really wanted a car; found them wasteful and expensive. I enjoyed my downtown city life. I walked to the market to buy produce for the café, picked up flowers for my apartment, knew all the shopkeepers and lived a full, urban existence.

I would peruse the classified ads of the local newspaper, looking for homes to buy. My family ethos was rooted in the American dream: buy a house and you will be financially independent. I never doubted it, I never questioned it. I needed to buy a house to have a complete life. Whether I realized it or not, even then I was striving for self-sufficiency: start a business, use the proceeds to buy a house, live autonomously. I've never expected my family to care for me in my old age, I intend to care for myself, and acquiring land and shelter was the next logical step.

I soon discovered that Vashon Island was a part of King County, the county of Seattle, and therefore had the same bus service. I could live outside of Seattle and ride the bus to work. I made a perfunctory review of the bus schedules and confirmed that there were buses that ran from downtown Seattle to the island, the buses boarding the ferryboats in the process. I couldn't really understand the schedules, knew nothing of the island and had never set foot on it, and yet proceeded to check out the local homes.

In the Seattle newspapers in the "Islands" section were advertisements for the local real estate companies. Today at the age of forty-seven I feel as though little has changed in the world, and yet as I look back, simply the act of being able to *look back* tells me that the world is different today than it was when I was in my twenties. I called one of the real estate companies arbitrarily—the name was pleasing: Channel West. I was very nervous and so had rehearsed talking to them, ready for what I thought would be asked: my name, address, phone number and so on. The youngish-sounding woman on the line asked me if I was looking for land and if so, how much. I stammered and pulled "four acres" out of thin air. I have no idea where that came from. I had never seen four acres, I had no idea what it entailed and I didn't know if that would cost ten thousand dollars or ten million dollars.

The real estate office sent me a small catalogue of listings. A thick manila cover and maybe twenty pages of listings with poor-quality black-and-white photographs, it had been photocopied at the local island office supply store. As it was late in the month when they sent me this booklet, many of the homes had *SOLD* written across them with a Magic Marker. It was hard not to look at those and wonder if I was two weeks late to find a lovely home for myself.

I made an appointment to see some houses and the agent agreed to pick me up at the dock. I was too embarrassed to tell her that I couldn't drive and that I didn't own a car. I took the city bus to the ferry dock and walked on the ferry.

The vessels that ply the waters of Puget Sound, crossing back and forth with their decks filled with commuters, are run by the state of Washington. The ships are large, solid beasts, with a lower deck nearly flush with the water and packed with rows of cars and trucks, and with the upper decks fitted with tables and chairs, galleys with food service and restrooms. The crossing from Seattle to Vashon Island is but fifteen minutes, even if the wait for a boat can be five times that. The interior of the upper deck resembles a cruise ship on the high seas, if the cruise line was a sad little government-run operation with a decorating streak stuck in the disco era. Although the distance from dock to dock is minimal, it takes just a quarter hour, the distance in mood and feeling and sensibility is tremendous. As the ferry pulls out of the Seattle dock, the present-day rush and modernity are left behind. Upon coming off of the boat, a feeling of calm, slow-paced island living always washes over me.

That first ride over was no different. I walked off of the large hulk of a boat, not knowing what to expect. My shoulders, held tight as if I were on a crowded city street, gradually began to relax. I quickly found the real estate agent waiting for me on the dock. I immediately felt comfortable as I sat in her ratty little car. She used a screwdriver to turn the ignition, which itself was lying on the floor, its wires stretched out on the wheel well. The days of real estate agents driving tidy Range Rovers had not yet arrived on Vashon Island.

We went back to her modest office in the center of the town of Vashon. Thumbtacked on the wall were photographs of all the houses available. The homes showed their flaws in color more clearly than in the poorly reproduced black-and-white photographs of the catalogue. In the black-and-white photos my mind filled in the blanks of what I wanted the houses to be; in the color photos I could see that the siding was bad, the lawns unmowed, the windows aluminum and lacking charm.

While in her office, I studied all of the photos and pulled one off the wall to get a closer look. The photo, which I still have, was of a small red shack, baby toys in the foreground, an old camper in the background and a scrappy apple tree framing the entire scene. The photo showed a house with little glamour or slickness. On the back was written: *One bedroom home, four acres, greenhouse, swimming pool, historic house*. The price, $125,000, was crossed out and $100,000 written below it in pencil. My mind was reeling. How could such a description match the image? I inquired further with the agent. She assured me that the description was true and that it was near town and we could go and take a look. The best part was that I could afford the $100,000 price; this was the cheapest property listed and the only one in my budget.

We drove the short distance to the entrance to the property and began the descent off the main road and down what barely looked like a driveway: overgrown with blackberries and willows, the gravel road rough and interrupted with large potholes. Her ratty car jolted up and down in response to the uneven road. When we came through the twisting and turning drive, we emerged in a clearing surrounded by brambles. There stood the small red house, still with the baby toys and the camper, together with old cars.

I hopped out of the car and began to walk around. When we passed through the long tunnel of the driveway I knew that I had found my home. I knew that this was the property I would buy. I explored the property, but only in a perfunctory manner. I had already made my decision.

There was nothing beautiful or gracious about what was to become Kurtwood Farms. It didn't look like a farm at all: it barely looked like a suburban homestead. Very little of the property was open, most of the land was covered in brambles. Sixteen old cars littered the property, along with a broken-down tractor, the camper and a variety of shacks and storage buildings. But the description listed on the back of the photo was accurate. On the property was a swimming pool, a greenhouse and a second home. The swimming pool was of a homemade flat-bottomed variety that could not hold water, its base cracked in half. The greenhouse was one of the fifty-some that were part of the defunct Beall Greenhouse Company next door. The surveyor had made an error earlier in midcentury

and as a result, part of one industrial greenhouse was on my
property, its roof caved in, blackberries now enjoying the run
of the space. The second home was a log house, said to be
the oldest standing house on the island, one that after many
years of work would end up being my home but which now
was a varmint-infested rotting hulk of Doug fir logs, held in
place by the English ivy that worked its way up the side of
the building.

I saw none of the reality of the property, but only its charms.
In hindsight, there were few charms to be seen on that June
day. I didn't have to convince myself, though; I was smitten.
What I experienced on that fateful summer day was a general
feel. Most of the island was covered in large Doug fir trees,
second- and third-growth tall, thin timber that blocked the
sun. Many of the island's homes were sited in claustrophobic
clearings in the midst of dense canopies of evergreens. For
over a century this parcel had been lived on; the log house was
built in 1880 and this was 1990. There was a sense of history
here, families had lived and died here, they had grown food
and cooked many a meal here. There were rampant blackberries that covered up the garbage and refuse of a hundred
years of human habitation, but it was cleared land. For a century the residents had worked hard to make this a home. I
was not only looking for a home for myself, I was also looking for a sense of family. The large family with a gaggle of
kids, the house with constant activity, the homestead passed
from generation to generation, that was what I saw in this
run-down property. I believed that if I bought this property, I
would become part of this legacy.

I spent the rest of the afternoon driving around looking at
other properties with the agent. I didn't have the confidence
to tell her that I had already made my decision. It seemed
too inexperienced, too humiliating. I knew what I wanted

to buy but rode around with her, feigning interest in other properties.

It was summer when I looked at the house and December when the deal finally closed. The ease of June was long past when I went out late that year to check on the home that I had quickly inspected months earlier. A friend drove me out to the island, and as we left the city late in the afternoon I made an important discovery: it gets dark at night.

The ferry dock was lit with the large mercury-vapor cobra lamps ubiquitous in cities; the glow was of an orange hue, flickering randomly like a loose fluorescent light. I had spent my nearly thirty years living in the city, first in a neighborhood and then in the heart of downtown Seattle. I had worked in restaurants for years, closing up late at night and walking home or taking the city bus well after midnight. I had the misguided impression that the darkness of the city was actual darkness. The streetlights in the evening give the impression that it is nighttime, yet you can see where you are going and walk around with no sense of darkness. I had never experienced the complete darkness of night except for the odd week or two of horse camp as a kid. Even then we stayed near the camp and never ventured too far from the buildings flooded with light.

We drove onto the ferryboat and parked on the lower deck facing west, and watched the sun drop as we crossed the channel. By the time we arrived on the island, the sun had completely set. I remember looking up at the hulk of the dark island in front of me and seeing no lights, except for those at the Vashon dock. In that short fifteen-minute crossing the atmosphere had changed. As we drove off the boat, the illumination of the city was at my back and the foreboding darkness of the sparsely inhabited island stretched in front of me.

As we drove down the highway toward my land, I was

conflicted: excited to be headed to my new place and eager to show it off to a friend, but also realizing that I was ill-equipped to deal with my future home. I realized quickly that I would have to change my plans for living on this unlit island. I was naïve and I had spent too little time in shopping for a house, guided only by my desire to own some land and a home. I was scared and excited, but tried to hide it from my friend. I plunged ahead and gave the perfunctory tour, despite the darkness that surrounded us. Staring into the immense blackness, I began to realize the enormity of my decision to move here. Like it or not, this was my life now, and I was going to have to figure out how to make it work.

Vashon, while certainly not uninhabited, only has street-lights in the town center. The rest of the island streets are not lit and the houses tend to be off of the road, well set back for privacy. Although walking the twenty-minute route from the bus stop on the highway to my new home would not have been impossible, it would have been difficult and not what I had in mind when I came up with the plan to take the local bus to work. I would have to learn to drive and buy a car.

I spent the next few weeks scrambling to make my new life possible. After quite a bit of effort, I got a driver's license and a friend offered to sell me a small truck. I would've settled for a little car, but thankfully my friend knew what I did not: that a truck was going to be a necessity. That pickup truck was the first of many such trucks.

Weeks later I moved into the small shack on the property. Built as a chicken house in the 1930s, it had a low ceiling, cracked foundation and was long and skinny. I still was look-ing at the property through rose-colored glasses, convinced I was living on the most beautiful place on the planet. Christ-mas came a week after the closing of the deal. As this was the first time I had bought a house and I was, as they say, house-proud, I invited my family to Christmas breakfast. Unaware as to what they were getting themselves into, they agreed, and on that wintry morning twenty years ago, my mother, my sister, her husband and their very young son journeyed out to the island to see what I was so excited about. I too had to ride the ferry from Seattle, as I had yet to move into the new home.

Little more had been done to the small chicken-coop-cum-house than to remove its rotted gold shag carpeting and three utterly unnecessary doors in the five-hundred-square-foot space. Immediately outside the large front windows was a pile of junk. In the week between the closing and Christmas I had heaved all of the rotten carpeting, greasy kitchen cabinets, moldy Sheetrock and rat-infested insulation out the front door. I wasn't sure how I would dispose of all of this, but I knew I needed it out of the house.

The floors were cracked linoleum on a broken, unleveled foundation. I had hooked up a small wood stove and had given the house a cursory cleaning. I had lit a fire in the small wood stove in a vain attempt to cook a pot of oatmeal with brown sugar and golden raisins. The fire never quite roared in the small chamber, the water never came to a full boil and the oatmeal resembled a muddy paste much more than the Scottish country breakfast that I'd had in mind. Undeterred by my family's lukewarm reaction, I persevered, convinced that this frigid, moldy chicken coop, situated in the middle of four acres of blackberries, was a bucolic dream reminiscent of the many pastoral British period films I had seen.

The next week I set about disposing of the rotting hulk of garbage in front of my new home. I had recently met a friend who had grown up in the rural part of the county and taught me many of his country skills. I assumed that I would need to load the large pile of rotting shag carpet into my truck and haul it to the garbage dump, at great expense and effort. He found my naïveté charming and proceeded to help me dispose of the pile by burning it. As it was winter, and had been raining in the weeks since I had pulled the carpet, the Sheetrock, the cabinets and the insulation from the house, the pile was quite damp. It would take a great deal of effort to incinerate this soggy mass. With a new burn permit from the local fire hall and a small tank of gasoline, we began my first lesson in country living. Looking back, I'm horrified by this environmentally irresponsible act committed on my own property, but at the time it seemed perfectly appropriate.

After a thorough dousing with gasoline, the pile eventually roared into flames, the sky above my rural retreat blackened by the toxic smoke the carpeting and plastics emitted. We continued on through the afternoon, throwing into the fire anything we could find from the area surrounding the house that needed to be disposed of. Oddly, my excitement was never dampened by the great noxious cloud above or the pernicious pile of ash remaining the next morning. I reveled in the grand fire and its ability to consume the detritus of the past. The farm was mine now.

Two

Growing the Farm

If I had planned this farm from the outset, it might have looked different, perhaps more deliberate. As it happened, the circuitous route of development gave this project a more "organic" style of growth. Through successes and failures the farm took shape and now reflects my interests and skills, the nature of this soil and the climate here.

Raised in a small, quiet family, I turned to reading early for direction and inspiration. I spent long, lazy summer days, weekends and afternoons after school lying on the plush rugs of the living room poring over books, dreaming of Europe and lands far off. Although I would have greatly preferred the idyllic family life that I saw on the sitcoms of the era, it was this isolation that contributed to and created my character. Books were my friends, my inspiration, my mentors. No one encouraged me, yet no one corrected my outrageous and unrealistic views of the world.

This upraising led me to this farm. I bought this land, moved here and transformed it because no one said that I couldn't. No one warned me that small farms never succeed financially. No one let me know that this junkyard of a plot would never be a rich, productive parcel of land. Granted, I created a farm that resembles the images I saw when I was ten or fifteen or twenty years old. I had never seen a farm up close. My visions of farms were from *Green Acres*, or from French cookbooks of the seventies and Time-Life books on the rural American South of the sixties. My goal was to re-create those photos from the large picture books laid out on my bed growing up. No matter that the photos in question were of Versailles, or Giverny, or a large plantation in antebellum Georgia.

I didn't intend to grow this home into a farm. The more honest history is that I spent the years working here on one project or another, making decisions that felt right on a day-to-day basis. Only years later would I be able to walk out my front door and realize that my goal was a farm; that each day's decisions led up to a farm. From the start I wanted the property to look good, I knew that, but I wasn't really sure what its function would be. My recollection is that I wanted it to look like a park. Large flat lawns, specimen trees dotting the landscape, long curving paved driveways, that kind of thing. As I began to work on the property, all I had as a blueprint was this phantom park.

My first task was to deal with the ubiquitous blackberries that held the majority of the land hostage. These vines were Himalayan blackberries, an invasive nonnative species. In 1885 Luther Burbank introduced the Himalayan blackberry plant from India to the United States for commercial berry cultivation. I envision one single half-dead plant showing up wrapped in brown paper, tied with a bit of string, a hand-written label glued to the side and shipped from the mountains of the subcontinent. This blackberry ran wild, breaking out of its commercial farms and running rampant across the Pacific Northwest. It is now the most notorious weed of this region.

Complicating the matter is the simple fact that the berries are delicious: thumb-sized morsels packed with juicy sweetness. The strong, thick, prickly canes can grow twenty, thirty feet in a season with adequate water and are not affected by the temperate northwestern winters. Each year they spread their empire, building on the prior year's unchecked growth.

These monstrous, albeit tasty invaders had colonized my entire plot of land through the benign neglect of the previous owners. The house lay in the very center of the property, the edges of the land shrouded in the tall vines. I could see no neighboring houses at the time, my view obscured by *Rubus armeniacus*.

The result, for the first few years, was a sense of physical isolation. The route from the main road was a tunnel of these blackberries that clung to the high cherry trees lining the driveway, their ever-growing tendrils scratching my truck as it plowed through them, my daily traffic the only thing that kept the blackberries from completely sealing off the route in and out of the property. Once inside the property, I could see no other homes, no neighbors.

Although Vashon has since started to catch up to the present day, when I first arrived the island was stuck about thirty years behind the rest of the country. Moving to Vashon in 1990 felt like going back in time to the 1960s. The stores were small and simple, three taverns as restaurants lined the main street, a large lumberyard, a few real estate agents, a Sears store, the Beauty Nook. The era of coffee shops, chain stores and art galleries had yet to arrive. The only glimmer of modernity came from the banks, although the people working in them had an attitude of disdain for the rules of their corporate offices, easily bending the rules for their neighbors.

I was still commuting to work in the city, but on my days off I would hole away in my small chicken coop of a home, heating with the wood stove, enjoying the evenings when the power went out and believing that I was living in the wilderness, the harsh elements just feet from my door. I picked up a kerosene lamp and an ax at the local thrift shop, where the

pricing was also stalled in the sixties. I believed, mistakenly
as it turned out, that I could chop my own wood, heat my
small, poorly insulated house with that wood and live by the
kerosene lights when the power dimmed.

I came to my senses rather quickly when I discovered that
a chain saw I bought from the local Sears store cut the wood
more efficiently than my dull ax. As it turned out, the dull
ax that I attempted to chop wood with was in fact a splitting
maul, its job to simply split logs and not in any way designed
to chop wood. The trees that I attempted to chop with that
maul I later determined were willow, certainly the worst wood
for heating, as willow is soft and spongy and it puts out little
heat when burning. A bit of scrounging through the woods,
and I eventually found cherry, birch, fir and alder—all better
suited to heating my small house than the willow. The chain
saw even made it a fun task.

The seed was planted in my head, though. I searched
through old Foxfire books, looking for ways to live off the land.
In these then-twenty-year-old books were methods and recipes for living in the backwoods of North Carolina Appalachia.
They referenced a way of life that had little in common with
that of my suburban tract, but I picked up the odd idea of curing hams, raising chickens and churning butter, ideas before
then unknown to me.

As I began to cut down the blackberries that covered the
ground, I found that some of the larger, taller stands of brambles were actually ancient apple trees that the blackberry
vines had climbed through in an effort to gain more sunlight. As the property was part of an original homestead, it
included fruit trees, among them many large apple trees and
the occasional Bartlett Pear. I hacked away at the vines and
found fruit trees, very much alive if a bit tired. I quickly discovered that the few fruits that did manage to bloom through

the cover of blackberry leaves were quite tasty. Although the trees were of course not labeled, I think the varietals included Red Delicious, Braeburn and Winter Banana. Week by week, month by month, I hacked away at the brambles, finding the apple trees, large piles of galvanized irrigation piping left from the greenhouses, concrete foundations from buildings long gone and a 1963 powder-blue Ford Ranchero, missing its engine and most of its tires.

I began with a pair of small pruning shears, quickly moving up to large loppers until I discovered an old riding lawn mower was most efficient at clearing the land, at least until it repeatedly hit protruding bits of pipe, bending the blades and putting the mower out of commission for that day until I could replace them, only so they could be damaged the next weekend. With time, I would need larger equipment to maintain my property.

With the apples and a few hazelnuts picked from large old nut trees found in the woods, my interest in food from this land was piqued. As I freed a bit of land from the blackberries, I would plant a pear tree or a walnut or a plum, without much plan, but knowing that I liked the fruits or nuts pictured in the shiny photograph on the tag dangling from the bare-root trees that I bought at the local nursery.

As I began to live on the island and work on the property, I still ran my restaurant. By this time, in 1991, I had grown my original four-table bakery into a much larger twelve-table café. The restaurant was open seven days a week, year-round, opening at seven in the morning and serving breakfast, lunch and dinner until midnight on the weekends and six o'clock during the week. Although I didn't work at the café every hour it was open, I kept up a feverish schedule to pay for my new home on Vashon. I was obligated to pay a high interest rate—at the time twelve percent—because the banks that I approached for a loan felt that this property was a poor bet. With most of the value of the property tied to the land and not to the structures on it, I couldn't get a standard residential loan. The banks couldn't even believe that I intended to occupy my little chicken coop; they were sure I'd tear it down and build a more customary house. It was not until years later, after I upgraded the property tremendously, that I was able to rewrite the loan to a lower and more standard interest rate.

Thankfully, the café was financially successful. Selling light lunches and dinners in addition to baked goods helped. It was the popularity and the profitability of espresso coffee that made my business so profitable. I was very lucky. I opened the first café in 1986 at the onset of the espresso culture. Seattle was the epicenter of the craze and my business benefited from it immensely.

In 1994, after four years running the twelve-table café, I sold it to buy a large, full-service restaurant. The full-service restaurant was on a busy street in a different part of Seattle and served full breakfast, lunch and dinner seven days a week, and included a cocktail bar and sidewalk tables during the warm summer months. My financial success depended on maintaining a high volume of business. The goal was to keep as many of the one-hundred-plus seats as possible filled from nine in the morning till midnight every day of the year, including Christmas Day.

Without realizing it, I had entered into a financial trap. I wanted the excitement of running a large, vibrant restaurant. I envisioned a packed house every night, every table seated, the bar filled with drinkers. Profitwise, the restaurant wasn't doing as well as my two prior, smaller businesses. I was terrified that if I didn't improve my balance sheet, I might lose my business and, by extension, lose my refuge: the small farm

I was growing on Vashon Island. Local and seasonal became far less important than the bottom line.

Anyone who runs a restaurant is used to seeing volumes of vegetables, meat, fish and fruit. Chicken breasts are a staple of a restaurant menu. They can be ordered from meat suppliers in nearly any size wanted: three, four, five ounces and so on. They arrive folded into an oval shape and nestled each in a plastic dimple, four across and five long, on a plastic flat. Each cardboard case has a couple of these flats in it. They are delivered frozen, and then the cooks flip the flimsy plastic flats upside down into buckets to defrost. Very much like ice cube trays, racking them just so, so that the ice cubes pop out into the ice bucket for your cocktail. After a day in the cooler, these chicken popsicles defrost into a slimy chicken product. Hour by hour, day after day, they are pulled from the buckets and placed on the grill to make chicken Caesar salads and the like. The unknowing clients at the pretty little tables are looking for a healthy, low-fat diet and have come to the idea that skinless, boneless chicken is their best alternative. They order chicken Caesar salads, chicken sandwiches, pasta with a grilled chicken breast on top or simply a chicken breast grilled and served with vegetables and mashed potatoes on the side.

We went through cases of these chicken breasts. The deliverymen would come through the back door of the restaurant two and three days a week with a hand truck stacked high with flat cardboard boxes filled with plastic trays of chicken breasts. I never thought about where the rest of the bird was, where the chickens were raised, what they were fed. I just knew that I could raise the price of a salad from $8 to $11 if it had a grilled piece of meat on it. I had a lot of rent to pay, plus a mortgage; I looked away when I needed to.

Over time, I began to think more deeply about food. Chicken

breasts were the first thing on my menu that I stopped eating. I doubt if anyone noticed. The cooks had worked for me for years and knew me well, but probably never noticed that I hadn't eaten chicken breasts in years. I never touched one of the flaccid pieces of meat in the last five years I was there, letting the cooks grab them and place them on the grill. The wet slippery white fluid on the meat never felt right.

Soon I started to think similarly about the pork loins. The restaurant was known for *schweineschnitzel*—a pork loin, thinly sliced, pounded flat, dipped in egg and flour and then fried in butter. Served with lemon wedges and garlic mashed potatoes, it was a filling meal. If pounded very flat and well cooked so that the breading was light and nicely browned without drying out the pork, it was a tasty dish and therefore sold well.

The pork was delivered in a way similar to the chicken, a twenty-four-inch-long loin Cryovac-ed in plastic. After the meat leaves the packinghouse completely sealed in thick tight plastic, it starts to weep. By the time it reaches the restaurant the pork is swimming in pork fluid inside the bag. The bag is cut open and the liquid drained out before the pork can be broken down to size. Since those days, I have butchered many pigs, prepared many pork loins. There is no pork juice to drain off of them.

Little by little I came to be unable to eat at my own restaurant at all. I told no one, especially not customers. It was a humiliating position to be in. I couldn't see the possibility of changing the restaurant into a more health-conscious business—the financial pressures were too great. The guy who sold hot baked goods from a tiny storefront had been replaced with a restaurateur disgusted by eating at his own establishment. My relationship with food had been shaken, and by proxy my own image of myself.

The farm became my haven from the troubling commer-
cialism of my city business. As my interest in quality meats,
fruits and vegetables grew, I realized that I had a large deficit
of knowledge. Growing up in the city, I had no experience
in agriculture. I began to read more about farms and small
agriculture. Down the street from the restaurant was a small
used bookstore and I would walk through it once or twice daily
when the dining room was quiet and buy up every book on
animals and farming and farm-based cooking. I would return
from my walks, sit at the bar and pore over the books, learning
how to grow corn, pluck chickens, make cider. Everything was
new to me and exciting. I wanted chickens, I wanted cows, I
wanted pigs. All was great; everything was possible.

The neighboring eight acres adjacent to my house came up
for sale and I decided to buy the parcel, not sure why I wanted
it or what I would do with it, but having the instinct to know
that I had only one chance to secure so much land for my own
uses. These new eight acres had also been part of the Beall
Greenhouse Company. When I took over the land, nearly all of
it was covered in small first-generation trees: alders, willows
and an understory of invasive plants: Scotch broom, blackberries, hawthorn. Once I began to have the land cleared, I
could see the terrain of it. What had appeared to be a plot of
original land, of undisturbed earth, had been in fact greatly
abused. I speculate that the previous owners, who had owned
the land for the prior hundred years, had bulldozed it, making roads, flattening hills for greenhouses and harvesting any
topsoil for use in the greenhouses. I also found vast quantities
of garbage: irrigation pipes, plastic bags, plastic pots, galvanized water pipes. Earlier clearing had pushed a century-old
garbage dump into giant heaps mixed with felled trees, the
trees rotting in the piles of plastic. Large empty oil drums

the size of trucks were hidden in the brush, a stack of pipes to their side.

The irony of all this garbage was that it was primarily agricultural garbage, the detritus of raising plants for nearly a century. I found the odd soda can from the 1960s, but principally I found horticultural refuse. While spending months picking up irrigation pipes and small plastic plant markers, I vowed to leave this land free of any negative mark from my enterprises when I would eventually leave the land.

To work my land, I wanted a tractor. Objectively, I may not have needed a tractor for a plot of this size. Many small farms don't use tractors; they raise crops better suited to hand work than tractor work. I had no idea what I would raise on this farm, but I wanted a tractor; I wanted to be taken seriously. Farmers have tractors, right?

I started at the largest John Deere dealer in the area, which boasted a giant, deeply masculine showroom. I'm not sure why I picked John Deere, but I knew the name and liked the color green. Really. I walked around and around and around, sheepishly pretending to check out this tractor and that, admiring the rows of implements, marveling at the new tractor models. None of the tractors had prices on them and the implements gave little indication of their intended use. I thought I would walk up to a salesman and engage him, but all that I had planned to ask was, "How much is that big green metal thing with the spikes on the bottom that rotate on the back side of it for mixing dirt or something?" Things could have become awkward, but no one even noticed me. I left with no tractor.

Undeterred, a few weeks later I searched out a smaller dealership. John Deere dealerships vary in their product lines. There are four distinct categories. The largest John

Deere dealerships sell large construction equipment: bulldozers, excavators and such. I knew enough not to set foot on these lots. Some dealers sell equipment for large agriculture, located in farming communities well out of the city; their tractors are huge hundred-thousand-dollar machines. The men who shop at these dealerships are older, have lived in the community for years and are well known. Other stores are closer to the city and sell "compact utility tractors." This is their classification for smaller-acreage-farm tractors. The prices range from ten thousand to upward of fifty thousand dollars. The fourth type of dealership sells lawn mowers and turf equipment. Their intended clientele run golf courses, cemeteries and parks.

I went to the fourth category, after starting at the second. I should have gone to the third. They were much nicer to me at the fourth, even though I clearly drove the wrong truck, wore the wrong clothes and talked the wrong talk. But they did have tractors for sale. I asked some poorly phrased questions about pulling trees with the tractor, the salesman responded ambiguously that the tractor could theoretically pull a tree if I set my mind to it and we had a deal. Only after buying the tractor in question did I learn that only a large piece of heavy equipment could pull out a tree.

These basic skills, such as which tractor dealer to go to, which tractor to buy, what to say, are hard to learn from a book and my only knowledge came from old, outdated books. In an ideal world I would have grown up on a farm, going to the tractor dealer to shop for new tractors, buy parts, look for implements with my father, my uncle, my grandfather. My father died when I was very young and even if he had lived long enough to take me shopping, to teach me the ways of the world, tractors were not his heritage. My grandfather had worked with cattle in the far northern reaches of British

Columbia, but my father spent his life in an office, keeping the books for small companies until he moved to the United States. I inherited bookkeeping skills, not tractoring skills.

Even though it wasn't suited to pulling trees, I quickly discovered that I liked my tractor. I liked it a lot. Part of the enjoyment was simply that the tractor was shiny and new. Driving a tractor is different from driving a car. In a car there is a disconnect between the driver and the engine. As you tap the gas pedal, the car accelerates tremendously. There is little sense, sitting in a car, of how or why you are moving. The engine is hidden, the interior of the car is designed to be like a living room. A tractor has no such disconnect. The engine is directly in front of you, the rear wheels high and just to your sides, and as you turn the steering wheel you can see the front wheels respond in kind. Tractors have little interest in speed, only torque; they have a goal of doing work. When I sit on the seat of the tractor and use the hydraulic controls, I feel strong. I can lift heavy objects, pull a huge weight, do more work than I ever could by hand. In a car I just feel as though I am on a sofa in a floating hotel room, gliding down the highway.

I had a book that showed how to cut a field. I would drive in concentric circles around the field, each circle one row over from the last, until I hit the edge of the field. I tried it out and it worked. The goal is to drive only in forward gear and never stop the tractor, nor change gears; to never put it in reverse, to not waste time backing up. After a long day at the restaurant I would rush home, hop on the tractor and drive around, regardless of whether I actually needed to perform a task with it. I liked the sound of the diesel motor, the bounce of the shockless ride, the noise of the brush cutter ripping through the weeds. As I drove up the hill toward the upper pasture, the oil in the diesel would begin to burn; smoke would come from the exhaust pipe that sticks straight up from the engine in front of me. I liked the smell, I liked to see the smoke; something was being done.

I was on my way to being a farmer and being thought of as a farmer.

Initially, I pursued growing food on the farm as a hobby, a way to stock my own pantry and explore the possibilities of the land. Eventually, I realized that I wanted to grow food full-time as a business, and that to do so I needed a business plan. I had to pick a business model that took into account what was needed in the marketplace, what I enjoyed growing and what the quality and the quantity of land I had could handle. By the time I began preparing to make the leap, I had owned my farm for a decade, but always as a restaurateur first and a farmer on the off days. With the eight acres I had acquired from my neighbor, I had twelve acres by then and a few sheep that friends had given me. I planted a garden every year and had started two orchards, one all apples and the other a mixture of nuts, cherries, pears, persimmons and plums. I was ready to stop working in the city and work the farm full-time.

I had attended a lecture given by a farmer named Henning from Lopez Island, north of Seattle in the San Juan Islands. In his lecture he described his farm where he raised grass-fed beef cows on a small scale. I was immediately inspired. I had never before met a successful farmer. Henning showed slides of his barns and cows and fields. They were all very tidy and well-cared-for. As I sat in the front row of the room, absorbed by everything he said, I began to notice the time frame that he was operating within. He spent ten years working on this project and ten years on that project and five years on the other one. As I looked at him I realized that he was far older than his body indicated. He was in great shape, trim, with a full

head of hair and a brushy beard and spry, healthy. He gruffly
called on me, asking me about what I grew, what animals I
raised; he put me on the spot as to my farming practices. He
thought I was a farmer. I liked what he did, I liked his life.
I left that lecture thinking that I wanted to raise cows, beef
cows. I had a hunch that there was a market for local beef;
customers were looking for healthier meats, and I thought
that the raising of beef cows could fit into my lifestyle. Beef
cows need attention, but not necessarily on a daily basis.

I went back and read Joel Salatin's book on grass-fed beef,
Salad Bar Beef. The challenge was that I had a small amount
of land for a cattle ranch and a large percentage of those acres
was not yet cleared; the land remained covered in small trees
and brambles. I simply didn't have the quantity of pastureland necessary to raise enough cows to make the kind of cash
that could cover my expenses. Feeding animals only grass is
a great system if you have a large volume of pasture. This is
the reason large cattle ranches tend to be in states like Mon-
tana: large expanses of inexpensive land. With the quantity
of land that I did have, either I needed a higher-profit crop or
I needed to find more pastureland.

I went off in search of more land to pursue my latest idea
of raising beef cows. Surrounding my farm were small parcels
with houses on them; there was no way for me to expand.
There were large pastures on Vashon Island, but none were
contiguous with my property, and all would have been pro-
hibitively expensive to purchase.

So I began a search for a farm near Seattle, but not on
Vashon Island. I considered selling my farm and relocating to
a more rural area. In the late 1990s, farmland was still available one hour's drive outside of Seattle. Today, it has all been
bought up, but at that time I still found old farms for sale at
decent prices. I came across a hundred-acre farm that was

more than an hour from Seattle, but at $300,000 the price was right. I calculated that if I sold my farm, I could afford to make a go of it. I made an appointment with the real estate agent and went out to see the farm.

The farm was a former dairy operation, located outside of the small town of Sedro-Woolley. A humble house, a very large hay barn, a milking parlor, loafing sheds for cows, equipment sheds, all of the trappings of a dairy farm were there, including many acres of beautiful pastureland. At the time I remember looking at all these structures and having no idea what they were used for. I simply stared at them, trying to imagine what they had to do with cows. The barns I could understand, and although I had never seen a milking parlor, its simple design made its function self-evident.

A river ran through the rectangular-shaped plot, meandering back and forth across the pastures as it made its way down the long length of the property. The county had changed the regulations and had instituted a one-hundred-foot setback from the river. Previously cattle were allowed to graze right up to the riverbanks. With new clean-water legislation the county did not allow cows to graze near the riverbank for fear of high nitrogen levels leaching from the cows' manure into the water, increasing the level of algae and decreasing the oxygen content, potentially detrimental to salmon. Because this river curved back and forth serpentinelike through the property, the owner was losing a tremendous percentage of his land. He had decided to sell.

If the owner were in his fifties or sixties this would be a story of a vital farmer forced out by ever-stricter county environmental regulations. This farmer, however, was ninety-five years old. I met him in his living room that morning. Not terribly mobile, but very much alive and active. He was ready to leave his farm.

After touring the pastures, checking out the barns and walking the river, I chatted with the real estate agent, who turned out to be a personal friend of the farmer. I assumed that he had been a farmer his whole life, and that he was coming to the end of a long run in the country.

She told me his story. He had been an accountant for many years in the city and when he turned sixty-five and retired, he bought this dairy farm and began a second career as a dairyman. Throughout his sixties, seventies and eighties he had run this dairy operation, taking care of his Holstein cows and milking them twice daily. When he hit his late eighties, he began to shut down his dairy, finding the work physically difficult. He continued to keep cows, now out of love, not necessity. With the pastures, barns and fences in place, he switched to beef cows, as it was less daily physical work for him.

Little by little his herd shrank as he aged, until just before he put the farm on the market he sold off the last cow. The pastures had no weeds and looked like they had been grazed that week. The barn still had old dry hay in the loft and it felt like the cows had just been in the milking parlor that morning.

The best part was that, even at the age of ninety-five, the farmer wanted to sell the property on a contract. He was willing to carry a thirty-year note and not rely on being cashed out by a bank on closing. I remember asking the agent to clarify this a couple of times because it was both so crazy and so sweet. He knew he would never live long enough to finish the contract, but for whatever reason he offered the option of carrying the paper. I want to think that he wanted a new farmer to take over rather than a residential developer.

After visiting the farm, I drove around trying to get a feel for the area, for the lifestyle and what it would be like to live there. North of Seattle by an hour and a half, Sedro-Woolley is located in Skagit Valley. The landscape is beautiful in this part of the state. Sedro-Woolley was a logging town, but by this point logging had all but disappeared. The small town and the neighboring area around the farm were economically depressed. In between the large, lush farms like the one for sale were small trailers, set off from the road, smoke rising from their metal chimneys. In front of the sad trailers sat clusters of old cars, baby toys and jacked-up oversized pickup trucks. It looked very much like my own property when I had found it: the same drab, moldy housing, the same junked cars.

The tone of the surrounding community, however, couldn't have been more different. On Vashon the old cars were derelict Volvo 240s, no longer running but still with bumper stickers for Carter/Mondale. On the back windows of those same Volvos were stickers announcing advocacy of world peace or membership in the Sierra Club. The broken-down pickup trucks parked near the farm in Sedro-Woolley also had stickers in their back windows, usually Confederate flags, clearly marking the politics of this northern county. Vashon has a history similar to Sedro-Woolley's—logging and agriculture—but Vashon gained a new lease on life in the late 1960s. With its proximity to Seattle, Vashon was colonized by hippies seeking what was at the time inexpensive land. Vashon went from being known for its lumber in 1900, to small fruits such as raspberries, strawberries and currants in the 1930s and 1940s, to premium-grade marijuana in the 1960s and 1970s. I liked the feeling on Vashon. It was a community of like-minded folks I wouldn't mind inviting over for dinner. When I was on that Sedro-Woolley farm, looking at the large hay barn, checking out the pastures, chatting with the wise old farmer, I imagined that I could live there. When I drove around the area, I knew that it was impossible. I instinctively knew that I would never be welcome and could never feel safe. I could never be a part of that community.

So I never put an offer on the Sedro-Woolley farm, even though it would have been an ideal place to raise cows. The drive home to my farm was the hour and half south into Seattle, then a short wait for the ferryboat, the quarter-hour boat ride and a short ten-minute drive down the island. In that time I had a chance to reflect on my trip. I had expected to sell my home on Vashon and use the proceeds to buy the northern farm. I believed that with the small amount of work I had done on my place and the increased real estate values on Vashon, I could clear enough money to afford the more expensive, larger farm.

On every level, the Sedro-Woolley farm was a real farm. The hundred acres were perfect for raising beef cows the way that I had been reading about. It was fenced and cross-fenced. There was a large barn for the cows to live in when the weather was poor. The pastures were in excellent condition and would feed a small herd of beef cows well. Water lines had already been installed, ready to keep the thirsty animals healthy on the warm summer days. All I would have had to do was move into the comfortable house, buy a couple of dozen beef cows, open the large steel gate to let them into the pastures and wait for them to gain weight on the lush grass. In a year and a half I could begin to slaughter great grass-fed cows for what I knew were waiting Seattle customers. I could be a farmer, a real farmer, in a very short amount of time. But I never could have called the community around the farm home.

I gave up this easy route to being a farmer. I chose the more challenging path. I would make my small, scrappy farm on Vashon Island a real farm. I realized that it had great limitations. There was not enough land to raise beef cows, my intended crop. I simply could never make a living raising beef cows on twelve acres of land, most of which was still covered by woods at the time. I would have to put that idea behind me and find a new model for farming that fit what I did have.

But I learned from the Sedro-Woolley farmer. He wasn't born into farming, he didn't spend his life as a dairy farmer and yet had pulled it off. When he was in his mid-nineties he looked wise and full of a lifetime of experience. Yet he had been an accountant and, as the agent told me, he'd probably gotten a book from the library and started reading about cows. I also want to believe that it was the obligation, the responsibility, the necessity of milking and feeding his cows every morning that kept him getting out of bed each day. He didn't have a choice; his cows were his great motivator. I want to believe that if he had kept milking fifty cows daily he would have lived forever, that only once his herd was gone could he succumb to old age. It is my fantasy of the power of the dairy. It wasn't his farm that I yearned for—it was his life.

My retirement plan is now to always have a dairy cow on my land. I might not always keep a herd of dairy cows and run this farm as a dairy business, but I like the idea of needing to be out of bed in the morning for a specific reason, every day, even if it is raining or snowing or if I am just tired. Some people keep doing crossword puzzles to keep their mind thinking and active; I plan on milking cows.

I was still running the restaurant but was now ready to take the first steps toward becoming a full-time farmer. I was naïve but committed. I enjoyed having animals and raising vegetables and thought that I could make it work on a full-time basis. *Salad Bar Beef* had captured my imagination, and the ninety-five-year-old former accountant had inspired me to pursue a farmer's life, but tackling cows was simply not feasible. I didn't have the land for beef cows, and constructing the facilities for a dairy would have been time consuming and expensive. Though I knew by this point that I was ready to sell it, I still had a restaurant to manage as well, at least for the short term. I would have to start small. I had heard from other farmers that vegetables are a good place to begin—cheap, quick and unregulated by the county, the state or the federal government. Plus, I knew there was a farmers' market on Vashon where I could sell my crop. It seemed like the most logical first step.

Farmers' markets are the face of small farms for much of the country. You see farmers and their helpers alongside their produce, their old pickup trucks parked next to the market. Every trip I made to a farmers' market either on Vashon or in the city, I mused on what the lives of the farmers were like. The farmers looked very similar: youthful if not young, dressed in very utilitarian clothing with obvious signs of work and wear, with hands dry and callused from working with tools. Their helpers were younger, presumably politically liberal and generally very happy and carefree. I liked the feeling, the look, the attitude. I wanted to be like them. I perceived a sense of honesty and integrity among the farmers.

But how could I be welcomed into this club? A couple of years earlier I had requested the guidelines and application forms from the largest market organization in Seattle, thinking that I could start selling vegetables there. Their guidelines—really more like rules—were extensive. They detailed the acceptable size of the booth, the appropriate tent over the booth, the amount of weight needed to hold down each corner of the tent, the minimum and maximum dimensions and content for the farm sign, the time you had to set up, the time you had to break down, where you could park your trucks and so on. I was overwhelmed.

Farmers' market managers are responsible for balancing the market. The goal is to give the customers a variety of product to buy and give the sellers a chance to sell all their product. If every booth at a market sells only tomatoes, few customers will show up, knowing that there will only be tomatoes. Furthermore, allowing multiple sellers with the same wares virtually guarantees that farmers will have to undercut other farmers by slashing prices. Everyone would lose. The result is a market manager that restricts what products come into the market and when. To this end on the application form was a long disclosure in which you detailed what you were planning on bringing to market and when. I had no idea if I could grow radishes and on which week they would be ready. I thought I would just plant some nice seeds and see what happened.

Restrictions aside, I still wanted to grow and sell, and as luck would have it, I met someone who would assist me in reaching that goal. While out having drinks with friends, I was introduced to a guy who had been an intern on a local vegetable farm. We began chatting and realized quickly that we had lots of common interests and similar goals.

Matt had worked on a successful farm a few miles outside of Seattle that was known for its quality vegetables. The farm where he had been an intern grew vegetables for Seattle farmers' markets and also had a subscription program. At the beginning of the growing season the farm would sell subscriptions entitling each subscriber to come out and pick up a weekly box of vegetables (or have them delivered) from the late spring through the early fall. This program is common in small vegetable farms throughout the country and is termed CSA, for community-supported agriculture. Matt had learned a great deal about growing vegetables during his year working at this well-run and profitable farm. He wanted to learn more; to raise animals, to make honey, to cook food. He was interested in farm animals and how they could be integrated into a small farm such as the one that he worked on. I had by this time started a small orchard, grown vegetables for myself and had a few sheep but had never grown vegetables in any volume to sell at a local market.

Matt had anticipated returning for another year to continue his internship on the farm. When his plans unexpectedly changed and he needed a job, we decided quickly to work together, to change my place from a home where I raised a few animals to a full-time vegetable farm selling at the local farmers' market. Until I met Matt I had no idea how I would ever break into the big-city farmers' markets. We would tackle this challenge together, with his knowledge, my land and a lot of sweat. For both of us, the stakes were high. I was already preparing to sell my restaurant, and our vegetable venture would be Matt's primary source of income.

We began getting ready for the summer growing season in the first week of February. I realized quickly how little I knew about growing vegetables. When I was growing up, my family often had a small garden. I had grown a respectable volume of food over the years—tomatoes, potatoes and strawberries, memorably. What I didn't know was that even small farms have different goals and have different strategies than small home gardens.

I was also struck by the difference between my vision of a small farm and the reality of a small farm in regard to harvesting. I would see the farmers in Seattle at their stands at nine in the morning standing behind high stacks of carrots and beets and lettuce and think that they had picked those vegetables that very morning. Actually, everything that went to a market on a Saturday morning was picked on Friday during the day and cooled, cleaned and packaged.

A farmers' market is a perfect example of an open market, in the economic sense. People come together to buy and sell products. A local farmers' market is really no different than the New York Stock Exchange or a large suburban mall. Sellers want to make the most money by selling at the highest price with the least expense. The basic method for achieving a high price is by selling unique products, through being either later or earlier than everyone else, or by having higher-quality products. Any of these factors can push the price up. If you sell ordinary green beans at the middle of the season when every other farmers' market stall is selling green beans, you will make no money. If you have beautiful, unusual tomatoes weeks before everyone else, you will clean up. There are tried-and-true strategies for producing vegetables as early as possible. Most of them involve plastic; others are simply farming practices that push the seasons. At a farmers' market, it is all about being first.

With Matt's help, I began a small vegetable farm. Overnight Kurt's farm was transformed to *Kurtwood Farms*—the *s* added at the end to make it sound grander than the humble reality. Together Matt and I ordered seeds, plowed and tilled two fields, installed an irrigation system, built one glass greenhouse for starting tomatoes and erected a long plastic greenhouse to grow tomatoes in the field.

Matt and I decided to sell vegetables at the local farmers' market and to grow tomato starts for sale to home gardeners. We also sold CSA subscriptions for our vegetables, taking advance payment in exchange for a box of produce to be delivered weekly from June until October. CSA is ideal for small farms in that the farms get much-needed cash early in the season and guaranteed customers for the entire season. The customers also win, receiving a weekly selection of the best vegetables of that farm without having to make the effort to go to the weekly market and shop. Quickly we sold enough subscriptions to get started.

Thanks to Matt, I knew we needed an early crop that would beat competitors to the market. We seeded tomatoes as soon as the greenhouse was completed in late February. Even though four hundred tomato plants would have been ample for our small farm, we enthusiastically seeded twelve hundred plants and quickly they germinated. The greenhouse was filled with flats and flats of small green plants. Matt made phone calls and in a couple of days we had a contract with a small chain of high-end gourmet grocery stores in Seattle to supply them with heirloom tomato starts.

Sitting in the dining room at the farm on blustery winter days planning vegetable fields and selling vegetable subscriptions was all good fun. In an effort to sell our vegetable subscriptions, I would make phone calls to potential customers describing weeks of fresh kale, verdant salad greens, cherry tomatoes sweet and juicy and boxes filled with winter squash and leeks in the fall weeks. I was a successful salesman, if an unproven farmer. Once we cashed the checks from the subscribers and winter turned to spring, we had twenty-five families expecting a box of vegetables delivered on June 1 and for each week after that into October. I knew these customers: they were friends and neighbors. The idea of failing them was inconceivable.

Following the tomatoes, we planted peppers, onions and leeks in February. Most of the spring plants started in March—cauliflower, broccoli, kale and salad greens. Then cucumbers in May, and squash in late May.

By mid-May the tomato plants had taken over the small glass greenhouse. The plants had been hardened off in the last week by bringing them out of the greenhouse for a few hours each day so they could get used to the cooler reality outside of the greenhouse. They had grown well, thankfully, and were ready to be delivered to the city grocery stores. I loaded up my dented old Toyota pickup truck with plants and headed to Seattle. With my cattle dog Daisy in the passenger seat and me wearing my filthy jeans, I felt like I had become that farmer I had seen all those years while shopping at the farmers' markets.

Although we had agreed to deliver a box of vegetables worth a specific value each and every week from June into October, the vegetables didn't always cooperate. Some weeks there were just a few vegetables ripe and ready to harvest, and some later weeks we had too much produce available. We had picked the start date of June 1 by convention, but that was not necessarily when a sufficient part of the garden would be ready to pick and deliver.

I was still working in the city at my restaurant a few days per week and, as many of our CSA customers lived in Seattle, I would deliver the boxes of vegetables to the customers. My responsibility was the subscriptions. The remaining vegetables from the farm Matt would sell at the local farmers' market on the weekend while I was in the city at the restaurant.

In lean weeks, when there weren't enough vegetables to harvest, the demand for vegetables for both the subscriptions and the farmers' market created tension. I wanted my customers to have their boxes filled with beautiful vegetables. Even if the box contained the requisite dollar value of produce, I wanted the box to be physically full. Matt wanted ample vegetables remaining in the field so that he could harvest them on Friday afternoon for the Saturday morning market. Working on a commission system, the more vegetables that Matt could take to market, the more money he could make.

In addition to the unevenness of our harvest due to weather and difficult-to-predict vegetable growth, Matt and I also confronted the limitations of my land. He had worked on an established vegetable farm; they had spent years amending

the soil, creating a rich, vital tilth. My fields, in their first
year of growing vegetables, had no such vitality. The soil was
thin, sandy and incapable of growing the bountiful crop I was
expecting. Our plants were hardly vigorous, and weeds and
predators quickly and easily overran many crops. The result
was fields that looked nothing like the glossy color photos of
the how-to books that I had read for years. We succeeded with
the easy-to-grow vegetables: those that didn't require rich,
healthy soil. The kale did especially well, carrots too. With
ample water pumped onto them, our tomatoes managed to
flourish. Overall, though, our harvest was thin.

At the end of the growing season, after the last pumpkin
had been delivered, the last tomato gleaned from the field,
the last bit of kale harvested from the tired plants, Matt and
I took stock of the year. I had worked part-time on the farm,
part-time at the restaurant; Matt had worked full-time at the
farm from early February until we finished up in late October. We added up the sales for the year: CSA sales, market
sales and sales of tomato starts. The total came to a measly
$17,500.

Our expenses were tremendous: I can't recall their exact
total, but in the ballpark of $10,000. We built a greenhouse, a
long hoop house, installed irrigation lines, bought seeds, flats,
pots, potting soil, packaging materials and so on. Much of the
investment would prove useful in the future, but our economic
model was flawed.

Kurtwood Farms' first growing season ended on a sour note;
we failed to crack the challenge of the vegetable farm. Matt
quickly quit to work on another farm on the island and I could
hardly blame him; he hadn't made very much money. Our
harvest had been far thinner than either of us had expected.
I had argued against taking disfigured, insect-eaten leeks to
market and for reserving the best produce for subscription

boxes, and as a result Matt made less money each week at the farmers' market. I had my restaurant income to fall back on, but vegetable sales were Matt's sole livelihood.

I wouldn't, however, be able to rely on my restaurant for long. Over the course of the growing season I had negotiated the sale of the restaurant, and just as we harvested the last vegetables, the sale went through. Although losing the stability of a city job was scary, I had no interest in abandoning my dream of being a farmer and returning to commuting. I would have to find a working model, and now without the safety net of my job in the city. As a result of the sale of my restaurant, I was going to be paid $40,000 per year for the next five years. At the time, it felt like a fortune that would last forever, but in retrospect it was barely enough to get off the ground. I've spent $5,000 to $10,000 several times to hire a crew to fell and burn trees in order to open up adequate pasture for my cows. Simply keeping my driveway functional was difficult. Although when I first drove down the driveway in 1991 I thought it a great asset, I've spent over $1,000 on many occasions to fill the four-hundred-foot length with gravel. I had a small cushion, but the money wouldn't last forever, especially operating at a loss.

I had a number of options before me. The infrastructure for growing vegetables had been installed. Parts of the farm were fenced for animals and I had a few sheep; pastures were seeded and growing even if they were a bit rough. Here and there were fruit trees that I had planted when I first arrived on the island; the orchard puttered on. Through Matt I had met young farmers-to-be who wanted to work for me as interns. Jorge, one of my old cooks from the restaurant, came asking me for work and I quickly hired him part-time. I knew that I couldn't run the farm by myself and more than anything I wanted someone here with me, if only for a few hours each

week. My goals of making this farm sustainable, profitable
and enjoyable would be a process of selection and elimination:
trying out sheep and goats, pigs and cows, bees and chickens,
vegetables and fruits. I was excited; I wanted everything, and
as much as possible. I would crack this nut.

Three

Bees

Beekeeping was the first project that I started on my farm, just a few weeks after I moved in, and long before my misadventures in farmers' market economics. I had always wanted bees, and now that I owned a house, I had no excuse for putting it off. I recall being terribly excited about the prospect of having bees. The restaurant in downtown Seattle was in a one-story building, and I had researched the idea of keeping bees with the intention of placing hives on the building's low roof in the hopes of collecting honey for the restaurant, which then I still owned, and for myself.

I looked into the equipment necessary and the city zoning required and how to keep the bees themselves. The city assured me that having hives in the city was not a problem as long as I kept them a few feet from the property line. As I remember, the people from the city were actually quite intrigued with the project and encouraged my downtown beekeeping. I collected beekeeping supply catalogues and proceeded to start my apiary when the deal came through with the Vashon property. The bees would now be country dwellers and not live among the buildings of the city.

I had no one to turn to for advice on keeping bees at the time. I had an old book—*First Lessons in Beekeeping* by C. P. Dadant—that my friend Michelle had given me for my twenty-first birthday. It is a classic volume that is reissued annually by the largest beekeeping supply house in the country, a slim book with a heavy manila cover and the most dated but charming photographs. She probably gave it to me for its vintage feel, not for its content, but I enjoyed both. I pored over the book, learning the names of the different bees, their seasonal food preferences, the old-fashioned methods of wrapping the hives in tar paper to protect them through the deep winters. I felt like I knew the young man in the book, dressed head to toe in a bee outfit, the long white thick fabric tied at the hands and feet to keep the bees out, a helmet with a veil to protect his face.

I found an ad for a beekeeping supply house in the back of a *Mother Earth News* magazine. The Brushy Mountain Bee Farm in North Carolina made beehives and sold them through the mail. I ordered their catalogue and when it arrived I studied it obsessively, choosing what I would need to begin my apiary.

Intimidated by the many choices in the slim catalogue, I ordered the beginner's kit. After all, I was a beginner. It contained a hive box, lids, base and frames, together with thick gauntlet gloves and that hat and veil from the photo in that vintage book. A hive tool and a bee brush rounded out the kit. I eagerly awaited the shipment.

When the large box arrived from North Carolina, I spread the contents all out on the floor of my humble chicken coop and began to assemble the pieces. Traditionally hive boxes are painted white; I went with a deep barn-red. I wanted my hives to have a bit more style, and I had a can left over from painting the outside of my house.

Also in the supply catalogue were advertisements for bee suppliers. These were bee farms located in the southern states that grew large colonies of bees and shipped them north for beekeepers. I had my pick of suppliers from Alabama, Texas, South Carolina, Georgia. All were a great distance from my home, but I choose a firm from Texas. I called up and placed an order for a box of Italian bees, a subspecies of honeybees. Carniolan are another subspecies of the honeybee used commonly in beekeeping, but I decided to go with Italian bees because of the familiarity of their name.

The first box of bees arrived in relatively good condition. A percentage of the bees were dead, but there were still many live bees in the box. The three-pound box that the bees are shipped in is fairly small—six inches by eight inches by fifteen—and contains around three thousand bees. The two longest sides are open, covered with tight mesh to keep the bees in but allow air to freely circulate. The other four sides are made of low-quality wood, similar to old food crates. Within the sealed box is a smaller, much smaller, box containing the queen. The bees are also given a tin can filled with sugar water to feed them on their journey north.

Once I received the bees I proceeded to install them into my freshly painted hive. I had read the books, spent time on setting up the hive and now I was ready to suit up and start raising bees.

I failed. It was a cool spring that very first year and I got the bees out of the box and onto the hive, but I couldn't put the covering lid of the hive on because the bees had not quickly entered the hive. Sadly, it began to rain that afternoon. Cool and rainy, not good bee weather. Fearful of putting the lid on their apparently delicate bodies, I left the lid off. My first decision in beekeeping turned out to be one of my worst. The next morning I returned to the hive to find the bees all dead from the rain and cold. I would have to start over quickly.

I made more calls to the southern suppliers and found one in Alabama that still had bees for sale and would ship them to me. I eagerly awaited their arrival.

Luck would not be on my side on my second attempt of that

first year either. I got a call from the post office informing
me that they had my bees, but as it was late on a Saturday,
they would not be coming out to Vashon Island for two more
days. I had the option of driving in to the main post office,
then termed the Terminal Annex, to pick up my charges.
Located in the industrial neighborhood south of downtown
Seattle, the terminal was a low long concrete building astride
the railroad tracks. Although it processed a majority of the
mail for the center of the city, it still felt like a remnant of an
era of large brown canvas mailbags and carts with large steel
wheels plying the concrete docks surrounding the building. I
headed down to the building and scurried up to the loading
dock, eventually finding someone who knew where the package was located. Although the bees were well sealed in their
box and then covered with a bag, the postal workers were
generally afraid of the parcel and left it on one of those high-
wheeled carts at the end of the loading dock. I ventured over,
found it and was immediately saddened. The box was lifeless, no noise, no activity. On the floor of the wooden box was
a pile of dead bees: dead from the heat, dead from the cold,
dead from the transport from Alabama. In an effort to salvage
something from the purchase, I was able to quickly show the
postal workers that the bees were dead and collect something
from the insurance. My first year of beekeeping consisted of
a pile of dead bees at the farm, a pile of dead bees at the post
office and a brand-new hive sitting in the yard, looking very
empty. I would begin anew with the next spring a year later.

The second year proved a tad more successful but was still
a failure. The bees made it to the farm, managed to colonize
my hive and lived through the year. Not a drop of honey, but
still I was hooked, convinced that I could make a go of this.
I liked the wardrobe, the simple design of the wooden boxes,
the smell of the beeswax foundations.

It would take a few years to get the basic skills necessary to keep a hive alive through the spring, into the summer, so that I could capture some of the honey produced. Once I achieved that level of success and tasted the result, the honey, all of the setbacks and lessons were worth it.

Fresh, local honey is an amazing product. Not sticky, not cloyingly sweet, full of delicate flavors. When I harvest the honey early in the summer it is light in color and light in flavor, simple, the product of bees on clover and spring flowers. By late summer the honey is dark brown, thick, complex and tastes of madrona trees and late flowers. Since that first year of success, I have kept hives every year. I have never been too successful, but have always harvested enough honey for myself and my friends. In a good year, gallons of honey fill plastic pails; in the lean years, a scant single bucket has to suffice.

Over the years I have slowly learned about the lives of bees. Primarily, I enjoy beekeeping because I will never understand it completely. Keeping bees is a task that is at first glance simple. With a bit of luck and some understanding of bee culture, you can be successful, notwithstanding the shipping of bees across the nation. In those first few seasons, I thought that I understood the colonies in my hives. I now know that I will spend my life with these small insects, never fully understanding their behavior, and yet I will always know enough to head out to the bee yard for another season.

A beehive is complex but organized. A few basic ideas: There are three types of bees—the queens, the workers and the drones. Queens and workers are females, drones are males. Each hive has one queen, the rest are mostly workers and a small percentage are drones. The queen lays eggs for future generations, the workers tend to the queen, leave the hive for food, make the honey, guard the hive, create the

honeycomb and keep the colony clean. The drones do essentially nothing except mooch off of the colony. The drones' one
and only task is to fertilize the queen. Only one drone gets
this job, but without a male on hand to fertilize the queen,
no eggs would be laid and the bees would die. This task takes
at most a few minutes and is performed once per season,
but the rest of their lives the drones drain the hives of their
productivity. Beehives are most certainly a matriarchal society; males have very little role. I wonder if the workers are
bitter at the arrangement: spending their days working tire-
lessly so that the larger, plumper drones can eat the wealth
of their labor.

The queen is the largest bee of the colony physically and in
presence. Nearly twice as long as the worker bee and slow to
move, she will spend her life gently moving from cell to cell
depositing eggs into the hexagonal cavities, the workers sealing the cells, feeding them and caring for the young bees. On
a good summer day she will lay two thousand eggs.

The essence of the beekeeper's task is to provide the colony
with a physical hive, the structure for growing their colony
in the most efficient way. Wooden boxes, open on the top and
bottom, form the outer dimensions of the hive. Within these
simple four walls are hung nine or ten frames: simple flat
panels, the outer framework of wood, the center made of thin
beeswax, pressed in with the indentation of the bees' hexagonal form. Each box resembles a hanging file folder common
in a modern office, the frames resting on the upper edge of
the wooden box; the frames can be moved freely back and
forth across the width of the box until the full complement of
frames fills the hive box.

The top and bottom of each box is finished with a wooden
base, the top with a series of lids to keep the bees in, the
weather out. Along the bottom where the wooden box meets

the base, a space is allowed for the bees to come and go, while larger creatures are kept out.

Bees are most particular beings. Their size is standardized. Unlike a pig or a cow or a dog, one bee varies very little from the next. In twenty days they reach full size and stay that way. This uniformity allowed early hive designers to create a hive with precise sizing, based on the measurement unit of *bee space*. Bee space is the amount of room needed for a bee to move through; larger than that volume and the bees will begin to fill in the area with wax and propolis until the space is back to their liking.

Once the beekeeper has provided a space for the colony, assured them of ample food in the form of sugar water if the weather and flora do not cooperate, then the bees will flourish. Through the spring and early summer months the bees will grow their colony; the queen will lay thousands of eggs, and those eggs will hatch into thousands of worker bees, all destined to collect pollen for the creation of honey.

At this stage beekeeping sounds like a great altruistic enterprise: create a perfect environment for these lovely insects to prosper. Sadly for the bees, altruism is not the goal of the beekeeper. Honey is the goal. The strategy for the beekeeper is to create a lovely home for the bees so that they will produce great volumes of honey, then to steal the honey and trick them into thinking that they need to create even more honey.

Honey is the bees' way of preserving the bounty of summer, much like the way we create cheese or jam or wine. They know that their only way of living through the cold and bleakness of winter is through the stockpiling of honey in the warm months of summer when the flowers are blooming. During the darkness of December they eat their stored honey for nourishment. Instinctively they are pushed to produce as much honey as possible to keep their colony alive. We capitalize on their industry. In a well-managed hive, the honey is removed regularly and replaced with empty beeswax frames, which pushes the bees to produce more and more honey.

Is it cruel? I don't think so. It is simply part of the social contract that we enter into with the bees. We provide for them, guarantee their survival through the year and in return we receive a part of the product of their labor. If I didn't love honey so much I would reflect more on the injustice of it all.

When the bees have filled a number of the frames with honey, capping them to seal them with beeswax, I can then go in and remove the entire set of frames to extract the honey. Entering a hive filled with bees is a delicate matter. I have little fear of bees. It is an essential trait needed to keep bees. A friend of mine wanted bees for years and finally started a small hive a couple of years ago. He loved the idea of beekeeping, certainly loved the honey and appreciated the concept of keeping bees. He was, sadly, not comfortable with the actual bees. His foray into beekeeping lasted a quick season. He would bundle himself up in layers of protection, gloves, hats, veils, tight shirts, and venture out to the bee yard. I think that they sensed his trepidation, his fear. They were most inhospitable to him. It was not a relationship destined to continue.

I enjoy bees, love to watch them. I often find myself on a warm summer day standing next to the hive, watching the bees fly in and out of the long slender opening at the base of the hive. I know what they are doing—flying to patches of flowers to harvest pollen to bring back to the colony—but I wonder if they know what they are doing. How can they possibly communicate with the hive as a whole? The queen is the center of the hive, but she really doesn't run the hive; she spends her days laying eggs. How do the bees pass on information? How do they make decisions?

The beekeeper's year is a relatively flat line with two, maybe three peaks—in a good year, four. The most exciting task involved with the keeping of bees is their installation in the spring. After those first couple of years ordering bees by mail from the southern states, I found a much better and more successful system. A small beekeeping supply store opened up an hour from my home. Their well-designed service involves driving a large panel truck down to California every spring and picking up hundreds of boxes of bees, then quickly driving them back up the coast to their eager customers. The bees always arrive in mint condition and it's a rare chance for beekeeping hobbyists to meet each other.

The date of arrival tends to fall on April 15. Easy to remember: the excitement of new bees, the dread of filling out tax forms. I order the bees weeks ahead and look forward to that date throughout the overcast early spring weeks. Once the bees arrive, flowers will bloom, the skies will clear and the pastures will grow again. It might not happen quite on schedule, but the hopes can be centered on one date: April 15 it is.

I order four boxes each year, enough for a season of plenty. Each year I have found that there is uneven success among the colonies. Inevitably one will do tremendously well, two adequately and one will be quite disappointing and produce no honey. Having four colonies spreads the risk well.

Before the drive to pick up the bees, I ready the hives for the new arrivals. I clean the boxes, stands and lids, scrape and repaint if necessary. I mow the lawn underneath and around the eventual placement of the stands; once the bees arrive, running the loud mower past them seems like taunting. By the end of the summer, long blades of errant grass surround the hives, the disorder of the exterior contrasting with the strict order of the interior of the hive boxes.

Once I return to the farm, the long drive behind me, I am

giddy with excitement and anticipation. I love this next hour; I wait all year for this time. I love to share this quick show with friends. It is a short performance, but full of drama. Everyone who is lucky enough to be at the farm for this afternoon gets immediately hooked; they order their own bees from their cell phones that afternoon or they pledge to start their apiary the next spring. Bees draw you in with their simplicity and their complexity, the mystery behind how their world operates.

I ready all the parts necessary: the bees in their boxes await on the back gate of the pickup truck, and the hives are already in their places, empty and waiting. I bring the tools from the toolshed: the hat and veil, the canvas gauntlet gloves, the smoker, the hive tool, a small scrap of cedar shake, matches, paper, twigs.

The challenge in the quest for honey, in my opinion, is the lighting of the smoker. Bees have a weak trait that keepers can exploit to their advantage. Bees recognize smoke in their hives as indicative of a serious danger to the future of the hive and immediately gorge themselves on the honey in their stores. Their vision, I suspect, is that they will need an ample amount of honey to start their new lives in a reborn hive after the fire. When they are full with honey, they have little desire or ability to contest the human invasion of their home. The smoke calms them and makes them uninterested in stinging, or at least less interested in stinging.

The tool used to smoke a beehive has changed little if at all in the hundred-plus years since its invention. A small cylindrical metal chamber holds the fire, a small wooden bellows with leather or false leather providing the hinges of the bellows. The action of pumping the bellows sends a stream of air into the base of the fire, keeping it lit, the smoke exiting from a spout at the top of the smoker.

Building a fire is straightforward—any Boy Scout can do it.

The trick here is to keep a slow fire, lit for an hour, but never letting it burn with any intensity. I'm looking for a source of smoke, not a source of heat. I build a small tight fire in the bottom of the can, get it started well and then cover it with a bit of dried grass. The fire will smolder a bit, the grass will filter the smoke and cool it off a bit and the bellows will provide enough air to keep the fire lit. I worry about the fire dying while I am working with the bees; as the smoker tapers off I imagine the bees springing to life and seeking vengeance on me.

Once the fire is well enough established, I begin to assemble the equipment and my kit. The hat is a sad white plastic interpretation of a muslin-covered safari hat, the thin veil draped over the top, a long string line pulling the veil together around the neck. I pull the string tight, tie a knot that will secure the veil well and yet leave a bow easy to disentangle if bees find their way into the interior of the space created around my face by the gossamer veil. A trapped bee, unable to find her way out, buzzing inches from your face, makes even a calm man shudder, hands quickly pulling at the string to release the prison that is the hat.

The gloves are elbow-length thick canvas: gauntlets. Regal in styling, they seem out of place with the plastic safari hat, cracked and soiled from years of use. They are thick enough to keep the stinger of a bee from piercing the skin with any depth, yet still thin enough to allow adequate movement.

In my side pocket is kept a hive tool: a small metal blade, eight inches long, an inch wide, with a tight bend on one end for prying and lifting, a sharpened edge on the other for invading tight spaces. This bar is a lever to open and pry and pull at the frames of bees stuck in the center of the hive boxes. Even with the clumsy gloves, it makes for dexterous handling.

The basic uniform I wear is always the same: long pants

with tight legs, long-sleeved shirt with tight arms and high collar. Early on I began a habit of always wearing the same shirt. A white cotton Oxford-cloth button-down shirt, it fits the bill in many regards. It is white, the color of coolness and calm, it is never as warm as a dark black fabric. It is made of cotton: cotton is a plant, familiar and unthreatening to bees; wool is of an animal and potentially a sign of aggression to the bees. It is also the same shirt that I have worn for years. The bees may be different every season, but I hope that they recognize me through this shirt. It is rarely if ever washed and most certainly has had no perfumes or cologne near it. I did make a tremendous mistake one early season. It was a bit chilly out when I went to check on the bees and wore a polar fleece jacket instead of the usual white oxford. The bees initially just checked out the jacket, but as the first guard bees landed on it their barbed feet got tangled in the fine hooked fabric. They let out some kind of bee alert, and when more came out to check on their sisters, they too got stuck in the fleece. In a few minutes I was covered with angry stuck bees, trying to sting me, attempting to release themselves, calling for more assistance. I dropped what I was doing quickly, ran through the pasture, trying to remove the pullover as I tumbled down the hill to the house, my arms and neck being stung repeatedly. The white button-down has sufficed since.

With the tools and garb assembled, I head out to the bee yard. I was told early on to site the hives in the sunniest spot I could. The first couple of years I placed the hives where I thought they looked right: at the end of a suitable grass path through the garden. The sun didn't hit that spot until midmorning and the bees never got a good start. Since I learned to locate the bees with more exposure, they have been happier. Bees are sensitive to temperature: they only forage when the temperature reaches an acceptable mark inside the hive (in the nineties, Fahrenheit), and the queen only lays eggs when the warmth is adequate. A few degrees here and there can mean the difference between bees making honey and bees relaxing and waiting for the sun to hit the hive.

It is the beginning of spring, the start of the growing season. All the boxes are cleaned and lined up, the outer covers are leaning next to the boxes on one side, the inner covers leaning on the opposite side. On the ground to the side of each hive box are the individual boxes of bees that will go into that hive in front of it. I only walk on the back side of the bee boxes; the openings where the bees come and go is on the opposite side, where I never walk. I was instructed that it annoys the bees, but I think it is more than that. It reminds me of being taught as a small child to only walk up to the altar in church and then turn and return to the nave—to never walk behind the altar. God would not strike you down if you did wander around the altar, but you knew that it was just wrong. Beehives are the same way. The front is for the bees, the rear for the beekeeper. Order is important.

When all these steps are prepared, then I begin to install the bees. The sides of the bee boxes are made of a tight metal screen. Through that screen you can see the bees, hundreds of them. They are not flying errantly around their smallish confinement, but rather are clumped solid. It is difficult to discern that these are in fact bees. They look like a large brown mass with the edges moving constantly, not a series of individuals. The mass of bees is hung from the top of the box, never touching the bottom of the wooden crate. They resemble an oversized ornate chandelier, hung in a tiny dollhouse room of a diorama. If you move the box to the left or right, the mass of bees moves as well, but with a bit of a drag, swaying in a drunk fashion, trying to right themselves back to their preferred position.

They are clumped together around the queen. As her survival is their survival, it is imperative that she live through the travel until she can take up residence in the hive. Cool drafts, the warmth of the afternoon sun, sudden movements— nothing comes near her; she is protected by her army of worker bees a dozen thick around her.

The queen is not loose in the box amid her subjects but rather is sequestered in a small wooden box. This small reliquary is made of the same cheap wood as the main bee box, covered in the same tight metal mesh, but one end is stoppered with a small cork, keeping the queen from leaving her confines until the hive is ready for her.

The top of the outer wooden box is stapled shut with a plank of thin wood, and underneath it lies a small metal can, a soup can sans label. In the can is a simple syrup of sugar water, a wet cloth in the small hole leaking out drops to feed the bees on their voyage. It looks like a Molotov cocktail, ready to light and throw toward the angry mobs. But no such violence will come from these bees.

The goal in the next few minutes is to install the bees and their queen into their new hive. Losing the queen would be the worst outcome. She is not designed for flight, but rather for slowly moving around the hive, laying eggs. The worker bees have the ability to create a new queen should something happen to their queen, but it would take three weeks. In those twenty-one days, many of the worker bees would come to the end of their lives, new bees would not be born and the strength of the hive would suffer.

The first task is to pry the staples off of the box lid that is holding the bees in, using the metal hive tool. Once the staples are removed, the lid is ready to be taken off. It is at this step that I stop and pause. I have done this many times, but I still get a kick out of it. I approach the act of getting the bees into the hive like I approach eating a really great chocolate bar (presently my favorite is a Scharffen Berger bittersweet). I know what the foil inside will look like, I know how the outer paper is folded, I can remember the smell of the bar and the feel of the bar and the way the back of the chocolate bar always has a bit of a swirl to it. Even though I know how the entire experience will go, I want to take my time, pull off the stiff outer paper, reveal the thin, wispy foil and then break off a corner of the bar. It is because I know the experience well that I can plan how I want to attack the chocolate bar to get the most enjoyment. Releasing the bees is the same for me. I know what will happen. I could rush through it to the finish, but it is great fun lingering.

Under the flat lid of the wooden bee box is the tin can. It takes up the full opening in the top of the box. It has to be removed before you are able to grab on to the handle attached to the queen's small box. As it is a tin can and it is level with the top of the wooden box it is very difficult to grasp with your thickly gloved fingers: the hive tool comes in handy to pry the rim of the can up.

The trick at this point is to pull up the can until it is entirely free of the box. Once it is out of the box, then the queen box can be quickly removed with the other hand. When the queen box is free, then I cover the hole with a flat piece of wood on the top of the bee box to seal it until the bees are needed. Now, the only challenge is that as soon as the can is removed, the bees will begin to fly out. Quickly.

There is an extra challenge that I mischievously forgot. The hundreds of bees are surrounding the queen in the bee box. It would be impossible to lift the queen's box out of the larger bee box while all the bees were grabbed on to each other, surrounding her. The solution is to untangle them from her so that she can be quickly removed. This is done is by slamming the bee box down quickly so that all the bees fall to the bottom of the box, confused and a bit angry, but having let go of the queen box. In this moment, the lid is removed, the can of sugar water removed, the queen box removed and then the buzzing bees resealed in their bee box. It is really quite exciting.

The fear is—actually, the only fear is—fear. Opening a box full of bees is not terribly difficult. It is like walking on an open train trestle over a ravine. The wooden trusses are large and ample to walk on. When the train tracks are on solid earth, I am calm and it is easy to walk along the tracks. I would never fall off. On an open train bridge, though, the fear overcomes me; I walk along the bridge, staring at the earth as it falls off deeper and deeper, my legs stiff and my feet leaden. I obsess over whether to turn back or to keep going. I am sure that I will fall through the gaps between the large wooden planks.

Working with bees is the same. Pulling a tin can out of a hole of a wooden box and then putting it back quickly is really quite simple. Throw in a few hundred or a few thousand annoyed bees, and it gets much more difficult. The exhilarating rush is achieved by overcoming your fear and skittishness. Then you are dancing down the bridge.

With luck, the bees have been kept mostly at bay within their screened box. The queen box has been removed and the few errant bees are so confused that they are not interested in you. The goal is to insert the queen into the new hive box without dropping her, stepping on her or entirely losing her. The cork on the end of the small confine is gently removed with the tip of the hive tool. She will have a tendency to move toward the opening, so work directly over the hive box. As I write this, I am reminded that the reason I can recommend

these things is because I have panicked while working with
bees and dropped queens, lost queens, even stepped on a
queen.

I try to wedge the queen box, with the queen still in it,
between the middle frames in the hive box. The frames will
keep the queen box from moving about, stuck right in the
center of the hive box, and will keep her from walking off
the side of the box and falling to the ground. The queen likes
the darkness of a sealed hive and will head down into the
darkness of the hive quickly.

Now for the best part. The queen is in her box, making her
way out of her confines. Her attendants are stuck in the bee
box, trying to find their errant queen. The bees need to be put
in the hive. The bees need to find their queen quickly before
she gets lost or gets chilled, if the spring afternoon is less than
cooperative. If the lid of the box were simply opened up, they
would certainly find her, but what is the fun in that?

The quickest way to get the bees to their queen is to shake
them out, covering the queen with thousands of bees. Pick
up the bee box, remove the wooden cover, exposing the round
hole where the tin can had been. The bees will immediately
begin to fly out. Turn the box upside down over the queen
and shake out as many bees as possible as fast as possible.
When the majority have fallen out into a big pile on the top
of the frames in the beehive, slam the box on the ground,
pushing all the remaining bees to the base, then invert and
pour them out as a confused pile of bees. It sounds a bit cruel
and forceful, but they recover quickly. Then there is this
moment: There you are, standing at the back of the hive,
an empty box in your hand, a large pile of bees covering
the queen, the bees slowly migrating down through the individual frames to begin their new life. The air is filled with
hundreds of bees flying around the hive, around you, land-

ing on you. It is spring at its best. The noise is not a simple buzz, but the sound of hundreds of bees buzzing all at once. It is glorious.

Once the bees trek down to the center of the hive and calm down, I replace the inner cover and the outer covers, and the colony is left to do its work. I take credit for the hive even though it is truly the bees that do all the work. The basic statistics for bees are incomprehensible to me: one hundred and fifty five trips to a flower to make a tablespoon of honey. I read this over often and cannot believe it. Is that even possible? I take for granted so much of my life that the idea of bees working so hard for such reward seems downright antiquated.

The rest of the bee season is generally anticlimactic after the original installation of the bees. I feed the bees additional sugar syrup to keep them alive until they can secure their own food source. I make simple syrup with 50 percent water and 50 percent sugar and fill a mason jar. I punch holes in the tin lid and place the inverted jar in a stand at the base of the hive. The sugar slowly drips onto the stand and into the hive, allowing the bees to access the vital sugar. I open the hive every few days to check on the bees, make sure the queen is laying eggs, look for any problems. In reality, I feel that the beekeeper is simply trying to gain a sense of purpose. I really have almost nothing to do with making honey. I collect no pollen, make no beeswax, fill no combs and yet I really want to take credit for the lovely haul a few weeks off. Opening the hive, pulling out a frame or two and doing a bit of inspection fills that need. It does little, I would say, except for the soul. The man who checks in on the hive is a beekeeper; the one who only collects the honey at the end of the season is a thief, a robber, a cad.

If the season goes well, the bees will perform a great deal of work to produce a sweet haul of honey. Weather has a large effect on the quantity of honey. A warm clear summer will feed the colony well, the queen will lay well for weeks and the hive will increase manyfold. With more workers comes more honey. If the spring is wet and damp, the result is a small work force with a correspondingly small bounty.

The first harvest is generally around June and produces light-colored honey; a subsequent harvest in the fall will yield heavier, darker honey. Experienced beekeepers are able to keep bees alive year-round, but mine die off when it gets cold. Since I enjoy ordering my four boxes of bees at the start of each season, and at $75 per box it's not prohibitively expensive, I've never investigated what causes my bees to perish around the first frost. Cold is the most likely explanation, along with the especially damp northwestern coastal air. It could even be varoa mites that invade the hive and slowly kill the bees—I really have no idea.

The official way to harvest honey involves adding small boxes of frames—*supers*—to the hive for the bees to fill with honey. When that box is full, another is added and the full unit is emptied of bees and the honey harvested and so on. I am simply not organized enough for this system, and it requires a greater variety of equipment at the ready than I have ever possessed. Instead, I have created a hybrid system of honey production and harvest.

On top of the main hive box I place another large box of frames. The frames on the base are separated from the frames on the top by a wire rack with thin spacing. The spacing is such that the worker bees can squeeze past, but the queen, with her longer thorax, cannot. The result is that she lays her eggs on the lower frames, which reserves the upper frames for honey production and storage.

When the upper frames are filled with honey, they can be

removed without taking any of the valuable eggs. I like to remove two or four frames at a time, maybe six out of the total ten frames in the upper box. The frames are quickly removed, the bees brushed aside and the heavy, honey-laden frames moved away from the beehives. A hot sunny day assures me that most of the bees will be out of the hive foraging, not in the hive to cause havoc as their honey is removed.

When I have a few frames safely away from the main hive, I take a dinner fork and scrape the thin layer of beeswax from the comb. The beeswax seals in the honey in its small hexagonal chamber. If the honey has been capped, it has been dried enough by the bees to be stored; if there is no capping, it is still full of moisture. Still tasty, but a bit wetter.

The honey is removed by spinning the frames filled with honey in a centrifuge. Although the name evokes university research labs, the centrifuge would be better described as an extractor. A large stainless steel cylinder, it holds two frames of honey vertically inside the chamber on a steel rack, spinning on a central axis. When the lid is closed, the frames are spun by a hand-cranked gear, whipping the honey out of the open-ended hexagonal cells to the side walls of the extractor. As the crank is well geared, it takes very little effort to gain a great deal of speed.

The honey flies against the side walls and slowly rolls down to the bottom of the extractor. When ample honey has collected, a side spigot is opened and beautiful golden honey flows out with great aplomb. Honey is thick, yet fluid. It flows, yet it flows with a certain reticence; with great formality. My prior experience with honey as a kid had always been the plastic honey bears containing a cup or two of honey, a small squirt on toast now and then. To see a gallon of honey flowing out of a two-inch valve is positively regal.

I strain the honey as it comes out of the extractor. Bits of wax from the cappings, bits of bees that got stuck in the process, are removed, making for a cleaner honey. Small bits of wax will remain in the honey, unlike in the commercial product found on supermarket shelves.

I continue to be amazed by honey and the bees that produce it. The sum total of labor that goes into the making of honey by the bees is incomprehensible to me. If so many bees make so many trips to so many flowers to make a single tablespoon, how can I even imagine how much work goes into five gallons of honey?

I am also confronted with spatial relationship issues with honey. A large frame from a beehive is nine inches by eighteen inches and an inch thick. It weighs a lot when filled with honey, maybe ten pounds. It feels like a large laptop computer. Bulky, but not like a carton of potatoes. When it is extracted, the honey flows down the sides of the metal extractor. When the frames have been spun dry, I look into the extractor and am generally disappointed. It looks like so little. The sides have a thickness to them, certainly, honey is puddling in the bottom, but it looks like a trifle. Then, as I wait a few minutes, the honey slowly collects on the bottom of the stainless can. I position a sieve and a large white plastic bucket, hopeful that I will need that large bucket. Then I open the valve and honey starts to flow out; a lot of honey. More so than seems possible.

The same feeling comes over me when I harvest corn or squash from the garden. When the vegetables are lying in the field, they look like a decent-volume crop, but never like when it is brought together in the barn. When a bin is filled with corn from the field it doesn't seem to match the volume of the rows in the garden. And yet with distance between each plant, the ears seem small and inconsequential. When placed one on top of another, they constitute real volume. Honey is the same. Each small hex cell is minute, a half inch by three-eighths by three-eighths, and might contain a quarter teaspoon of honey. Miraculously at harvest time the pail at the base of the honey extractor is filled with golden honey; the miracle of the loaves and fishes lives on.

Four

Fruit, Apples, Vinegar

In the center of this farm are fruit trees—an orchard, if you will. Oddly planned rows of trees, not quite straight, not quite parallel to the house, of a motley variety, my orchard makes me smile.

This orchard began when I first started to hack away at my blackberry forest, and continued as I bought bare-root fruit trees one by one at local nurseries and hardware stores. Occasionally I ordered a special tree by mail, something cheap with a grandiose description. I spent very little on the trees. Twenty dollars here, maybe thirty dollars there; a small price to pay for a tree. I would quickly plant them in the ground, expecting no fruit for many years. My hope was that these twenty-dollar expenditures would grow into something of value over time, much like a business investment, one that would hopefully be more successful than my foray into farmers' market retailing. Like a 401(k), fruit trees grow with compounded interest. The first year, nothing; the second, still nothing; maybe the third year the odd fruit here and there. And then they take off. The volume of fruit starts to increase dramatically after five or seven or nine years and the abundance continues for many years.

Looking back now, I realize with some amusement that I was predicting my future. I put little stock in financial institutions, have little time for IRAs, bonds and other esoteric financial concepts; I value earthly institutions, solid investments that I can see and touch: fruit trees. My vision was that when I am old and gray I will have very little cash in the bank; I never expect to be financially rich. But rather, I will have rows of fruit trees in their prime, producing lovely fruit. There I'll be at eighty, sitting in the log house, enjoying fresh apricots, peaches, cherries, persimmons and all the rest. For me, wealth is having these luxuries.

I also enjoy working on Kurtwood Farms' portfolio of trees. A quince that just isn't performing as I would like will be pulled this winter to be replaced with another variety; the present one is simply too small and flavorless. A cherry tree that was grazed by an errant goat is long since gone. I have a long-term approach to the persimmon, which is years from producing even after a decade in the ground. The yield is worth the wait, however, as a tree full of fresh persimmons brings greater joy than the simple cherries that bear within a couple of years.

The greatest long shot is a loquat tree. Planted a decade ago, it is just now beginning to take off. Although I have seen loquat trees fruiting in Seattle, it is likely that there simply is not the warmth for this tree to thrive in this location. Loquats thrive in more southerly climes, producing an exotic fruit similar to a lychee. I stick with my tree, pruning it and feeding it and keeping it watered in the dry summer months. I'm not sure if Warren Buffett would believe in this system, but for me it's as valid as any money market account, hedge fund or 401(k).

Above the house, kitchen and small orchard is the larger, main orchard. The area is flat, fully open to the sun and fenced in to keep the cows and sheep from nibbling on the leaves and breaking the overhanging branches; this orchard holds over 130 trees.

When I first bought the second parcel of land a decade ago,

I needed to figure out a use for the new acreage. I decided to plant apple trees, hoping to produce apples for hard apple cider down the line. It seemed perfect at the time; the climate is perfect for apples here. Kingston Black, Ashmead's Kernel, Cox's Orange Pippin, Roxberry Russet. Every bit of good land on this island has an old apple tree on it, planted decades prior and still producing great apples.

The schedule of growing apples and making cider appealed to me as well. Pruning in the winter, thinning in the spring and picking in the fall. A few weeks of intense work and a lot of breaks in between. It sounded very patrician, very noble: the pruning of trees in the cool chill of winter, picking the fruit of that labor months later.

I had also heard about a bit of federal legislation that made producing hard apple cider even more appealing. A Vermont senator, Patrick Leahy, had introduced a bill that would make hard apple cider exempt from any federal laws if it only contained apples and no other ingredients. Designed to protect the small cider makers of his home state, it could never be taken advantage of by big producers because of the strictness and it appealed to me entirely; freedom from the oversight of the government. Perfect.

I set about researching the varieties of trees needed to make cider, the nurseries growing such trees and the methods of making the cider. I ordered 130 trees, mostly Kingston Blacks, and waited for them to arrive. I was confident that I would persevere. I had spent months planning this orchard, this business, on paper. I had read the books, read the nursery catalogues, made plans for ways to produce and sell the cider. I had never put my hands in the soil. It was a most ungrounded project.

When the trees arrived, I laid them out, pruned them a bit and warmed up the brand-new tractor. I used my shiny green tractor to dig the many holes, its first real test. The planting of the trees gave the tractor a reason for being; a function. The soil was mediocre at best, and no soil at all could be found in some of the spots. I puttered on, digging hole after hole, planting the young whips. At last all the trees were planted, and staked and labeled with their variety.

The weather changed from the cool days of winter when the trees were planted to the much more hospitable warmth of spring. The days grew longer and my young trees budded out. Although the trees grew slowly at first, my books had told me they would put on a foot of growth the first year. I kept them watered and kept the weeds at bay. Every couple of days I would venture out to the upper pasture to check on them. Summer had arrived and they looked like trees. Like small, barely growing trees, but still there was hope.

And then one day I got to the first row of trees and realized that they looked a bit different than they had. All the leaves were missing; simply gone. The young, tender branches were also absent. I thought this was an isolated problem, until I began frantically running from tree to tree, realizing that most of the trees had been chewed on, their tender growth fodder for the deer of the island.

Over the course of the next few days almost all of the trees would be chewed to their small stems. I felt despair, anger toward the deer, and utter disbelief that my trees were essentially ruined and all my work for naught. I had not understood the damage that deer could inflict on young fruit trees, the height of which is ideal for young deer to feed upon. The leaves were perfect for them: tender, easy to access and far enough from my house to escape detection until the light of the morning when the deer would return to the woods. I had thought, naïvely, that the deer would ignore my fruit trees because I was a nice guy; because I had planted old French heirloom cider varieties to make into cider.

In my less-than-scientific approach, I believed that if I did good work—by reclaiming old tired land that had been disrespected by the prior stewards and planting trees—the animals of the kingdom would somehow be privy to that knowledge; that nature would allow good things to happen.

The deer debacle of the apple orchard quickly taught me my first lesson as a farmer: Nature is cruel. It is neither fair nor equitable. Animals die, the weather does not always cooperate and everyone is out for themselves. The deer did not care that I was planting apple trees. To them, food was available for them to eat and their only responsibility was to feed themselves and their young.

The deer destroyed most of the trees, but left a few here and there. The survivors continued to grow and branch out. The next fall, I placed another order with the fruit tree nursery and in the winter replaced the trees most unlikely to recover. This pattern continued, and, well, it continues to this day.

I began a series of projects aimed at restricting deer access to the orchard. All were successful on some level; none were completely successful. Small battery-operated motion sensors that turned on powerful sprinklers to spray the deer when they walked through the orchard was the most ridiculous project. Although the sprinklers did startle the deer, they learned quickly to simply walk to other trees that were just outside the radius of the spray.

A large, expansive fence surrounding the orchard proved difficult to erect, time-consuming to maintain, unsightly and impossible to keep free of weeds and brambles. One small breach and the deer would find their way in. At this point it seemed personal. One of us, either myself or the deer, was going to win. To get all the apples. To outwit the other. To be the master of this land. I was determined to win. At least on a good year, I was determined to win. Some years I was simply too discouraged to believe that I could triumph. Three or four years after the initial setback, I stopped walking past the orchard. Simply couldn't look at it. I denied it existed, walked another way to get to the sheep pastures beyond the apple orchard. I had pinned my hopes on this orchard, this business plan, and I had failed. Again.

Large fences, short fences, portable fences, all were tried. Oddly, benign neglect has been the most successful. There are two blocks of apple trees here. The first has one hundred trees, the second thirty. I concentrated on the large block and ignored the smaller. The smaller filled with blackberries, Scotch broom and tall grasses. The deer could not find the apple trees in the midst of these invasive plants. One day I gained the fortitude to take a machete to the block and see what had occurred in the preceding half decade. To my amazement, the trees were still there, and had grown though not exactly prospered, but they had found enough sunlight to persevere. I was thrilled. I spent a day hacking through the brush to find the trees. One stick looks very much like every other stick, so it had the feeling of looking for thin needles in a large haystack of nearly identical needles, but eventually they were all found. What made it possible was I knew how they had been planted. Not randomly, but in a laid-out grid, five deep and six across. I would sight the lines of the grid and then thrash about until I found a stray leaf that looked like an apple leaf and begin to excavate from there.

The small block was restored and has done well; a few trees have matured to produce apples. The majority are slowly growing thanks to an increase of sunlight and water after the removal of encroaching plants. A couple have been replaced.

The larger block has followed a similar pattern. Simply by

the volume of trees, the odd tree would be neglected by the deer and prosper. Once the tree obtained a height above the reach of the deer, it could escape the attention of the grazing deer. Many have been replaced, some more than once. If all of the trees would die or be badly damaged, I could move on, plow the ground and plant a nice bit of pasture for the cows. I have been kept on the hook, unwilling to give up on the trees that have done well, committed to replacing the trees that have been damaged. It is a long-term commitment, with an outcome expected of a full 130 cider apple trees mature and producing fruit. Potentially in my lifetime, but there is no certainty with apples.

There are enough trees producing in the large apple orchard on the upper pasture, together with a few producing trees in the smaller, mixed orchards near the log house and old trees planted decades ago on the property, to realize a large volume of apples in the late fall. When summer comes to a close, I go from tree to tree picking the apples, thinking little of their value as table fruit, but only of their juice. They are scrappy fruit—bruised, scabbed, small, bug-eaten—but they are tasty, juicy and full of sugars.

The apples are brought down to the kitchen bucket by bucket and piled on the back porch, waiting for a sunny, dry day to press the fruit. The large old wooden apple press is rolled out from the farm shed and rinsed of the spiders that make it their home over the winter.

With a friend's help, I rinse the apples of any errant dirt and begin to load them into the wooden hopper, as the more energetic of the pair mans the hand-cranked grinder. The whirling wooden spool with sharp knives pulverizes the apples into a slurry of skins and pulp and cores, juice flowing out all the while. Positioned below the grinder is a slatted wooden basket to hold the pulp as it flies out from the whirling blades.

The basket is lined with a loosely woven bag that will hold the pulp during the pressing, allowing the juice to pass through.

When full, the basket is slid out from under the grinder and placed beneath the large screw that will slowly wind down to press the apples. With a bit of muscle, the screw turns and the platen pushes down on the bundled apple pulp and the juice begins to flow freely into an awaiting bucket. It is miraculous. The juice is fresh and sweet and golden. It is alchemy, this transformation of knobby, warted fruit to golden, clear, sweet juice. To stand and look at the remaining apples piled on the concrete, the grinder chewing the apples into bits, and at the old, wooden, much-used and not the least bit hygienic press, and then to pick up the bucket of apple juice and fill my mouth with this juice: it doesn't add up. The juice is far greater than its parts.

My pressing partner and I will greedily drink as much fresh apple juice as possible, keeping in mind that the lion's share must be saved to be preserved. Part will be saved for vinegar and the rest for *apple redux*, which is made simply by boiling fresh apple juice. A large kettle is placed on the range and filled with as much apple juice as I can budget to the endeavor. The three uses of the juice—fresh, vinegar and redux—are all worthy. It is hard not to favor one over the other two. I want so much of each and yet there is a limited amount of apples to press; a finite volume of juice. My original goal of growing apples to make hard cider never panned out; the apples are now in demand for the new uses.

With luck, at least ten gallons of fresh juice are poured into the hefty caldron and the juice is brought to a boil. The juice will boil through the afternoon. If the apples were picked early, the weather will still be warm and the windows of the kitchen full open. If fall has already arrived, the kitchen will be sealed against the chill and the windowpanes will quickly fog over from the constant boiling; soon the sills will be puddled with water as it condenses on the cold glass and drips down.

The juice is kept on the stove for hours. Slowly the level will drop in the kettle, although the apple juice will appear to be essentially the same as when it came out of the press earlier that day. I keep an eye on it as it gets lower and lower, fearful that I will miss the point when it has reached the desired viscosity. Once the majority of the water in the apple juice has boiled off, what will remain are the sugars, the apple flavors and a deep caramel color. I pull a spoonful out from time to time and dribble it on a clean plate, letting it cool and observing the juice as it sets. At first it will simply run off the plate with little or no thickness. With time, however, the juice will stick to the plate, yet maintain a liquidity. The kettle is then shut off, the apple juice gently poured into half-gallon jars and stored away for the winter months when we are hungry for sweetness and the depth of flavor that the redux contains.

When the apple trees have long lost their leaves and there is no chance of leaving the windows open, I love to pour a generous serving of the redux on hot, steaming pancakes fresh from the pan. This syrup is our local version of maple syrup: brown, thick, sweet and of the land. A half gallon left on the kitchen counter is often picked up by a weekend cook and used to sweeten a pork braise, or mixed with apple cider vinegar for a taste of *agrodolce*—known to me as sweet 'n sour, from my years of eating mediocre Asian food.

The apple juice that is not boiled down for this winter syrup is destined to be transformed into apple cider vinegar, changing the sweet, light, simple summer beverage of fresh apple juice into a complex, acidic vinegar; preserved.

Off to the side in the kitchen are three large barrels. Made of French oak, they vary in size: three gallons, four gallons and fifteen gallons. Each is filled with vinegar. One, red wine vinegar; the second, apple cider vinegar; and the last, an attempt at apple "balsamic" vinegar.

Vinegar is essential. Acid is a most necessary part of cooking. Without acid, food is flat, simple and lacking depth. Ample salt and seasoning are always needed, but acid makes good food great. Inadequate-quality vinegar—store-bought vinegar—makes for less-than-fabulous cooking. We have collectively come to rely on commercially prepared vinegar, while vinegar is such a simple product to create.

Vinegar comes from alcohol. Alcohol is the by-product of the fermentation of a sugar-based liquid. Generally that sweet liquid is grape juice. That juice is fermented by yeast added to the sweet fruit juice. The yeasts eat the sugars and produces alcohol. Wine is created.

When that wine is given a vinegar culture—a *mother*—the alcohol is transformed to acid. The higher the alcohol level, the greater the acidity. The mother, the culture that is added, is a strange beast. It is thick, gelatinous and appears to be a living thing. I am fascinated by it. It isn't pretty, neither clean nor tidy. It is slimy, slippery and unclean-looking. It does, however, produce lovely results. I often pull a glob of mother from the barrel, place it in a canning jar and pass it off to someone who wants to start their own vinegar. My first mother came to the farm in this same way: a friend gave me a start.

I started barrels of vinegar because of one man. I never met him and he has recently passed away. Richard Olney, the editor in chief of the Time-Life *Good Cook* books during the late seventies, kept vinegar in barrels on the mantel of his fireplace in Provence. I was completely captivated by this and couldn't wait to try it myself. I now have such barrels some thirty years later. The mother lives on the bottom of the

casks, transforming the alcohol into acid. The bung that seals
the barrels is left ajar to allow fresh air to circulate. Unlike
wine making, in which the goal is to seal off the vessels, vinegar needs air to live. Sadly, fruit flies love this vinegar as
much as I. The constant struggle to keep them away from
the fruity juice makes for a challenge, the opening often kept
covered with a linen napkin, a towel, some screen.

When the apples have all been pressed, the press hosed
down and rolled back to the shed, the fruit juice that I manage to keep aside and not drink is poured into five-gallon glass
carboys. A bit of juice is set aside in a small glass and a packet
of fresh wine yeast is pitched into it. When the yeast has
proofed—shown that it is alive and bubbling—the yeast-juice
mixture is poured into the carboys, which have been filled not
quite full with sweet fresh apple juice. An air lock is attached
to keep stray strains of yeasts away and the large heavy glass
jug is stored away to allow the mixture to ferment for a few
weeks.

Slowly the juice will begin to bubble, in a couple of days it
will foment, a week later the juice will bubble rapidly. The air
lock will be active, bubble after bubble of air let off from inside
the glass jug. The apple juice will have begun to ferment.

Once the bubbles have ceased—the sugars in the sweet
cider have been fully eaten by the yeast—the hard cider is
drawn out of each carboy. The clear upper portions of the hard
cider are transferred with a siphon and a hose to the awaiting
barrel. The lees, the dredges, the dead yeast cells are left in
the bottom of the glass jug. If it is a new barrel, a mother is
brought in; if it is an active vinegar barrel, the mother is kept
on the bottom, always waiting for the new year's fresh hard
cider. In a few weeks it is ready once again, full of flavor, tasting of the apples of the cold fall, sharp with acid.

My newest project is to use this basic method, but to adapt

it in the manner of the Italian balsamic vinegar procedure. In that tradition, the juice from Trebbiano grapes is boiled down to concentrate, to make it sweeter. Once the juice is of a suitable sweetness, the yeast is pitched and the process continues as for a regular vinegar. In the case of balsamic vinegar, a complex process of transferring the vinegar from barrels to ever-smaller barrels of different woods over a period of many years further concentrates the flavors and the sugars. Paul Bertolli gives an excellent description in his book *Cooking by Hand*.

My interest lies in trying this process with apple juice. I have taken the fresh apple juice and reduced it by half through boiling, heightening the sweetness of the juice and leaving it a dark mahogany color. The yeast has been pitched and the juice fermented. The barrel is full with the mother making her transformation. Only time will tell of its success.

Red wine vinegar follows a more modern course in my kitchen. Few grapevines prosper on the farm, and yet red wine flows freely at this farm's table. As is often the case, it runs too freely. The bad bottle, the disappointing vintage, the glass filled when a half a glass would suffice—all contribute to the red wine vinegar barrel. Every night those extra bits, an ounce here, an ounce there, are poured into the cask. Every night the vinegar is topped up, kept full, ready for the next salad. The acids in the vinegar keep it all very healthy and nice. I must use those extra bits of wine. Wasting food is the greatest sin; all must be used.

I cherish these casks; the vinegar in them provides the punch to the food prepared in this kitchen. Without the needed acid, the salads would be flat and bland, the sauces simply sweet. The original goal was an orchard of apple trees for bubbly hard cider. I do not expect to ever meet this particular end, but the sweet apple redux poured on my morning pancakes and the tart apple cider vinegar are an ample goal, and one I value. As I walk across the upper pasture, I still often cringe at the uneven orchard: some trees tall and flourishing, filled with fruit, some struggling along and others continually nipped down by the deer. Each spring a carton of new apple whips, first-year starts, will arrive in the mail and the process will continue.

The journey of building hives and an orchard, of producing my own honey, cider and vinegar, has proved immensely enjoyable for me. Though both the beekeeping project and the birth of my orchard were relatively time-consuming, I was still working full-time in the city. These endeavors amounted to elaborate, delicious food-yielding hobbies, not viable business models. I never sold any honey or cider, I was more than happy enjoying it with friends. Down the line I would have to reconcile my love for producing food with a need to cover my expenses and earn a livelihood, but at the time I was content to revel in the wonders my land had produced.

Five

Sheep, Goats, Pastures and Grazing

Ah, sheep: the eternal symbol of the pasture. I always visualize rolling green pastures somewhere vaguely in England, with sheep spread out, grazing for as far as you can see. In the distance, they look calm and peaceful and without problems; living their peaceful, pastoral life.

And they are lovely creatures: simple, content and at peace.

Sheep are gateway animals. They are the first farm animals many, including myself, have, and are a smart way to get started as a farmer and to get a feel for animals. My first two animals here were a ewe and a ram that friends gave me. They believed that they were going to raise sheep and realized quickly that they would stick with raising children and sent the sheep over to me. I really didn't want them. I was looking for pigs and hadn't been able to find any. But I did have a fenced area and figured putting sheep there was a good start. I put little thought into it. I had no idea what sheep ate or what I would have to do to keep them alive.

I had fenced a large area, probably an acre in size in anticipation of the pigs that would not arrive for years later. The sheep could live in this paddock. There was a bit of grass in it, but of very low quality. Early on a visitor came to my place and I gave him a tour. I knew that he had some experience in horticulture, working as a landscape architect in the Bay Area. When we came to the paddock in question I noted that the grass was in the process of going to seed, its stalks high and a seed head about to form. With feigned authority, I explained that this was *"timothy grass."* I had no idea what timothy grass was or what it looked like and was basing my assessment entirely on a passing comment by a friend of mine who said he fed his horses timothy grass. It sounded of high quality. The landscape architect in question gently took me aside and whispered, "Actually, Kurt, it is not timothy grass, but rather feather grass, with almost no nutritional value whatsoever; you might consider seeding some pasture grasses." I felt a bit taken aback, and thankfully the sheep chewed it down and somehow found some merit in it.

For water, I ran a series of hoses from the houses to this far pen. Twelve acres is small in comparison to most commercial farms, but when water is needed on one end of the property and the only water connection is on the other end, it is a formidable task to connect the two far points. I went to the hardware store and picked up two seventy-five-foot hoses. One hundred and fifty feet had to be adequate to reach the far sheep. Two more drives to the hardware store, two large armfuls of plastic hoses, a sizable addition to my credit card, and the sheep had water.

Surprisingly, the sheep lived. Poor-quality food, little or no shelter from the sun except the shade provided by the odd tree on the edge of the property and intermittent ignorant attention by myself, all led to a surprisingly good outcome. The ram succeeded in breeding the old ewe. Come spring after that first year, the ewe gave birth to twins.

There is nothing like a young animal to inspire, or maybe to cloud the judgment of, a young farmer-to-be. Baby lambs, much like baby goats, calves, and piglets, are supremely endearing. They reek of innocence and goodness. Fresh-faced, bright-eyed and with an intoxicating optimism, they drew me in. I wanted more, more sheep, so that I could have more baby lambs. I am reminded at this point of Michael Pollan's *The Botany of Desire*. The central premise of his mind-altering book is the idea that the most brilliant species, both plant and animal, create ways to use humans for their continued existence. Tomatoes are guaranteed existence with little or no chance of extinction because they "convinced" us to love them, to plant them the world over. The animal, the plant, that does not have this persuasion will be ignored, extinct, dead. I now think of most agricultural animals this way after reading Pollan's book years ago.

Unlike their young, sheep are not particularly endearing. Large, loud, less than bright, smelly, needing to be sheared yearly, they have little in the asset column. And then once a year, generally on a sunny, fine spring morning, they produce one, two, three lovely lambs. Suddenly the other 364 days of loud, loutish behavior on the part of the sheep is forgotten as we pick up the baby lambs.

I fell for it entirely. That one ewe with her twins became two, which became four and so on. Originally I fell for the cuteness of the baby lambs, the way they bounce unbelievably higher than their bodies, their nonstop playfulness with the other lambs. Months later I realized that the time of cute had expired. Not yet a year old, these lambs had less lamb, more sheep to them.

As these lambs' intended function was not just to be cute and bounce across the pastures, but rather to provide meat for the farm, I called the butcher out to slaughter the lambs. He quickly dealt their death and handed me the carcass of meat. Having little sense of the preciousness of lamb, I threw a barbecue party. We roasted two lovely, large lambs on a spit: four hind legs, a couple dozen chops and four fore shanks. Turned on a spit over a small fire, basted with rosemary and fat, the meat cooked splendidly: juicy, rare on the interior, charred on the exterior and tremendously tender throughout. I loved it. Everyone there loved it. I needed more lambs; I had eaten my year's supply in an afternoon.

And so I had learned that sheep have two enduring reasons for remaining on this planet: the cute factor of lambs and the superb meat that follows a few months later. In my world, sheep have a place at the table; they will not go the way of the dodo bird, the homing pigeon.

The first animals that people generally acquire are not sheep but goats. In my opinion, this is a poor choice. I hear from many people who think they will move out of the city, quit their jobs, buy a few goats and make goat cheese. I try to react with an enthusiasm that matches theirs. They seem to believe that they are the first to come up with the plan to make goat cheese and leave their jobs in the city. Thankfully, I was too timid to announce my plans to anyone all those many years ago.

Goats really are beautiful animals, very clean and tidy and full of personality. Goat cheese is especially tasty and reeks of the French countryside. Little rounds of white cheese, often with some ash or a few flower petals or cracked pepper—it's a lovely pastoral daydream. But the reality of keeping goats is much different. They are beautiful and full of personality, but also can be quite pesky. They have an uncanny ability to outwit any fence, gate or confinement. If they just escaped and wandered around with their sweet demeanor it might work, but their wily intelligence leads them right to the best tree or your favorite plant and they nip it down to the ground. Quickly. Effortlessly. Silently. If you are lucky they will stay on your property and only wreak havoc on your favorite trees. If you aren't so lucky, your neighbor's favorite trees will fall victim to your cute goats as well.

I think they plan it out. Spending their afternoons chewing their cuds and looking over their fence, getting a sense of which plants you really care about. Watching you prune and water and fawn over a beautiful specimen that is close to blooming, something that would break your heart if it were to be eaten.

When they get a chance to jump a fence or squeeze through a space in between fence boards, they head directly for that predetermined tree. Their goal is not nourishment, but rather to inflict punishment upon you. They want you to know that they are in charge, that you are merely there to assist them in their life on your farm.

Beneath the hooves of sheep, goats and certainly cows lies the breadbasket of the farm: the pasture. Pasture is simply grass, the lawn that the ruminants eat for sustenance. When I look at the bulk of a thousand-pound cow or a hundred-and-fifty-pound sheep or goat, all those bones and flesh and hide, I'm awed that they are the product of daily grass nibbling. The lawn deserves respect.

Following the north road of the farm up the hill, through a bit of woods, one comes out onto the upper pasture. A canopy of large trees darkens the north road; it is an intimate space. And then the trees end and all is open; the full, expansive pasture stands before you. It is dark green from years of being fertilized by cow manure, the grass nibbled flat and even by the large selective tongues of the cows grazing. The pasture is not flat, but rather rolls in large hills. Not perfect land, but it is the pasture that I have to work with, and years of maintaining it have improved it greatly.

Dotting the pastures are a few large trees that I felt were worth saving when I cleared the land. Mountain ash, madrona, Himalayan birch, Pacific Coast dogwoods. Because of these trees, some solitary, some in groups, the pasture looks

unlike a customary pasture at a dairy farm. Most dairy farms
are located on flat land, river-bottom land, down in the valley.
My pastures are on the highest point of the island, no rivers
run through them, no mountains rise up from the sides; so
trees remain. If a pasture is designed to maximize grazing
and to facilitate ease of tractoring, trees are quickly removed.
It is slower and more difficult to drive the tractor around the
trees and between the small groves of birches. I prefer a bit
of visual beauty over the loss of efficiency, and the cows enjoy
the shade from the trees as well.

Pastures contain a variety of grasses and legumes among
lesser weeds and other plants. Grasses in pasture are generally perennial, spread by rhizomes. Grasses make up the bulk
of the pasture; legumes, which are of the pea family, a much
smaller percentage.

The grasses have long roots: the rhizomes. Although grasses
can also spread through seeds, in a pasture setting it is rare
to ever let the grass go to seed. The pasture fills in through
the spreading of the roots. They grow underground for a few
inches out from the crown of the plant and then emerge from
the soil as more grass. Over time, the grass becomes a solid
mass of roots and crowns and the green blades above the
surface.

The crowns of the grasses contain the sugars: the energy
of the plants. The act of the sun hitting the green grass is
photosynthesis: the energy of the sun converted to sugars in
the crown of the plant. This energy, this sugar, is what gives
the plant the ability to grow. Ideally the plant has large roots,
a healthy crown and an equally large top of grass. The plant
would be balanced at this point. When the top of the plant is
cut, or chewed down by an animal, then the crown must spend
part of its stored energy that was captured from the sun to
regrow.

The more grass that needs to be replaced, the more energy that needs to be expended. In order to replace that energy, the plant needs green grass for photosynthesis. If it has all been chewed down, then the time to capture the requisite energy is longer. If the grass is still long, then the crown can quickly recover from the loss of grass.

This basic concept of the regrowth of grass is paramount to understanding how to manage pastures. The quantity of land available is generally fixed; that is, it is very difficult to gain more pastureland. Land is expensive, in short supply, and more likely than not in use and not available. Better management of pastureland, in effect, gives the small farmer more food for his animals.

The result is the basic concept of rotational grazing. Not new, not revolutionary, but still rather difficult to accomplish well, despite its wide use. I fail miserably most of the time.

Rotational grazing takes this basic concept of grass and leverages it to the benefit of the pasture. If the grass is kept long it will quickly rebound from grazing. If the grass is kept short, it will be very slow to rebound from grazing. The trick is to feed the animals without letting them graze the grass too far to the crown. Easier said than done.

The method that has been developed is to only allow the animals to graze when the grass is of adequate height. The minimum height is generally two inches tall. Less than that and the animals have overgrazed the pasture. When they have grazed down to two inches, then they must be quickly removed from that pasture until the grass has regrown to adequate length.

What has made this possible in the last couple of decades is the invention of flexible, movable and inexpensive fencing. What now exist are portable electric fences and wires that can be moved often, quickly, and still manage to confine large or small animals. These fences are relatively lightweight and manageable. Paddocks can be defined, the grass within grazed and then the paddock left to regrow, while the animals are moved to another quickly defined paddock.

The procedure is thus: the large pasture is divided into individual paddocks with the flexible fencing. Each paddock contains the amount of pasture that the animals on the farm can eat in one day without overgrazing. At the end of every day, the animals are moved to the next paddock. Ideally, when they are at the last paddock, the first paddock in the rotation is ready for the animals to return to.

If the paddocks have not recovered by the time that the herd comes back around, then the animals are returned to a "sacrifice" area. In this smallish paddock, the animals will live chewing the grass to the nubbins while they are fed hay or other feed. Only when the other paddocks return to ample height will the animals be returned to pasture. Depending on the climate, this time frame could be all the months of fall and winter when the grass is not growing at all, or it could be simply an additional day while the fast-growing summer grass catches up.

The result of this rotational grazing system is that the animals take the best of the pasture and leave it in a state healthy enough to quickly regrow. If the animals are left on pasture continuously, then they will graze the pasture to the ground and it will take weeks or months to recover rather than days or weeks.

For the past ten years I have read about rotational grazing, most notably in Joel Salatin's *Salad Bar Beef*, the most complete book on the subject. I understand how it works. I embrace the concept. I took a class from the local county extension office. I get it. And yet, I never seem to do it well.

The fine details are in order. Pasture is needed: real pasture. Not lousy grass on even worse soil, but pasture that can grow grass. The most heartening part of Salatin's book is his description of the history of his family's place, Polyface Farm. When his father bought the farm in Swoope, Virginia, in 1961 and began to set up portable fences, they used fence posts set in old tires filled with concrete, as the ground was too rocky and compacted to hold a portable fence post. Now, decades later, Salatin's pastures are deep, rich and loamy, with a fence post easily tapped in. My pastures are closer to the tire-concrete years than the rich-loamy years.

Without vibrant pastures, the animals are relegated to the sacrifice paddock for most all of the year while you wait for the scrubby grasses to grow. If they're confined to a small paddock, the animals' manure quickly piles up. For reasons of health, the manure must be removed daily. Emotionally, keeping animals in a small paddock is difficult. Here are the animals that you care for, both literally and figuratively. They are living in a paddock of bare earth, pockmarked by manure, and yet feet away is a large pasture. A pasture unable to support them year-round, but nonetheless, a pasture. The temptation is always there to open the gates and let them graze free.

I am too soft to corral my animals in a sacrifice area. I have taken a different approach: a lazy man's rotational grazing. The pastures here are not valley, nor river bottom, nor sandy loam. They are the result of years of misuse and bad bulldozing. Although they improve every year, they cannot support the use that I demand of them.

My compromise is to feed the cows and the sheep on the pasture, regardless of its condition. Twice daily I carry flakes of hay out to the upper pasture to the waiting cows. I choose a destination for the hay based on the neediest ground, and there the hay is dropped and the cows are fed. As they chomp their way through the bundle of hay, they leave the woody stems and parts that they find unpalatable. As they feed, they also leave behind their manure.

Day by day the animals are moved around the pasture, their manure and hay fertilizing it. The areas with the direst need get the most attention; the more vibrant sections, less.

In this way the pastures have a chance to become pastures and not remain weedy dirt lots. The grass remains overgrazed in this system. After the animals have consumed the hay, they begin to nibble down on the surrounding grasses. But little by little the fertility increases. As the cows lay down the manure as they graze, the crows, wild geese and chickens follow, pecking out the grain that the cows have not digested, spreading the cow pies over the pasture so that they can be easily broken down by the soil.

A system of rotational grazing has gradually been implemented here at this farm. Large sections of pasture are roped off to prevent the cows from grazing, allowing the grass to recover. With time and luck, a classic system of rotational grazing will be fully operational.

Time, as it relates to soil fertility, works in years and decades, not days and months. Taking on the task of improving my soil, I began to see myself less as an owner and more as a steward of the land. During my initial period working the pasture, I was still a part-time farmer and I couldn't afford to pour huge amounts of cash into improving my land. Thus, I had to make decisions that benefited my soil and my pocketbook. I've never used fertilizer on my farm—partially because I don't believe in it, and partially because I don't want to pay for it. Rotational grazing appealed to me immediately because it's a method—in fact, the only method I know of—to increase the tilth of the soil without chemical fertilizer. By allowing my farm's avian residents to eat the grains that the cows fail to digest, I get the most value for the feed I buy. The manure that gets spread on the pasture is highly valuable, and even more so because I don't have to labor to move it around. It's easy to discuss the "best" environmental practices in farming without a budget, but implementing good systems with limited funds is a challenge, and rotational grazing is one of the best solutions.

Like the rest of the farm, my system of rotational grazing is a work in progress. I would love to achieve a fully operational classic system of rotational grazing, but getting there has meant a healthy dose of experimentation. Thankfully, I'm not in it alone, as the animals play an important role in the cycle and, like me, put up with a setup that isn't quite perfect. Except for the occasional escapee goat, everyone seems content with the way things are working out.

Six

Cows

In my attempt to find a viable niche for this farm, I have tried many different animals, a variety of crops and on dreary winter days even contemplated going back to work in the city. Eventually, the beast of choice for this farm became the cow. It all started with a cow I named Dinah. I wanted a cow for a variety of reasons. One was that I wanted this small, until this point unprofitable business to be thought of as a real farm. Sheep and goats always had an air of hobby farm to them. Cows were farm. If I had a cow, then I would be a farmer.

When Dinah first arrived one fall day five years ago, I was excited. I had looked for a cow for months, made many calls and had finally found one for sale. I borrowed a truck and trailer to transport her to the farm. I had driven off the island to a small farm that raised replacement Jersey cows for small dairies. As I loaded Dinah into the back of my friend's horse trailer, Jackie, the woman who sold her to me, began to cry. Driving down her long driveway headed to the ferry back to Vashon, I could see her in the rearview mirror, watching sadly from the middle of her driveway. I was convinced I had found the perfect cow.

With the addition of a cow to the farm, things changed quickly. Growing vegetables is a time-intensive business for a few months of the year with virtually no work needing doing in the off-season. Sheep, goats and pigs take some daily attention, but really very little work for most of the year once the fences, sheds and watering system are installed. With vegetables or small animals, it is still fairly easy to leave the farm for a few days here and there; easy enough to get a neighbor or friend to stop by and feed the pigs, check in on the sheep. Dairy cows are different. They need daily attention. Raising them requires a commitment.

Suddenly, with Dinah backing out of that horse trailer that day and walking into her new paddock at this farm, I had a revelation. I no longer had a hobby, I had a job. I couldn't back out—you can't just return a cow for a refund, and I couldn't afford to just write off the $1,500 I had paid for Dinah. Even if I decided I didn't want Dinah, what was I going to do with her? You can't drop a cow at the pound like an unloved mutt, or let it die during the winter like my bees. She was stuck here, and so was I. I was a full-time farmer.

Discovering what I had become was one of the most terrifying and gratifying moments of my life. I could no longer retreat to a city job if I stumbled, and I didn't want to. I wanted to be that ninety-five-year-old waking up every morning to milk his cows. After years and years of yearning for a farmer's life, it was mine. I would have to make my twelve acres work. There was no turning back. My vegetable business had failed. Matt was gone. My payouts from the sale of the restaurant were keeping the electricity on for the time being, but they were dwindling. I was dirty and tired and I loved it. I was happy.

Dairy cows in this country are generally of two breeds: Holsteins and Jerseys. Holsteins are the most familiar-looking dairy cows: black, with large white spots. Holsteins comprise approximately ninety percent of America's herds and Jerseys the remainder. A few other breeds—Guernseys, Milking Shorthorns and Brown Swiss—round out the list of dairy cows. I wanted a Jersey cow because they are beautiful: small, light brown and with a streak of curiosity running through them.

Holsteins are known for large quantities of milk and low butterfat, Jerseys for low volume and high butterfat. Jerseys are ideal for my small homestead dairy: smaller in size, more gentle and producing high-quality rich, creamy milk.

Dinah was a gorgeous cow, with a distinct, inquisitive personality. She was larger than most Jerseys, and I was immediately smitten with her. This was going to be wonderful.

I milked my first cow by hand for the first three months after I got her. I thought doing so would be a lovely old-fashioned experience. Buy a cow and a pail, and in a few minutes you'll have the best milk you have ever tasted. So I bought the cow, got her back to the farm and then realized I actually had to milk her. Myself. Twice a day, every day, and starting immediately. When you buy a cow and drive her home, you have to milk her within a few hours, at the most, of her arrival. Once she arrives, she is ready to be milked, and milked completely, immediately. I was not ready.

I brought her back to the farm and all was set. I would begin milking her that afternoon and the milk would begin to flow. As I look back now, I am grateful that I didn't know what was to come, for fear of never starting out.

Dinah had a large frame to her and was strong of spirit, yet had unusually small teats. Never having seen a cow before, I did not notice her teat deficiency while checking her out prior to purchasing her. The process of hand milking her should have taken a few minutes, twenty minutes at most. In Dinah's case it was closer to an hour, forty-five minutes with a bit of luck. Each squeeze of her substandard teats yielded a tablespoon of milk, with the eventual goal of nearly five gallons a day. Do the math: five gallons is equal to 1,280 tablespoons. That is a considerable amount of hand milking.

For the first few days I stuck with it, spending a considerable part of every day sitting on a small child's stool I'd bought at the local thrift store, attempting to squeeze out the full volume of milk that Dinah kept in those pendulous udders. The basic premise of milking is that the cow believes her phantom calf is drinking the milk she is producing. As long as there is a demand for that milk, whether for an actual calf or by draining the udders manually, then the cow will continue producing milk. If the milk is not fully captured daily, then the cow begins to slow down her production of milk. As the gestation period of cows is nine months and there is considerable difficulty in breeding cows, there is a great deal of pressure in keeping the cow in question thinking that all of her milk is needed. I feared that she would dry up, a process in which she would begin to limit the amount of milk produced. That fear kept me sitting on that miniature stool day after day attempting to drain her udders completely.

Physically this was difficult. My hands ached, my wrists hurt, my pride was wounded. I couldn't quit. Fall moved to winter, and there I was sitting on the stool, as it poured down rain outside, surrounded by mud and manure, milking this cow. I had to do something to fix this. I called around to people who might have milking equipment, hoping to find an affordable used vacuum pump and milk can that I could use. I had the option of ordering a new piece of equipment from a supplier, but the price was exorbitant, and the shipping fees compounded the problem. After three months I finally found a small used vacuum pump and a milking can on the island and got everything set up for daily milkings. My daily task went from a two-hour ordeal to a pleasant ten-minute chore.

As miserable as this initial period was, it did yield one big positive. I spent two hours a day with a cow. Previously I had never even spent five minutes with a cow. I had seen the odd cow in a field while driving through the countryside as a child, but never such an intimate experience with a cow as I did in those first few weeks. That experience has done me well. I bonded with Dinah, for lack of a better term. I know her, know how she moves, how much room she needs, how to converse with her, and by extension cows in general. I sang to her every day as well. A bizarre variation of "Someone's in the Kitchen with Dinah." My voice would trail off after I sang out, "Someone's in the kitchen I know-o-o-o. . . ." Unable to remember any other words to the song, I filled in any spaces with whatever came to me. After an hour of my singing a nonsensical ditty, both Dinah and I were exhausted. I want to believe that the singing calmed her down, made her more open to some kind of relationship with me; that we were friends. Truly amazing, where the mind goes when you're locked in a small, damp, cold shed with a cow for two hours a day.

Now each morning of the year, after the alarm goes off, I slip on some muddy jeans, an old fleece jacket, a pair of muck boots, and head off from the house to bring the cows down to the milking parlor for the morning milking. The ritual begins with the assembly of the milking equipment that has air-dried overnight, the making of a bucket of warm soapy water to clean the teats of the cows and the leading of the cows into the milking parlor. It is a ritual that is practiced every day, even if it is Christmas, or pouring down rain, or even if I am terribly hung over, with no interest in ever seeing a cow again in my life.

These rituals have become my practice—in the Buddhist sense of the word. Every day of my life, I do the same thing, in exactly the same way. I do not need to think of what I am doing. It has become a part of my body: placing the milk can on the right side of the cow, reaching over with my left hand to grab the vacuum line, reaching back with my right hand to grab the inflation plugs from the shelf where they always sit and so on. I don't expect to achieve enlightenment through cow milking, but the daily practice is important to me. That time of the morning and the late afternoon is the short piece of the day when my mind can wander without care. No part of my brain is needed to operate the equipment. Occasionally Jorge will have mistakenly moved a simple object, a pail, a towel, a soap dispenser, and I am completely helpless; suddenly I need to think of what I am doing instead of simply acting out the daily ritual.

Part of milking is waiting for the machine to pump out all the milk from the cow. It takes just a few minutes, maybe five. The ancient 1940s vacuum pump is whizzing away in the attic, the pulsator pumping on and off, and I can stand at the door and look out onto the farm, or sit and watch the cows chomp the buckets of grain before them. This is my time to plan for the coming day, reflect on yesterday's experiences and watch the sun break through the trees to the east of the farm. No one is ever with me in the milking parlor in the morning, it's just me and the cows. The dairy building with the radio playing is too far away for me to hear what is being said, although I can usually make out the theme music played by NPR, which lets me know that I am running late, or that I managed to get started on time that morning. This is my favorite time of the day.

I have milked the cows here with a machine since that first brief hand-milking period, with the exception of the odd power outage. While I do have friends who milk by hand and wouldn't do it any other way, I am partial to machine milk-

ing and think it is a superior method because hand milking is
physically very difficult. Cows have four teats. Seems basic,
but if you have never reached down there, there are four. You
have two hands. So, you have to move from front teats to back
teats or near teats and then far teats. The process is repetitive and uses only a few muscles in the hand. By the time you
finish milking out a cow, you will feel it. I have a friend who
grew up on a farm in Mexico and as a young child milked a
small herd of cows every morning and night. To this day the
muscles in his hands are damaged. I have no interest in permanent hand damage.

I also worry about the cleanliness of milking into a pail.
The bucket is partially open on top to allow the milk to enter
the pail. Above the pail are the teats, the udder and the belly
of the cow. She has been potentially sitting in dirt or manure
prior to coming into the milking parlor and although the teats
and udder are first cleaned, dirt can fall into the pail from the
belly or sides of the cow.

Here is how a basic small milking machine operates:
The parts are a vacuum pump, a bucket and lid, a pulsator,
inflations and the milk lines and vacuum lines that link the
vacuum, the cow and the bucket. The inflations are rubber
sleeves that slip over the cow's teats. The milk flows down
the inflations and into the milk lines to the bucket. The milk
is sucked out of the teats of the cow by the vacuum pump.
Although the original inventors thought that they could
just run a constant suction to extract the milk, the incessant vacuum quickly damaged the teats. The vacuum has to
be interrupted, mirroring the action of the calf's mouth on
the teat. The result is a pulsator, a mechanical contraption
that breaks the constant vacuum pressure into a series of
vacuum cycles. This gives the teat a chance to rest in between

moments of pressure. The level of vacuum determines the number of cycles per minute.

Essential to the good hygiene of the milk is the proper cleaning of the cow's teats and udder. In the hours preceding milking she may have slept in manure, which is loaded with coliforms. The teats, and especially the tip of the teats where the milk will be drawn, are generally cleaned with a towel soaked with an iodine-based cleanser. The use of iodine has the ability to disinfect the teat better than other methods. A clean dry towel finishes the procedure by assuring that no moisture runs down the udder and into the inflation, potentially contaminating the milk.

The bucket milker is assembled, linking the can with the vacuum line, then the inflations with the cow's teats. Small plugs temporarily fill the ends of the inflations to create a complete vacuum. Without a completely tight system, a vacuum will not be achieved and the inflations will fall off the teats of the cow. If there is a leak somewhere in the system, either from a loose hose or a misaligned lid gasket, the vacuum can never be achieved. It is a frustrating moment, as you rush about trying to find the leak before the cow runs out of the grain that occupies her attention. With an unruly cow, quickly concern can turn to panic as the cow begins rustling about looking for more grain.

Acquiring my first cow—Dinah—gave me insight into the dairy business, something I knew nothing about beforehand.

The dairy business is by nature reluctant to change. Many young interns join small vegetable farms, bringing new blood into market farms every year. The cost of starting up a small intensive farm to sell vegetables at a farmers' market is relatively small in comparison to that of a dairy business. The need for large tracts of land for pasture,

cows, barns, milking equipment, along with a steep learning curve, make the entrants to dairy farms traditionally
the offspring of established dairymen and not new young
farmers with fresh ideas. Tradition has a real value in preserving the old ways, but it robs the industry of a chance for
much-needed innovation.

The dairy business is also a rather closed community. The
investment needed to start a dairy is huge, even for a small
one-hundred-head dairy. Finding a quantity of land needed to
pasture a large herd is even harder today near a metropolitan
area. Often the dairies have been passed down from father to
son for generations, frequently in families of Dutch origin. As
a result, an outsider showing up to buy a cow is immediately
suspect and not necessarily given access.

There is always a steady stream of young female calves,
and the dairies are constantly retiring their older or less-
productive cows. The new heifers (female calves) will replace
the retired cows. If the dairy is trying to expand, they will
retire fewer cows and keep all of their young heifers; if they
are trying to decrease their herd, then they will retire more
of their older cows.

The smart dairyman therefore has cows to shed constantly:
the older and less-productive cows and often the sick and dis-
eased cows. He has to swap them to maintain or increase his
productivity and quality standard of milk. If he sends the cow
to auction, he will get a low price from someone looking to
slaughter the cow to produce ground beef.

Along comes the young idealistic farmer-to-be, making a
call to an established dairyman and looking for a cow to buy.
The dairyman sees his opportunity to unload an unwanted
cow at a higher-than-auction price. He may be honest and fair
and sell a cow that can't produce enough to earn a spot on the
high-productivity farm and which would be a perfectly good

cow for a small farm, or he may take advantage of the situation and sell as a viable milker a cow that actually belongs in the slaughterhouse. The problem is that to the inexperienced eye, cows all tend to look the same. In fact, some cows are really pretty, endearingly pretty.

With that said, a bit of cajoling, some homework on bovine health and a great deal of luck can lead to finding a great cow.

Another way to buy a cow is from a farm that only breeds and raises heifers and is not in the dairy business. These farms have an interest to sell only healthy cows; their reputation is at stake. They will still sell the best animals to known buyers and more likely sell the newer farmer their lesser quality, but are more likely to be honest about it.

The last and worst way to buy a dairy cow is at a livestock auction. In fact, it shouldn't even qualify as a way to purchase a cow. Auctions are dumping grounds for sick animals. There is no reason for a healthy dairy cow to be at a livestock auction. Possible reasons for auctioning are an inability to breed, extreme mastitis that cannot be cured, very low productivity that doesn't cover eating expenses, lameness or chronic disease. A young male cow in good health could be for sale at an auction, but never a female.

The basic idea of a dairy is this: a female cow is bred and nine months later she will produce a calf. Two months before she is to calve, her body will begin producing milk in anticipation of her offspring. When she calves, her body is ready with milk to feed her calf, sustaining the young animal through its early months. In a dairy, the young calf is taken from the mother to be raised with other young calves and the mother will continue to produce milk, her body thinking that a calf is drinking the milk as the udder is emptied every day by the dairy. Slowly, over the course of a year of twice-daily milking, the cow's production of milk diminishes, mirroring the smaller needs of a phantom calf that would have moved on to grazing grass for nourishment.

The offspring of a cow is either a female *heifer* or a male *bull calf*. Their gender seals their fate. Females will be raised to live out their life on the farm, producing milk. Males will most likely be castrated—at which point they will be known as steers and raised to be slaughtered for meat. On a large dairy farm, the heifers will often be sent to heifer replacement farms, only to return to a dairy farm after they are bred. Bull calves are sent immediately off the farm to be raised for veal or "baby beef." On the small homestead farm, the animals would most likely stay on the farm regardless of their gender, the heifers to raise for milking, the bull calves to raise for eventual slaughter.

Although cows generally have one offspring at a time, occasionally they produce twins. If both of the young calves are of the same gender, all is well. But if one of the calves is a female and one a male, a unique situation is likely. Before birth, the young calves exchange hormones through their blood. The female gains male hormones and is born infertile. She can therefore never be bred and will never produce milk for the dairy. She is termed a *freemartin* and is raised for meat.

Although I consider the cows, their calves and the pastures to be the dairy, in reality "the dairy" refers to the physical structure on the farm. The dairy is actually three buildings: the milk room, the milking parlor and the milk processing plant—the creamery. I wish that I could say I named them, but no, these are their official names, shared in dairies all across the nation. Tradition abounds in an industry as slow to change as dairying.

My milking parlor is a simple building: a concrete floor, a

galvanized tin roof, the same metal sheets on the walls and
a large sliding metal door on the south side. It is the room
where the cows come in one at a time and are hooked up to
the milking machine. In the simple loft above is the vacuum
pump that runs the milking machine; down through the ceiling run the vacuum lines. An old metal stanchion hangs from
the ceiling. As a cow puts her head through the steel doughnut in an effort to get at the grain kept in a box on the floor,
the stanchion is locked around her neck, giving the cow plenty
of room to move around, but not so much that she can back
out and exit her confinement.

The building's design is intentionally simple, to meet its
function: it must be hosed out twice a day after the cows come
through. The concrete slab is often wet during the day, but
always clean. It is the first step toward keeping the milk
healthy and clean. As soon as the milking of the cows is completed, the milk is removed from this room and taken to the
milk room a few feet away. In the milk room, the milk is
stored, well away from animals and their manure.

The milk room is in a larger building, more complete and
finished than the milking parlor. The milk room's functions
are to cool the milk, store the milk and house the milking
equipment. Constructed of insulated concrete, it is a big box,
smooth on the interior walls and floors, more rustic on the
exterior. The ceiling is tongue-and-groove pine, whitewashed,
which always reminds me of milk, like milk paint.

When I am in this room I think that a dairy is a simple
place: simple, straightforward and wholesome. Then if I turn
from the three walls of sinks and counters and the bulk refrigeration tank and look at the fourth wall I see the large shelf
standing there. On it are stacks of paperwork, inspection
reports from the state Department of Agriculture, large bind-

ers of federal milk protocol, bound reports of a farm plan written by the county soil conservation corps, state dairy nutrient
management plans, veterinarian results and bills, artificial
insemination receipts, private milk-testing lab results, state
milk-testing lab results and an assortment of gallon jugs of
cleaners, disinfectants, acid cleaners, iodine and bleaches. I
find it more comforting to look in a different direction and
keep that wall to my back.

Sharing a common wall with the milk room is the creamery.
Here the milk is transformed from the cool liquid stored in the
bulk refrigeration tank to the finished cheeses aging in the
coolers lining the walls. In the center of this room stands the
squat, heavy steel cheese vat, its sturdy thick, short legs supporting the round, shiny vat. The vat is connected to the walls
of the creamery by hoses bringing cold water to the heating
elements and the robust electric cord to power the machine.
Slinky cords connect temperature controls from the milk to
the recording device attached to the back wall. It all looks
very high-tech, albeit with a 1950s conception of technology.
There are no digital readouts, no bells, no whistles. Atop the
vat is a bulky, oversized motor to stir the milk, with the same
midcentury design.

Within sight of the dairy buildings are the cow paddocks,
the small courtyards where the cows wait to be milked each
morning and afternoon. Cows are miraculous creatures. Quiet
yet stubborn, strong yet gentle, they have personalities far
richer than their initial appearance suggests.

I love cows. Large, solid, beautifully color-toned, gentle, the
symbol of a dairy, a farm. I think it is their size, their bulk,
that gives them their cultural value, their heft. Pigs, certainly
lovely; chickens certainly tasty; but cows, they command your
attention. They are larger than we are, yet we control them,

rule over them. I feel important and valid standing next to my cows. I am strong; I am powerful.

And then they knock into me, refusing to go where I want them to go, and I swing back to reality: they are in charge.

Cows are a mystery. Are they bright and in control or acting instinctually with little thought? When I got my first dog, very soon after I moved to the farm, a friend of mine who'd had dogs for years explained that same mystery with canines. He said that from the day you get your dog to the day he dies, you will never know if he is dumber than a stick or if he is brilliant, spending his life pretending to be simple in order to convince you to feed him well and take care of his every need. Cows, to me, exhibit that same perpetual mystery.

Cows are not the brightest animals on the pasture but they possess a certain sort of intelligence. They carry a calf for nine months, give birth, spend a small amount of time with their calf before it is separated from them and then they continue producing milk as if they still had their calf. So far it appears as though the farmer is in charge. But then the cow slowly begins to produce less milk. A little less each day, not really noticeably, but still less. Ideally the cow would be quickly bred again to keep her carrying a calf nearly all year long.

The cows here have managed to get me to order in the finest alfalfa hay from Eastern Washington, store it in a beautiful French barn to keep it from getting wet and then carry it out to the field for them. They do need to go through the whole milk production lifestyle, but it still seems likely they got the better end of this deal. But then again, they might have no idea what is going on. I may never know.

Throughout the winter, and parts of the early spring and late fall, I feed the cows hay, specifically alfalfa. In those cooler months, the pasture grasses cease to grow and

I must supplement the cows' diet with hay brought onto the farm.

On the eastern side of the state of Washington are vast hayfields. The land is cheap, flat and fertile. Thousands of acres are devoted to hay production, for feeding horses, dairy cows and curiously for export to Japan for racehorses. Hay is one of the largest crops of this state, and yet nearly all of it is grown in Eastern Washington. Western Washington is simply too wet, with inadequate heat in the summer to dry the cut grasses before they can be baled for storage.

Every few weeks a large hay truck pulls up to the farm to unload five or six or seven tons of premium alfalfa hay. It is not certified organic hay. The haulers that I hire do not grow the hay, they simply broker the transaction and transport it over the mountains and stack it in my barn. Therefore, it is difficult to know exactly how it is grown. I must assume that growing this much needed hay consumes great quantities of water, fertilizers and diesel fuel to run the tractors that cut, gather and bale the alfalfa. After it is baled, then it is driven across the state, over the mountain pass and into my county and eventually onto the ferryboat, across the water and down the long driveway to the farm. There are few haulers willing to come out to the island. It is costly, annoying and time-consuming. I have never found one that can source organic hay and so I must settle for the hay that I can get.

Situations like mine with hay make the discussion on raising food "green" interesting. Sitting at my kitchen table, reading the current books on farms and food and health, I sincerely desire to supply the best-quality feed for my animals. When the reality of actually trucking that feed onto the island comes into the equation, it becomes more difficult. Quickly my ideals fall and I end up contributing to the chemical fertiliz-

ing of Eastern Washington farmland. Few choices in farming
practice are black-and-white.

The daily life of a cow is very predictable. I love to watch
my cows as they go about their prescribed pattern. They are
awake far earlier than I, but not necessarily active till sun-
rise. On those rare days when I am awake as the sun rises, I
find the gals in the pasture, sitting, looking content and very
much awake. They have yet to stand up, might be relaxing,
chewing their cud a bit. They take their time getting going
in the morning. I think of the cows at this time of day as my
paperweights, precious trinkets I remember seeing at fancy
homes. Made of glass or brass or ceramic, those paperweights
were heavy, squat on the base and always had a bit of faded
green felt on the bottom to protect the smooth polished end
tables where they resided. My paperweights are more substantial, yet I imagine that I have positioned them just so, to
hold down the *tapis vert* of the pasture.

Once the day has begun, they stand up and begin grazing.
The grazing is haphazard at this point, a light search for food,
knowing that the bulk of their feeding will happen in the next
hours. Once I finally show up on the scene, they focus on me
and getting to the milking parlor for grain.

The cows appear to have no interest in getting milked, but
the grain appeals to them. They love the sweetness of the corn
and oats and barley. It is easy to eat and there is no competition from neighboring cows to keep them from their allotment
of grain. There is pressure on their udders from the milk that
has been produced and if they were not milked for a number
of hours or days they would feel that increasing pressure. On
a twice-daily milking schedule I don't sense that they have
any desire to rid their bodies of their milk, but rather simply
the desire to get a bucket of grain while the milking machine
whirls above them in the attic.

After the cows are milked and returned to pasture, either they are left there to graze for the day or fed hay if the grass is low and there is not enough for them to eat. For the following three or four hours they will work their way through the pasture, munching on this clump or that clump, generally keeping in a herd, with the odd cow going out on her own for some time, but always returning. Seemingly on cue, the cows will be satiated, their many stomachs full, and they will one by one drop their bulky bodies to the ground, all within a few feet of each other, and begin to chew their collective cuds.

The basic idea of a ruminant is thus: all ruminants, whether cows, sheep or goats, have four stomachs. The first two, the rumen and the reticulum, perform the function of predigesting the feed that the cows eat. The grass goes from one stomach to the other and then is brought back to the mouth of the cow to be chewed and returned to the stomachs and so on. The cows spend a few hours filling the rumen with grass and water and then sit down, relax in the grass and pass the digesta back and forth. It is a picture of contentment; they have found their own bovine enlightenment. Another hour or two later and they are up again, the morning's grazing having passed on to the later stomachs: the abomasum and the omasum. It is a well-designed system and generally functions smoothly.

The most common hiccup in the cow digestive track is bloat. Occasionally, and usually in the springtime when the young grass is plentiful, the digesta in the rumen will create bubbles that it cannot break. The bubbles of fermenting grass become too tight to break and expand. The cow cannot break the bubbles and the rumen will start to expand. It is a remarkable sight. On the left side of the cow near the spine, the hide will be taut and huge, the entire upper side sticking out from the normal silhouette of the cow. To a light tap, it feels like a finely tuned drum, full of pressure and stretched to the limits of the skin. Although amazing to watch, bloat also has the ability to kill the cow. The pressure can increase and press against the cow's lungs, making it difficult to breathe. The cow will also stop chewing its cud and stop eating, a sure sign of bloat.

I first encountered bloat on the morning of a party here at the farm. Guests were sure to arrive a few hours later and I had a cow that I was certain, in my nervous state, would die.

The death of an animal, especially a favored dairy cow, would have been sad to say the least, but the sight of a large dead cow carcass in the front paddock in clear sight of everyone arriving that afternoon was not one that I could live with.

Eliminating dead animals is an issue. Jersey cows, the breed that I have, are the smallest bovines and yet still weigh eight hundred pounds minimum, an average Holstein cow twice that. A half ton of dead weight, with legs extended, is not an easy load to move. My small tractor could never pick up such a weight and the sheer bulk of the animal could not fit in the tractor's bucket attachment. In addition to the inability to move such a carcass, digging a hole to accommodate a large animal is an equal or greater challenge. Digging a pit six, seven, eight feet deep and eight to ten feet across would take hours if it could be done. The only option is to hire a small excavator or backhoe operator to dig a pit and lift the dead cow into it. An easy and quick task for a hydraulic-equipped tool, but getting the operator and equipment to the farm on a Sunday afternoon with hours to spare before a party was not how I wanted to spend the afternoon.

I called the woman who sold me my first cow for advice. She

was shocked that I didn't have a supply of anti-bloat medicine at the ready, but gave an alternative therapy: butter. I took a pound or two of butter and balled it up in my hand, lump by lump, and forced it into the mouth of the unappreciative cow. With one arm around her head to steady her and the other as deep into her mouth as possible, I attempted, rather unsuccessfully, to get her to swallow the butter. Most ended up on the ground or spit at me, but I was successful at getting some down her gullet.

The logic is that the fat of the butter will break the surface tension of the bubbles in the rumen, relieving the stomach of its air. After a few stressful minutes of walking the cow around the paddock, the pressure on the side of the beast had subsided. I really wanted a loud, eventful belch to signal the success of my butter-stuffing, but had to be content with a slow relaxing of the stomach and the health of my much-beloved cow.

Since then I have come to rely on vegetable oil instead of butter as a bloat reliever. A liquid is much more likely to be swallowed by a cow than lumps of yellow butter. Even if the vegetable oil didn't work as well, it's hard for me to give up great butter. The cows deserve it, but a less precious alternative is welcome.

The curing of bloat early in the history of my dairy was a small success that I was most thankful for. I wish I could say that all illnesses associated with cows could be so smoothly remedied. Immediately after the farm became a licensed grade "A" producer of raw milk, the state Department of Agriculture came to the farm and took a milk sample to send off to the state laboratory for its monthly testing. I had never tested the milk and had no idea what to expect, but needed a positive result to maintain my licensing status.

A day later the inspector called me to let me know that

there was a problem. The somatic cell count of the milk was extremely high and well over the legal limit. The somatic cell count—SCC—is an indication of the number of leukocytes or white blood cells present in the milk and therefore in the udder. A low number indicates that there is a low level of infection; a high number indicates a high degree of infection. My count was so high that there was an obvious and serious problem.

Mastitis is the most common disease that can plague a cow. It is a bacterial infection of the udder. The udder becomes infected when bacteria enters the teat canal. After a cow is milked, warm milk remains in the teat while the cow walks back to pasture, the ground potentially littered with manure and other contaminants. The low-hanging teats touch the manure and bacteria are drawn up into the udder. The result is an unhealthy cow, lower-quality milk and a potential spread of mastitis throughout the herd. There are a few ways to diagnose mastitis. The first is through a strip cup, a small stainless steel mug with a stainless screened lid. The teats are milked by hand before the milking equipment is attached into the strip cup, with a small amount of milk from each teat hitting the screen. Any milk contaminated with bacteria will show up as small clumps on the screen.

The infections can also be transmitted from cow to cow through the milking equipment, with the potential for widespread disease through the milking herd. Milk that is highly infected, although not considered dangerous to humans, is of poor quality. The milk can be clotty or stringy and cannot produce good cheese.

I took samples of the two cows that I had at the time and sent them off to a lab to be tested individually. The milk sample that is taken monthly from every dairy is a sample of the milk that is mixed together before being sent to a pro-

cessing plant or before bottling. It is the responsibility of the
dairy to check the health of each individual cow. In the case
of a dairy such as mine, only two cows were in the sample and
therefore the health of one cow can skew the results dramatically. One very sick cow in a one-hundred-cow herd would
alter the collective sample, but not as dramatically.

The milk sample came back from the lab with the results
that one cow was heavily infected and that she was infected
with *Staphylococcus aureus*. I had no idea what that meant
until the state inspector explained it to me. *Staphylococcus
aureus* is a bacterium that is extremely difficult to control. In
humans it is known as methicillin-resistant *Staphylococcus
aureus*, or MRSA. As it happens, the procedure for treating
humans and cows is different. Humans get a bit more attention; cows are immediately slaughtered, considered impossible and unwise to treat. I made a few calls to dairymen and
my veterinarian, who confirmed that it wasn't worth it. The
price of the antibiotics and the possibility that they might not
be effective was too high relative to the chance of my other
cow catching the infection as well.

I removed the cow, Bella, to a separate paddock. I now
had a problem that I did not anticipate and had to deal with
quickly. I didn't have the equipment to transport her either
to a slaughterhouse or to a livestock auction. I didn't even
have the equipment to kill her and bury her on the property.
She still had value as meat and I didn't want to lose that.
The only good part of this story is that the udders of a cow
are very separate from the body of the cow and that each
of the four quarters of the udder are separate from each
other. Even though the udder was infected with the *Staphylococcus aureus*, the meat on her was considered healthy to
eat. I couldn't waste that meat; to do so would have been

even sadder, more wasteful and more disrespectful of the
animal.

An adult dairy cow such as Bella weighs in the neighborhood of a thousand pounds. The block and tackle that I use
to hoist animals to skin, gut, hang and butcher can hold five
hundred, maybe six hundred pounds comfortably, but I didn't
have the confidence to raise a full-grown cow with this simple rope block and tackle. I knew I'd have to call in a mobile
butcher.

We scheduled the day for him to come and slaughter Bella.
It was in three weeks, so I had to look at her every day knowing that she was to be slaughtered, but could do nothing about
it. I kept her apart from the other cows, which only seemed to
make it worse. Not sure if it made it worse for me or worse for
her or both, but it just had a bad feeling to it.

By this point in the history of the farm and my evolution as
a farmer, I had slaughtered a few animals myself and had no
problem with it. It could be sad, certainly, but it was never an
emotional moment, rather one of necessity. This was different. I had spent every morning and every afternoon with this
cow, chatting with her while milking, through the heat of the
summer and the rain of the winter. She was a good producer
of milk and had a lovely disposition. Even now, two years
later, I have fond memories of this cow. When the day arrived,
I saw the butcher's large panel truck pull into the driveway
and begin its drive past the paddocks and toward the house.
Two young men hopped out of the cab with long rubber aprons
on. Each had a rifle in hand, ready to go to work. To them it
was business, another call at another farm on a busy schedule, hoping to make the early boat off the island and back
home at the end of their day.

I went to the paddock where I had left Bella to graze, put a rope harness over her head and led her through the gate and toward the large gravel parking area in front of the house. I chatted to her briefly, thanking her for her life and apologizing for her early demise. I handed the rope lead of the halter to the main butcher, mumbled that I had to head off for errands, told him I would speak with his boss back at the butcher shop later and thanked him. I hopped in my truck and drove out the driveway toward town. I wanted to make sure that I was well enough away before they made their shot, before she fell to the gravel beneath her. I didn't want to look like a complete fool; a sad romantic trying to be a farmer and failing in the eyes of the two seasoned, tattoo-adorned butchers with their rifles and chew and logging boots. I walked crisply but quickly and drove in the same manner. I tried to look like I was a busy man, with many errands to take care of in town, instead of an emotional mess too fragile to watch my favorite cow slaughtered in front of my eyes.

There was a chance that I could have saved Bella with a lot of antibiotics and a lot of luck, but not likely. Slaughtering her was the most logical alternative, and yet it was a decision I didn't want to have to make. My impression of a small dairy was of wholesome goodness: gentle creatures casually walking into the milking parlor to effortlessly produce gallons of pure, white, clean milk. Premature death wasn't part of the equation. I learned quickly that dairy cows come and go, sometimes not in the best circumstances.

An important component of producing milk on a dairy is breeding the cows. The cows come into lactation in anticipation of their having an offspring to feed. If they do not get pregnant, then they do not produce milk; they are dry. A dry cow is still a lovely cow, good for that pastoral look. Such cows do, however, eat hay or pasture every day and, without any milk being produced, they are a financial drain on the farm.

Every day that they are not in milk, they are a loss on the
balance sheet. The easiest time to breed a cow—for her to be
"bred back"—is two to three months after she has calved. At
that time she is at the peak of her milk production for the lactation cycle and she is most fertile. In a commercial dairy this
is when she would be bred. The tricky thing is to determine
if she is in heat.

When I had just started the dairy, I had just the one cow:
Dinah. She had just calved at the farm I'd bought her from
and she and I were just getting used to each other. I had no
idea how to breed her, when or how it was all going to work.
She was producing lots of milk, so it was really the last thing
I was worried about. People had warned me that it would be
difficult to tell when she came into heat, as she was all alone.
I really didn't understand what they meant.

One February morning a few months after I had gotten
her, I learned more about cows than I needed to, very quickly.
The morning milking had been finished, Dinah had been fed
and I was headed up the pasture to attend to the sheep, to
get them watered and fed. It was foggy and cold, a mist in
the air. There are some mornings when I love this job, it all
makes sense, I feel good about what I do and I am confident
that I will continue. This was not such a morning. Wet, cold,
trudging up the hill to the sheep, I was looking forward to
quickly finishing and heading back to the kitchen to have a
hot breakfast and move on to other tasks for the day, preferably inside.

I was lost in my own thoughts, walking across the field,
when I realized, all too late, that Dinah was immediately
behind me. She rose up on her two back legs and proceeded,
or at least attempted, to mount me from behind. Her body
knocked me to the wet ground, one of her front hooves smack-
ing me from behind, cracking my ribs in the process.

She immediately moved on, walking off in search of some more grass to graze, thinking little of her action. I stayed on the ground for a moment, unable to move, rethinking this farming thing completely in the couple of minutes I lay in the grass. At that moment, the farm had had no glamour: a single cow grazing weedy pastures, a few sheep and a couple of pigs. I had no choice but to get myself up and head down the hill to the house, wondering what I'd been thinking. Why had I given up my comfortable city job?

Dinah had most definitely cracked my ribs. For three weeks I had to roll out of bed in the morning; it was too painful to lift my body up. Carrying anything of weight was very difficult. If I could have found a way to get rid of the one cow at the time, I would have. It was too humiliating to quit and I had no idea how to do it. Buying a cow had taken a lot of time and effort. I didn't have a horse trailer or a truck that could pull a trailer. Even if I could have moved her, I had spent too much money on Dinah to drop her off at the auction and get a minuscule recoup of my investment. Dinah and I would have to learn to love each other.

What I didn't understand was that Dinah had acted like all cows do in heat. I had always thought that the male mounts the female. Period. During my brief experience with a farm as a kid (two weeks at horse camp a couple of summers), I remember seeing the male horses mounting the females in the pasture near the arena where we would ride. The horses on top were obviously males, the ones on the bottom obviously not males. I thought I understood the nature of the world.

Cows in heat will either mount or be mounted. Therein lies the confusion. The one that is in heat will show "standing heat." That is to say, she will allow the other female not only to attempt to mount her, but additionally will stand there deferentially while she does. The cow in heat will also attempt to mount, unsuccessfully, other cows who are not in heat. In the case of Dinah, alone in the field, she attempted to mount me. She was in heat, I was not. I ended up, however, in a great deal of pain.

With a small herd of cows, luckily, I am now out of the heat equation. They mount each other as they each go through their cycles. Watching closely and with a bit of experience, I can tell who is coming into heat. I look for a "slick," a long drip of thick mucus trailing out of the end of the cow. The slick is the best indicator of a cow in heat. There are times when this slick is tremendously long and full. After a cow has walked around the field for a while, her tail switching away at flies, the slick will be tossed onto her back to dry in the sun.

This is the time when a cow should be bred. In a perfect world, a bull would be available and she would be most receptive. In a more difficult and modern time, artificial insemination is a suitable alternative. The benefits of a bull are that cows have a much better understanding of when they are receptive to breeding than I could ever gain through observation. A bull, if he is functioning properly, will do the deed without question at the right time, and do it right. The downside of bulls is that they are bulls: full of vigor and dangerously strong. They are needed for a few minutes a year, and yet eat heartily every day and can potentially cause serious problems. The chance of gaining a top-quality bull is slight; most available bulls of are of lesser quality.

The upside of artificial insemination (AI) is that the best bull in the nation can be bred with your cow for relatively low cost. The AI providers are national companies that have access to the finest bull semen nationwide. Although this is for the most part a positive thing, there is also something disturbing about most all of the dairy cows in America being the progeny of a handful of bulls. They are collectively getting more and more inbred every year. The sperm facilitators also are creating calves that are bred for production and high fat, and not necessarily for the qualities that are important to a small homestead farm like long life, temperament and ease of handling.

When I see a cow come into heat I make a note of it on the milk room calendar. It is very difficult to schedule the AI breeder to come out in time for the actual heat cycle. It is possible, but a great deal of planning is needed. The other alternative is to manipulate the heat cycle. Cows will come into heat every twenty-two days. After ten to twelve days they can be given a hormone, Estrumate, that will bring them into heat in a very specific time frame, generally seventy two hours after an injection. This gives me a very tight window to schedule a breeder.

I sometimes fear that AI from such a limited pool is manipulative of nature. Should we be using artificial insemination and hormone shots to breed cows to the same bulls that are used to breed most of the other cows around the nation? The diversity of dairy cows will diminish as more and more are bred from the same genetic pool. Presently I am working on using a bull from a neighbor's farm, but the logistics are tricky. Transporting a docile dairy cow isn't easy, but it's nothing compared to moving a thousand-pound bull with a mean streak.

After the cows have been bred and the nine-month gestation period has elapsed, it is time to get ready for the cow to calve. The calendar in the milk room here is a special one. The cow breeders give them away with advertisements for their bull semen on each page. Each day has two notations printed on the date: one is the date twenty-two days forward when the cow should come into heat again after the present day, and the second notation is the target date nine months hence when a cow bred on the present day will calve. The photo at the top of the calendar for each month also depicts bizarre cow fantasy scenes: a perfect cow, groomed excessively, standing on a verdant piece of grass with an impeccable barn in the background and a caption at the base of the photo like: *Miss Sharpshooter April Sun, Grand Champion 2007.*

The calendar is covered with my marks, dates when the cows have come into heat, or when I think they have come into heat; the dates when I think they were successfully bred, or might have been bred, and when I think they will have their calves.

As with all mammals, when the cow is close to giving birth she will begin to produce milk in preparation for feeding her progeny. In a dairy cow, this is readily apparent. She will "bag up," meaning her udder, which had hung loosely for the past sixty days, will begin to fill out.

With my newfound knowledge, I love chatting with women about cows. It is my great entry into the private lives of mothers in my community. Generally we would have little common ground. Conversations thrive at the local coffee shop about mastitis, colostrum, switching from milking twice a day to once a day, ovarian cysts and other milk topics on which the thirty-something women love to compare notes with me. I have quickly learned, however, never to use the terms *bred back* or *bagged out* to describe females of the human race, though it's of course standard fare for the bovine crowd.

If a stall is available in the barn, or a paddock is empty, I will move a pregnant cow there to keep better track of her and so that she doesn't calve far from me. A common part of every animal husbandry book I have ever read is a series of drawings showing all the different ways a lamb or calf can get stuck in the birth canal of its mother. Then there is a long description of how to right that position, pulling this leg or pushing that leg and turning the body around and so on. The most pressing worry concerning a dairy cow, however, is not that there will be a breached birth, but rather that she will have milk fever.

Milk fever, or hypocalcaemia, is especially prevalent among Jersey cows. The basic idea is this: The mother produces milk to feed her calf. Once the calf is born it will begin to drink the milk from her. Her body needs to quickly jumpstart milk production immediately after she has birthed this animal and expelled its placenta. The calcium needed to produce this volume of milk needs to be able to come from the bones in her body. If she tries to draw it only from the food she is eating, she will not be able to produce enough with sufficient speed. The result is a dramatic loss of nutrients in her body.

The reaction comes very quickly to her. She will fall to the ground and not be able to get up again. In a few hours without help, she will be dead. The remedy is to inject calcium supplements intravenously in a controlled manner. Too much too fast will cause damage to the heart and even kill her by stopping her heartbeat. Too little and she will die from the milk fever itself.

I worry every time a cow has a calf. My third cow, Francesca, came down with milk fever. Of course, it happened on a Saturday afternoon when the regular large-animal veterinarian was off the island. I did manage to find another vet who agreed to make a farm call and administer the IV. The farm is located very close to the town of Vashon, a short drive from this vet's office. After making the call and chatting with the doctor, who assured me that she would head out, I began the wait for her to make the three-minute drive. After thirty minutes I started to panic, sure that my beloved cow would be dead before the vet arrived. She did show up close to an hour later, and after a long and slow IV drip of calcium solution the cow popped back up.

Luckily, milk fever is preventable. The preventive steps are intriguing and counterintuitive. I would think that feeding a cow about to calve with alfalfa hay, which has the highest concentration of calcium, would be the best idea. My logic goes that if she needs calcium, make sure there is plenty in the animal's food to cover the quick production of milk. On the contrary, if a cow is fed only alfalfa in the last few days, then she will rely on her diet to produce the calcium and not adapt her body to utilize the calcium in her bones.

Immediately before she calves—the night before or early that morning—I give her a large tube of calcium paste. A calcium gun looks like the caulking guns that that you buy at the local hardware store. I come around the head of the cow, and with one arm and my shoulder I steady her head, opening her mouth with that hand. With the other hand I stick the caulking gun in her mouth and quickly start pumping the handle, sending the white paste as deep into her throat as possible. As expected, she is not happy about this, but with luck a suitable proportion of the paste will go down her throat to be ingested. The remaining paste will invariably end up all over me as she tosses her head and spits it out, calcium flying through the air.

When I began this farm venture I had no idea how to do any kind of medical work. When I was growing up, my mother worked in a pediatrician's office and I would spend my weekends hanging out in the lab playing with the autoclave and the syringes—sans needles, of course. I never wanted to be a doctor, always felt too nervous around medical work. When I had blood drawn for tests I would invariably pass out, unable to deal with the sight of blood, or my blood, at least.

As I began to have livestock here at the farm, I needed a veterinarian. I am most fortunate to have access to a great one here on Vashon Island. Like many semirural communities across the country, this island has a lot of horse enthusiasts. Horses are finicky animals and need veterinary care often. Having a large-animal doctor nearby is a boon for me. Treating dairy cows and the odd sheep or pig is a welcome change for the vet and, as he is a mobile vet, farm calls are all he does. I had never seen or heard of a mobile vet before and was quite intrigued the first time Mark pulled up my driveway in his full-sized pickup truck. Fitted into the back of the bed is a large fiberglass box that spans the width of the bed. Inside the box, accessed by lids that open on either side, is a compact veterinarian's office. A small refrigerated compartment holds a variety of medicines, and small shelves and drawers hold the requisite syringes and ointments and salves. A tank of clean water with a pump guarantees an ability to keep the whole operation hygienic and tidy.

The relationship I have with Mark evolved in a way that I never expected. I thought it would be like going to my doctor. You make an appointment, you have the office call, he treats you, you pay him and you go on your way. Working with a mobile vet is a different procedure. I do make an appointment, he drives out to check on the animals, but then he gives me ideas about what is wrong with the animal in question and the pricing of different options. After years of coming out to the farm, he will now give me some medicine and syringes and tell me when to give them, where to give them and expects me to step up and administer the doses. Often now he will simply leave the medicine for me at his home

without ever even coming out to the farm after I call him
with an animal problem. I know now what specific medicine
I need for a variety of problems and how it is to be adminis-
tered. It has been a slow learning curve, not one that I had
expected in the least, but very rewarding.

The most frequently used skill I have had to acquire is giving a cow an injection. I had watched Mark take the syringe
and stab the cow in the ass quickly and precisely several times
before he left me a small bottle of medicine and a baggie of
syringes to administer the next few days' worth of medication,
but I really had no idea what I was doing.

The next morning I went out to the barn, brought the cow
in question into the milking parlor and fed her a bit of grain,
locking her in the stanchion to hold her in place. Although she
had been milked just an hour before, she happily took to the
uncharacteristic routine: more grain is always a pleasure to
the cows. And there I stood. The cow was chomping away at
the grain in the bucket in front of her, unaware of my apprehension. When she ran low on grain she lifted her head and
turned my way, silently requesting additional feed. I refilled
the grain buckets a couple of times before I opened the Ziploc
and reached into the small plastic baggie of the type generally reserved for a lunch sandwich, and pulled out a syringe. I
picked up the small bottle of medicine with the flat rubber top
where I expected a screw-on lid. I removed the plastic sleeve
that guarded the sharp needle of the syringe and pushed the
point into the rubber top, piercing it, the needle going into the
clear glass bottle. The needle was rather sharp, but I expected
it to pop in a bit easier. How was I going to get the needle
into the cow? I pulled back the plunger of the syringe, draw-
ing the liquid into the chamber, and withdrew the needle from
the bottle, slowly and deliberately. Then I held the syringe

vertical and pushed the plunger just a bit, until a bit of medicine squirted out the tip of the needle. I have no idea why I
did this, except that I had seen Julie London on *Emergency!*
do it in the emergency room on every episode. I also tapped
the syringe quickly with my finger, just like Julie. This made
me feel like I knew what I was doing. And then I stood there
again and stopped, with the loaded syringe held straight up,
the cow looking over at me for more grain.

I had no idea how much pressure it would take to get the
syringe into the cow's hide. It had been tough just getting the
needle into the small medicine bottle. Mark had mentioned
to me that one way to administer an injection was to take the
needle off and push just that in first, then, if no blood came
squirting out, attach the syringe cylinder and administer the
medicine. The needle seemed way too small for me to hold on
to and to jam into the cow, so I took my chances and hoped
that I wouldn't hit a vein. If I hit the vein, I would dose way
too fast and my cow would be dead in minutes, all on my first
attempt.

The longer I stood there in the milking parlor, the more
grain the cow ate, and I would have to stop and grab another
scoopful of the oats, then walk back to the other end of the
cow, pick up my syringe and try to get the nerve up again. I
finally tried a much larger scoop of grain in hopes of buying
myself a longer bit of time.

At last I mustered up the confidence to proceed. I grasped
the syringe in my fisted hand and jabbed it as hard as I could
into the thick hide on the side of her hip. It went in well—not
gracefully, but well. I had watched Mark enough to know that
the cow would move around a bit, quickly and with strength.
I stood back right away as she felt the needle hit, letting go of
the syringe in the process, and it stayed put, embedded in her
hide. When she calmed down a bit, I pushed the medication

into her and quickly pulled the needle out. With my newly
acquired confidence, I rubbed the area where I had poked my
cow, not really knowing what function this performed, but
thinking it seemed like the right thing to do. By this time she
was bored with her excessive second breakfast of the day and
was ready to return to the other cows in the paddock, thinking
little, I presume, of the entire experience.

The administering of an intravenous calcium solution into
the vein of a dying cow to save the cow from milk fever is one
procedure I have never done. It takes much more skill than an
intramuscular (IM) or subcutaneous (sub Q) shot. I get very
nervous when my cows are down, when they can't get up and
they need help quickly and proficiently. I look at injecting an
IV calcium solution as my final exam in the caring of cows,
and I hope to perform it one day.

One of my favorite bits of cow lore is the concept of *hardware disease*. The term is both perfect for what it describes
and highly cryptic. The basic idea is that as cows graze grass,
they eat very close to the ground. With their powerful lips,
they might try to ingest any item that is on the ground. If that
item is a rock or a stick, not a big deal; but metal, such as a
nail, is a much bigger deal. They would have to pass a nail
through their system with the risk of puncturing one of their
stomach chambers or their intestinal tract.

When I first began fencing my pastures, a friend came to
help who had experience fencing, from growing up working
on his family's farm. Part of stringing fences is to pound large
staples into the posts to hold up the woven wire. I tend to
be rather casual about most chores and downright sloppy at
times. He insisted on keeping track of each and every staple
to make sure that they were all accounted for. In the process
of hammering, staples tend to fly off from the post if they are
hit slightly off. The result is a heavy one-inch staple flying

into the grass. I wanted to move on and grab another one; my friend would make me grovel around on the grass until the errant staple was found. He knew cows would eventually find them and possibly ingest them. He had been raised right.

Beyond making sure you don't add metal to the cow fields, there is a strange additional precaution you can take. In all the livestock supply catalogues and often on the counter of feed stores are torpedo-shaped magnets. About two inches long, a half-inch around, with tapered ends, they are fed to cows and remain in their stomachs to catch errant metal objects.

Even though I have never fed one of my cows one of these magnets, I recently slaughtered an older dairy cow that I had bought from another farm. When I put the numerous large stomachs into the metal bucket of the tractor to haul them to the compost pile, I heard a clunk of a sound, and found that a bullet-shaped magnet had stuck to the side of the steel bucket. Attached to that magnet was a mishmash of small wires, brads and nails. I am still a bit confused how it all works, but I can confidently state that it is indeed a sound system for keeping those errant ferrous bits from lodging in the intestines of a cow. I do wonder why the ferrous bundle wouldn't pass as a whole, making the cow's experience that much worse, but I trust that this has worked for so many years that it has become a part of the bovine procedure.

Just when I thought I knew everything about cows, I learned one more crucial fact: they are tremendously sensitive to electricity.

Inside the milk room is a cooler that chills the milk from the temperature of the cow at ninety-eight degrees to the legal maximum of forty degrees. It is a large, powerful cooler that consumes a great deal of electricity. A few months ago I noticed that the cooler was blowing its internal circuit breakers and acting strangely. It appeared as though there was an electrical short.

The first morning of this unusual cooler activity, I led the first cow onto the walkway surrounding the dairy building. My dear cow Francesca immediately reacted as she placed her first two hooves onto the concrete, her trailing two hooves still on the wet winter soil.

The reaction was swift and dramatic. As her front two hooves hit the concrete she convulsed, her body writhing. She didn't make a sound, but quickly moved across the walkway to get off, as if her hooves were on fire. As I watched her in horror, I thought that she was having some sort of heart attack. I have no idea if dairy cows even have such afflictions, but that was the conclusion I jumped to. I took her in to be milked, thinking her behavior was odd, but she seemed to bounce back and I wanted to assume that it was behind her, never to show up again.

Then I brought the next cow through, passing by the milk room on the way to the milking parlor. Boo, an admittedly sensitive cow, headed onto the concrete slab to make her way to the milking parlor and had the same reaction.

My first thought was that there was an electrical problem in the concrete. I got on my hands and knees and felt all over the slab. I could feel nothing. I bent my head down low and tried licking the concrete, thinking my dry hand was not conductive enough. Although I was the only one at the farm at this hour, I still had the fear in the back of my mind that someone would pull up and see me crawling around with my palms flat to the floor, my tongue on the concrete, trying to feel something, anything.

It tasted like concrete. I couldn't reconcile the idea of electricity in concrete. Concrete is like dirt; it is of the earth. Copper conducts electricity. Aluminum, steel, tin, those kinds of things.

Still worried about my cows, I called a friend who does electrical work for me on the island. I was nervous about leaving the following message on his cell phone: "Jason, I think I have electricity coming through my concrete, can you come and check it out?"

To his credit, he agreed right away to come out to the farm. He pulled out his voltage meters and checked everything. As it happened, he did find a small amount of electrical charge—up to one volt in the metal gutters and metal roof—but was unable to find anything in the concrete.

After he made a few phone calls, he gave me insight into something called "stray voltage." Evidently, a large section of the standard electrical code is devoted to electrical work on dairy barns. As it happens, cows are deeply sensitive to electrical current. We did manage to solve the crisis in the milk room, but the problem worked itself out in a different way as well. In addition to being very sensitive to electrical current, cows are unable to forget anything. Cows are large, stubborn beasts; difficult to move, challenging to motivate to try any new path. The only part of their personality that makes moving them and milking them easy is their love of repetition and their excellent memory. They remember where the milking parlor is, what time they can go in and what their favorite route is.

Once Francesca and Boo realized that walking over the milk room slab on their way to the milking parlor was painful, they would never return there. They quickly found a safer, albeit longer, route to the milking parlor. No amount of pushing, shoving or coddling could get them to return to their old, painful path. The fact that the electrical problem has been solved was inconsequential to them; they had learned a new route and would stick to it, thank you very much.

Perhaps I enjoy cows because, like them, I'm a stubborn creature of habit. I began milking a single cow every morning five years ago, and I've never wanted to stop. Four cows at $1,500 each was a serious investment for this small farm, and one that I knew I had to figure out how to earn back. I didn't want to give up my glorious mornings with the cows, so I had to turn them into a viable business. My city life, with its security and compromises, was over. I was a farmer, and if I was going to stay one for long, I had to become a profitable one. I would become a dairy farmer.

Seven

Dairying

Keeping a cow is a lot of work. They eat a lot, they create a lot of manure and they're rather expensive to buy. Although nice enough and attractive, they won't thank you for feeding them and milking them twice daily. The rewards, therefore, center around the milk, in addition to the joys of working with cows.

Fresh cow milk is amazing. Full of fat, flavorful and sweet. When I was a child, my mother would often buy powdered milk during the tougher economic times of the early 1970s. I'm not sure that it was that much cheaper, but we bought it nonetheless. The irony that I now produce exceptional milk is not lost on me. The trick to making acceptable powdered milk was to remember to mix up a new batch at night in antici- pation of finishing off the older batch the next day. A jug of freshly made reconstituted milk was warm and unsavory. The chill was what made it palatable.

The odd thing is that I love fresh warm milk today. Not fresh milk in the sense of a few days old, but really fresh milk: out of the udder by a few minutes. It is certainly not chilled, but closer to ninety degrees, and rich and creamy. Warm milk is more dessertlike; chilled, more milklike.

Milk warmed even hotter, more like one hundred and fifty, two hundred degrees, mixes well with honey for the ideal bev- erage to solve all the problems of the world. I can think of nothing more soothing and ideal. Biblical references to the land of milk and honey ring true.

Milk has a thickness, a body, because it is filled with fat. Without the fat, milk is tasty, but the fat makes it rich.

Modern production milk is not only pasteurized but also homogenized. Pasteurization is the heating of the milk to kill any pathogenic bacteria present in the raw milk. Milk that is not pasteurized is termed *raw*. Homogenization mixes the fat and the milk together so that the fat will not rise to the top of the milk. Essentially all of the milk in this country has been pasteurized since before the Second World War. Homogenization is a relatively new part of milk technology, showing up around the middle of the last century. I have never really understood why we need it. I like the cream rising up to the top.

Milk is homogenized by forcing it mechanically through minuscule holes to break up the fat globules in order to make them less likely to coalesce and form a fat layer. Luckily, my dairy does not have such an apparatus. The cream rises up and collects on the top of the milk.

Milk is highly enjoyable, but butter is different; it is transcendent. It's more than just an enjoyable food, it enlivens the tongue, fills the palate and makes food cooked with it special. When I was growing up in the 1960s, our table was graced—maybe not graced, but occupied—with plastic tubs of vegetable-based margarines. On the odd holidays of each year, a stick of butter would show up on the table, its rectangular shape out of sorts with the customary swirl of pale yellow fat in the tub made to vaguely resemble a country crock. My recollection is that both the sticks of butter and the margarines were vaguely fatty and pale, devoid of color and flavor.

Fresh raw butter has no pale characteristics. As Jersey cows do not completely process carotene from their grass diet, but rather pass it through in their milk, the cream and resulting butter are bright yellow in color; they appear to be dyed. The result is a fullness on the tongue, without the fattiness.

I was intrigued by raw milk, but I yearned to make raw butter. The cows have held up their end; an actual crock of raw butter now always commands my table.

Butter, simply described, is the collection of the fat globules of milk into a solid. Churning butter is fairly straightforward and has remained unchanged for generations. The fat is suspended in the milk and rises to the top. The cream congregates on the surface little by little. After a few hours some cream will be visible, by twenty-four hours there will be a goodly amount and in two days there will be a full thick layer of cream.

The longer the wait, the less milk and the more cream that you can easily skim off. Keeping a backlog of milk is difficult, however, as it takes up a great deal of space, and twenty-four hours works well enough to capture the cream necessary to proceed.

A large ladle lowered into the surface of the milk will pick up the cream that runs into it without disturbing the milk below. Moving the ladle around the surface will complete the process, getting as much cream as possible without dragging too much milk along as well.

Best to save up the cream until enough has been collected. Usually a gallon or two of cream makes enough butter to make churning worth the effort. Luckily, old butter churns can still be found in the odd antique store or online. New ones exist as well, but the price always seems a bit high to me. The owners of the antique shops tend to be rather relieved to sell a butter churn. Not a lot of demand for them these days.

The basic design of the butter churn is this: a large one-gallon or two-gallon glass jar, often with an odd design to encourage the moving of the cream. The jar is threaded on the top to accept a lid mounted with a motor. The motor is used to rapidly spin a metal shaft with a blade at the end. The jar is filled three-quarters of the way full, at most, and the lid is screwed on tightly, with the metal shaft entering well into the cream.

Many factors challenge the cream to give up its butter; temperature is big. Too cold, and the churning can take an exorbitant amount of time. Room temperature is ideal. The quality of the milk affects the resulting volume of cream as well. The purity of the cream and how much milk is pulled into the churn along with the cream also contribute to the quality of the butter.

Over the course of the week, I skim the cream from the milk in the dairy cooler. Each day another quart of cream, a half gallon of cream on a good day, goes into the butter churn. By the end of the week, the churn is filled with rich Jersey cream.

The churn is then left out in the morning for the cream to temper, to come up to the room temperature. Oddly, as a pastry cook, I was always taught to keep the cream as chilled as possible when whipping cream, to ice down the mixing bowl and the whisk to assure a chilled cream to whip the best cream. For butter, warmer is better.

Once the churn filled with cream has come up to temperature, I attach the motor to the top and hook up the paddle. Using an old cook's trick of placing the glass churn on a moistened towel keeps the churn from sliding around the counter while the motor is rapidly spinning. I have to admit that I learned this from experience; bad experience. When I first started making butter I left the churn running on the counter while I worked on other things, confident that I had a few minutes before the butter would need my attention again. A large crash as the glass churn filled with cream hit the concrete flour taught me to keep my eye on it, and to use the towel beneath. Thank God for eBay to keep us in outdated appliances not readily available at the local hardware.

There are two basic styles of butter: sweet cream butter and cultured butter. I stick with the sweet cream style. The basic difference is the time the cream is left to settle at a temperature where the cream will begin to culture, or sour. If the cream is churned quickly after it reaches room temperature, the butter will taste "sweet" like the taste of fresh cream. If allowed to sit for hours at room temperature, it will begin to sour; the lactose (sugars) will begin to turn to lactic acid. When that cream is churned, the resulting butter will have a more cultured taste. Delicious, but with raw cream as the principle ingredient, I shy away from it. As the lactose is converting to lactic acid, bacteria also are given a chance to regenerate. Good bacteria, fine. Pathogenic bacteria, dangerous.

Making butter is something that is done here each and every Saturday afternoon throughout the year. The butter that I make on Saturdays lasts through the week until the next batch is made. I like that this is predictable; it makes me feel old-fashioned, like my grandmother making cookies every Saturday.

Churning cream into butter varies every week. Some weeks, the cream will quickly churn into butter in a few minutes. Other weeks, close to an hour and that churn will be still be going, the motor getting hotter and hotter. I am not really sure why there's a variation. Possibly it is the fat content of the cream in the churn or what the cows ate that week. Maybe it is the quality of the milk or the health of the cows. But it changes every week. Keeps me on my toes. I can't time it, can't expect it to act a certain way.

The cream at the beginning of the process is liquid, consistent and slightly yellow. After sitting in the cooler all week, with additions made every afternoon, the milk has fallen to the bottom. A half inch of lighter colored milk shows off the yellowness, the creaminess of the higher eight inches.

I plug in the churn and the cream starts to move. Very little changes. It swirls and swirls and appears to do nothing. This is the part that can go on and on and on. Often I feel as though it just won't ever come together. Can it really just keep swirling? Is there any fat in this cream? The glass jar of the butter churn is not quite filled, maybe three-quarters or two-thirds filled at most. Once the motor starts, the cream immediately fills the jar, the sides are completely splashed with cream. There is no headroom left.

The cream will whisk around, with seemingly little change, until it happens. The sound of the cream hitting the sides of the churn will vary a bit. The level of the cream at the top will change just a bit. If you lift up the lid, the consistency of the cream will be slightly different; a tad thicker.

And then a shift will occur. Quickly, the level of the cream on the side of the glass will drop, the sound will drop, the cream will begin to transform into butter. Most indicative of the change will be the consistency of the cream. While the cream is being whisked around it will coat the inside of the glass churn, rendering it opaque.

Once the change takes place, the level will drop and the liquid whisking around will not coat the inside of the glass, it will hit the glass and fall. It is no longer thick, no longer opaque. It still won't be butter, but it will have changed.

Rapidly, this liquid will begin to break. The most apparent

sign after the dropping of the level and the cleaning of the glass is a thin top layer of the cream will be bluish, not yellow. Just the edge, the top edge will be thin, non-cream-like; blue. Below will be yellow and creamy still.

And then it will all happen. The blue liquid will move from the top to the entire jug; the milk will separate from the fat, from the butter. The contents of the jug will move from a swirling cream mixture to bits of fat in a thin liquid; it will move faster, swirl faster.

And now it can all go very well, or go too far. I look for this ideal time, this ideal situation when the fat, the butter-to-be, resembles rice floating in milk. Little beads of golden butter, buoyed in the swirling milk. Too early, the beads will be too small and you won't have butter and milk, but just fatty milk. Too much churning, and the butter will clump up, potentially churning the milk back into the butter. But neither is an unfixable disaster.

At the rice stage, I stop the motor, open the churn and take a look. Big rice. Big golden rice. I can picture the butter on the table now, taste the hot bun broken open, the butter melting into the bread.

I ready a colander, a tight sieve atop a large pot. I want to save the buttermilk as it drains from the butter. I quickly pour the contents of the jug into the sieve. If it has churned enough, the butter will remain in the sieve, the buttermilk draining below. If not, if it is too early, I pour it all back in and let it go some more.

In the colander the mixture drains for a while, ridding the butter of buttermilk. What amazes me at this stage is the look of buttermilk. For most of us, buttermilk means one thing: those quart milk containers found in the store. As a baker I used quart after quart for biscuits, cakes and frostings. If you read the fine print on that carton the correct name is *cultured buttermilk*, or, for some reason, *Hungarian buttermilk*. Cultured buttermilk simply means that it has been inoculated with some culture. Similar to that used for yogurt, the culture quickly and completely regenerates throughout the buttermilk, making it thick. But the buttermilk that comes out of making butter looks nothing like the store-bought version. Homemade buttermilk will be thin, with no fat left in the milk, very little color, and unless you're making cultured butter, it will not be very sour.

I save the buttermilk that drains off the butter. I save it because it must be saved. The cows were well fed with beautiful alfalfa, lush pastures and sweet grains, and they produced this product. It must be saved; it must be kept in the farm. I have tried to make ricotta out of it, but it is rather odd, I must admit. The dogs will drink a bit of it, but get bored with it quickly. The pigs will most likely get the lion's share of it and enjoy it tremendously.

Once the butter sitting in the colander has drained adequately, it must be washed. Butter really doesn't go bad. I am sure that the United States Department of Agriculture, the Centers for Disease Control, the Food and Drug Administration and every local health department would disagree with that, but I stand behind it. At the very least, butter is always eaten before it can turn. The buttermilk, however, can sour in the butter and make it go off. Removing the residual buttermilk is essential.

If you stop the churn at the rice stage, the butter will be loose and fluffy and light. A spraying of water over the colander of butter will rinse it completely. Too much pressure, and all of the butter can go down the drain; hot water is a certain disaster. A cool stream of water will work. After rinsing, let it drain well.

Now the fun begins. I have never been a big proponent of

latex gloves. Health departments the nation over find them to be a great hope of cleanliness in commercial kitchens. My opinion lies in the idea that messy habits don't change simply because they are wrapped in plastic. The latex glove can contaminate food just as easily as the bare hand. Wash your hands, and the food should be fine. In this case, however, gloves work well; I embrace them.

I like to salt the butter. Salt is always a good thing. Brings flavor. Unsalted butter is a sign of sophistication, I suppose, but I find it dull and drab. Add some salt. Originally salt was added to assist in preservation, but flavor is a better reason. A couple of tablespoons per pound of butter seems about right. More can always be added.

Flip the butter out of the colander into a bowl ample enough to hold the butter and then some. With your gloved hands, begin to squeeze the butter. Begin to pull the butter together into a ball. Immediately liquid—half buttermilk, half water—will emerge from the butter, filling the bottom of the bowl. Pull the butter to one side of the bowl and tip the bowl to its side, eliminating the liquid. Continue balling up the butter and pouring out the liquid until no more liquid percolates out from the butter. Then the butter can be formed. Squeeze the butter with your fingers. It will move from bits of fat to a large, golden, dry mass. I like this part. It is food, good food, and it is in your hands, made by your hands.

Suddenly the early winter mornings with the cows in the rain and mud seem long forgotten; now there is butter. Butter for warm bread, for pastries, for sautéed carrots. Nothing better.

I will stick with that. There is nothing better than great butter, but there are a few close runner-ups. Yogurt, ricotta, *cajeta*. All great. All better when made by hand than when store-bought. I am of the belief that because of the nature of dairies and the potential health risk of milk, dairies have been industrialized more than any other part of the food industry. You can grow your own carrots, buy them at the farmers' market from a small local farmer, or even from a grocery store that ships them in from out of state or out of the country. A Mexican-grown carrot is still essentially the same as the carrot you pull out of your garden in the backyard. Your own carrot is better, no question, but the process of growing each is essentially the same.

Dairy products just aren't like that. Cheese made by Kraft Foods is a completely different product than cheese from a small artisan cheese maker. Ricotta, yogurt, butter, all are really very different. Pick up the product in the supermarket and read the ingredients list. I have no idea what those chemicals are. I am confident that I do not have them in my larder. I am certain that I don't need them. My favorite is supermarket cream cheese; what is that big white block shrink-wrapped in plastic? No relation to actual cream cheese. It is some kind of milk product suspended in guar gum.

I have found it difficult to find descriptions of original processes for dairy products. Yogurt recipes certainly exist, but finding a really good recipe for butter is extremely difficult. Recipes for cheese making exist, but not as many as one would think. We have collectively lost the ability to process foods in a nonindustrial manner.

As we lose this ability, we also lose part of our culture. For hundreds of years we have processed milk to preserve it, to enjoy it. In the last fifty years we have given the role of producing food to large corporations; we have lost our culture. Culture is now Philadelphia cream cheese, Kraft singles, and Yoplait, not farmstead butter and cheese.

Yogurt is a simple craft: turning milk into a cultured

product by inoculating it with live cultures. Understanding how cultures work helps greatly in creating a high-quality yogurt.

The cultures that the milk is inoculated with vary, but are all variations of *Lactobacillus bulgaricus* and *Streptococcus thermophilus*. The easiest way to find these cultures is in supermarket yogurt. They are often listed on the container. The smallest producer is generally the best, although, surprisingly, not all are the same. As yogurt is a rather basic product, I expected all commercial yogurts to resemble one another. I look for small regional Greek yogurts. I get the best results with those. The flavor and texture of the eventual yogurt depends on the specific cultures. The large national yogurts have so much going on in them that they scare me. Try a few different ones; it is surprising which you will enjoy and which you will eventually avoid.

I studied very little biology in school. It really didn't interest me. Since my entrée into the dairy world I have had to pick up a basic working knowledge of biology. I realize that I have absorbed quite a bit since that first day Dinah came off the truck and I started milking her.

The *Lactobacillus* is a bacterium. *Bacillus* refers to the shape of the bacterium; it is always described as rod shaped. With the bacterium *Streptococcus*, *coccus* refers to its spherical shape. These bacteria, being fragile as most are, have a specific range of temperatures at which they're comfortable. For *Lactobacillus* and *Streptococcus*, that range is between 100 and 110 degrees Fahrenheit. Too hot, and the bacteria will simply die; too cold, and they may still grow, but too slowly to be effective.

The milk could simply be heated to 110 degrees and the culture added, but thanks to Harold McGee and his book *On Food and Cooking*, I have learned that heating the milk before adding the cultures to 185 degrees Fahrenheit alters the casein proteins in the milk to create longer proteins. The result is a more custardlike, thick yogurt. Sadly, I should have listened more in biology class and could explain why this happens. Take it as fact that it works; I do.

The procedure is to heat the milk to 185 degrees Fahrenheit and then allow it to cool to between 100 and 110 degrees. In the process of making yogurt the cultures eat the food in the milk and expel their waste. In this case, the bacteria eat the lactose—the sugars in milk—and create lactic acid. The result is a sour, thick milk product: yogurt. By way of comparison, when yeast is added to bread dough, the yeasts eat the sugars in the flour and expel gas, which causes the bread to rise; when making wine the yeasts added to grape juice eat the sugars of the sweet grapes and expel alcohol and carbon dioxide.

Once the culture has fully consumed all of the sugars available it will die, having no more food. The yogurt will be finished. Depending on the temperature, this could take a few hours; keeping it warm overnight is always a good idea. Once it is complete, the yogurt is chilled, further firming it and creating a finished custardlike sour product. For an extra touch, draining the yogurt at this stage in cheesecloth, allowing any moisture to drip out, gives it a more refined texture. It will be drier, thicker and will not resemble custard but rather a moist cheese.

The volume of milk produced by a cow fluctuates during her lactation. When she first calves, it is not at its highest point. A few weeks later the cow will come into her full production and then slowly the volume will decrease until she has dried up.

In an ideal setup, each cow is in milk for ten months of the year and dry for the remaining two months while she waits to calve again, giving her a chance to revitalize her body after being taxed by heavy, constant milk production. Cows also respond with increased milk production to large volumes of high-quality grass. When the pastures are at their best, the volume of milk is highest. The result of this variable milk supply is that there are times of year when there is way too much milk and times when there is way too little.

A normal quantity of milk produced by a Jersey is five gallons per day; a Holstein, potentially ten gallons. When the milk is being used daily at about the same rate, all seems just fine. The cow is milked, the milk is cooled, then stored, then sent out as milk or butter or cheese, and the process keeps a nice equilibrium.

When the balance is off—and it doesn't have to be off a lot, but just by a small amount—everything backs up. Five gallons of milk is a fair amount of volume. By dimension, approximately twelve inches by twelve inches by twenty. By weight, also substantial: more than forty pounds. When the milk leaving the dairy drops below the amount of milk coming in, the cooler starts filling up with milk. Quickly. If I can't get around to making cheese for a couple of days during a period when there is a large volume of milk being produced, suddenly the coolers are full. Full of ten, twenty, thirty, forty gallons of milk. It is very difficult to quickly get rid of thirty gallons of milk, especially if you take time to deal with the problem. Every twelve hours, more milk is produced, chilled and needs a place to go. Sounds like a good problem to have, but when it happens, it can be overwhelming.

By contrast, if the cows simply aren't producing an adequate amount of milk to fulfill your milk needs, then the milk supply diminishes very rapidly. Simply put, a balance between supply and demand is quite important, and difficult. The result is the co-op system.

Generally, throughout the United States, dairies are each a

part of a specific co-op. The dairies raise the cows, milk them, chill and hold the milk in a large bulk tank and then sell the milk in bulk. Every day, or every few days, depending on the volume of the dairy and the size of the bulk tank, a large milk tanker shows up at the dairy and removes the milk. The tanker continues on its way from dairy to dairy, eventually returning to the milk bottling plant to pasteurize the milk, bottle it and distribute it.

This system solves all of the varied volume challenges a dairy faces. The volume produced can vary every day, and yet with a large number of dairies in the co-op, the volume is evened out and remains fairly constant. A dairy can concentrate on producing as much milk as possible without any waste from overproduction; the bottler purchases all the milk.

Co-op production demands pasteurization. The milk from all of the cows from each dairy is first mixed in the bulk tank at the dairy. Then the contents of the bulk tanks from all of the dairies are mixed in the tanker truck, and then the milk from different tankers is conceivably mixed at the bottling plant. If one cow was sick, if one milking machine contaminated with coliforms, the entire co-op batch could be contaminated. Granted, the bad milk would be hugely diluted, but the possibility of a huge public health incident is too serious to risk, and so pasteurization is needed.

With pasteurization, the entire volume of milk is treated to eliminate pathogens in the milk. Without pasteurization, the dairy industry could not have expanded from small, local independent dairies delivering their own milk to a nationwide system of large dairies shipping milk all over the United States.

At least in the state of Washington, raw dairies are required to bottle their own milk. They are not allowed to sell their milk to a bottling plant. This is logical, as the large factory could not be confident that it could keep the raw milk and the milk to be pasteurized separate throughout the process.

Making cheese is the answer to a simple problem: Milk has a short shelf life. It needs constant refrigeration, a large challenge up until the Twentieth century. Grass that cows eat to produce milk is most prolific in the summer, and the option for feeding cows in the winter—hay—is difficult to produce and therefore expensive. Finding ample sources of protein for people to eat throughout the year, made difficult by cold winters, gave cheese an added bonus.

Cheese solves all of these challenges. When cows are eating lush spring, summer and early fall pastures they can be milked, and the milk is transformed into cheese, which can be stored throughout the year with minimal refrigeration to be used as needed.

You can look at cheese making—and charcuterie as well—as the result of a challenge that plagued people living off of the land. Their solution is a pleasing culinary delicacy, but its roots lie in a basic need: preserving food through the winter. The various riffs on the basic idea of cheese all relate back to cheese's preservation function. Coating cheeses with ash helps keep flies away; smoking has the same function. Ricotta is a way to utilize more of the proteins in the whey to get the most from the work of raising the cows.

The cheese cooler in my kitchen was manufactured as a chocolate cooler, the supplier tells me, the thermostat set from the customary forty degrees of a normal refrigerator and lower to the more comfortable fifty-five degrees that chocolate prefers, and, as it happens, the temperature that cheese prefers as well. The shelves have been adapted from their standard kitchen aluminum to the much more friendly pine to house the cheese. Aluminum could leave a bad taste in the cheese and its inability to temper the moisture of the cheese makes it inappropriate.

Seeing the rows of hard cheeses that will spend their year-long life in this case gives me comfort; it is the equivalent of a savings account. Financial times may be strained, but we will always have cheese to grate on the dinner noodles.

Cheese making is similar to other simple pursuits. There are only a few rules, a short list of ingredients and yet the results are infinite; some cheeses are really quite bad, most are adequate and every so often a fabulous result arrives. The blocks of dyed cheese shrink-wrapped on the supermarket shelves are in fact cheese—or so I want to believe—and they have the same basic preparation as a lovely raw-cow's-milk Camembert from an artisanal French producer.

The basics of cheese production are: changing the acid level of the milk by adding cultures, adding rennet to coagulate the milk, cutting the curds to expel the whey, forming the cheese and aging the cheese. There are certainly variations to this simple procedure, but all cheese making follows this basic idea.

In order for the milk to have the ability to curdle from the addition of rennet, the pH must be brought down. The addition of a culture to the milk performs this function. The culture pitched into the milk converts the lactose to lactic acid. Conceivably milk could be allowed to sour on its own over time. If left at a warm temperature for a few hours the milk would sour and culture on its own, equally changing the acid level.

Immediately after the bacteria culture has begun to do its work, a rennet is added to the milk. The purpose of the rennet is to curdle the milk; to gather the casein proteins in milk to coalesce together.

Although vegetable rennet also exists, the classic rennet

is from the stomach of a calf. When a calf is still suckling from its mother, its stomach needs special enzymes to break down its mother's milk for digestion. When the stomach—the abomasum—of a young calf is removed and cultured with the addition of a liquid, the result is the rennet. The capturing of rennet and its use in the making of cheese is one of the reasons for the existence of veal. The other is simply the need to breed dairy cows yearly. Dairy cows produce an abundance of young calves each year.

A small volume of rennet is poured into the warm milk—as little as a teaspoon per ten gallons of milk. Within minutes the powerful enzyme pulls all of the casein proteins in the milk together, creating a thick jellylike substance. The whey begins to be pushed out along the edge of the curds.

In order to expel the whey from the curds—the basic idea of cheese making—the curds are cut to create more surface area. Long-bladed knives or wires slice through the thick jelly at designated intervals to create individual cubes of a desired size. The more cuts and the smaller the cubes, the more whey is extracted; the fewer cuts and the larger the cubes, the less whey will be able to seep out from the curds.

Once the curds have been cut and the whey begins to pull away from the individual cubes, the curds are formed into a shape to become the final cheese. Round, square, squat, tall, pyramidal or cylindrical—each shape and size has some implications for the final nature of the desired cheese and also plays on certain cheese-making traditions. The curds can be pressed, layered and cut, or simply ladled into a mold. Curds may be salted while curds, or salt can be added later on the surface, or the whole cheese can be brined by submersing it in highly salted water. The cheese can be consumed immediately or aged for days, weeks or months, depending on the desired outcome.

That is the basic procedure for making cheese. Milk curdled, the whey removed, the curds brought together and formed into a cheese. All the many cheeses of the world follow that same procedure and yet they are completely different. It is the variations that make the spectrum of cheese vast and interesting.

The choice of milk is fairly straightforward, whether cow, sheep, goat or possibly water buffalo. A combination of two or three of these types of milk makes cheese even more complex and unusual. Personally I have no interest in milking a sheep. They are just too smelly and uncute for my taste. I can't even comment on water buffalo. Life is difficult enough without milking a water buffalo every day.

The temperature at which the milk is coagulated can have an effect on the final outcome. Lower temperatures produce lighter, fresh cheeses; higher temperatures make for a tighter curd for hard cheeses. Once the curds have been cut and the whey begins to be expelled, the curds are often cooked as well, though not for fresh cheeses. For harder, aged cheeses, the curds are cooked up to 125 degrees. This creates tough, firm curds. The whey is completely expelled from the curds and the resulting cheese will be firm and dry.

The choice of shape for the cheeses is varied and probably the most evocative of the final product. We all know by sight what a Brie looks like or a Stilton or a Parmesan, without ever taking a bite. The shape is what mostly informs the prospective eater, although the color helps as well.

The shapes are not as arbitrary as they look. The basic idea is that smaller cheeses ripen faster than larger. Brie wheels are very wide and yet very thin. The cheese is never more than two inches thick, and will therefore ripen quickly and over the entire area. Parmesan cheeses are tall and round. Very little of the mass of the cheese has any surface area. The Parmesan will age for months without completely drying out. Fresh goat cheeses are often formed in muslin bags, to be quickly drained and used as fresh cheese spreads immediately, therefore a mold is not necessary.

The most difficult part of cheese making is the aging. The basic variables are temperature, humidity and cultures in the air. As it happens, these three qualities are connected. The type of cultures present, or the type of cultures that can be presented, are dependent on a suitable combination of temperature and humidity. Without the appropriate physical conditions, the desired molds cannot live.

Of course, this is a basic explanation of cheese. Some cheeses are coated in wax, some brined, some curds are washed with warm water to cook them, some are smoked and so on. The variations in preparation and presentation could easily fill a book, and certainly have.

Whenever there has been an overabundance of milk at my farm, I have experimented with making different cheeses. Some have been successful, others really quite poor. The former are enjoyed here at the table, the eager pigs consume the latter.

I love to sit in the kitchen, tasting the cheeses right from the cooler. They are tasty, full of flavor and nourishing. More importantly, however, they are unique and of this farm. I can look through the open French doors out to the pasture thirty feet from the doors and see the cows. Lily and Boo and Dinah, Luna and Andi, are there grazing, watching me as I watch them. It is their milk that is the basis for this cheese. It is their cream that is the basis for the butter that lurks in the crock in the cooler as well. It's a long voyage from pasture grass to raw milk to fresh butter or aged cheese, but every stop along the way is fascinating and can be tasted in the final product.

As I immersed myself in the world of dairy, I started to

mull my business opportunities. Unlike beekeeping or managing an orchard, one can hardly manage to dairy as a hobby. The time commitment is enormous, and on top of that, the equipment and facilities require a very serious financial outlay. Conservatively, I would guess I spent in the ballpark of $50,000 on the buildings alone. Owning an operational dairy made me feel like a real farmer, but in order to keep my fledgling dairy afloat, I would have to figure out how to start turning a profit.

Eight

Raw Milk

When Dinah arrived here five-plus years ago, I had put little thought into how she would fit into the overall scheme of this farm. Keeping a cow, milking her and selling the milk seemed simple at the time. In the end it was more complicated than I could have imagined. I thought I would pour her fresh milk into mason jars and sell it to my neighbors. Raw milk is simply that: milk that it is not pasteurized. The vast majority of all milk sold in this country is pasteurized, milk that is heated to a high enough temperature to kill any possible pathogenic bacteria or diseases present in the milk.

I started down the road toward having a licensed raw dairy much by accident. I had visited a farm on the island owned by a friend who had cows and who was selling raw milk. He related to me that he couldn't produce enough milk to satisfy all the demand he had for raw milk. He was getting a decent price for the milk, so at first glance it sounded ideal.

Raw milk is in demand throughout the nation. It constitutes a very small percentage of total milk sales, but the people who are looking for it are fervent, willing to pay for it and will do what it takes to get it. No large national company supplies raw milk; it is illegal in many states, and controversial in all states. Thus we have a great demand, no supply and little competition. From a business perspective, selling raw milk is excellent.

Soon after this initial visit to my friend's farm, I began

my hunt for a dairy cow. Within a few months I was milking
Dinah and selling the milk.

I would milk Dinah into large plastic containers and then
place the warm milk into the cooler to chill. The next day I
would open the container, find the milk chilled, pour it into
half-gallon canning jars and deliver it to friends on the island.
The milk was tasty, the glass jars harkened back to simpler
times and my customers were happy.

Unfortunately, I had no license to sell milk. I knew that
selling raw milk, or any milk for that matter, without a license
was illegal. Oddly, I managed to put that fact out of my mind.
Collectively, the impression among those of us who sold raw
milk and those who bought it from us was that the state had
no interest in granting a raw dairy license and that contact-
ing them would lead to the sudden demise of your dairy. The
intrinsic nature of the business kept me from thinking too
deeply about the nature of my lawbreaking. All I was doing
was milking a cow and selling the milk to people who wanted
it: how could that be against the law? Lawbreakers were people who practiced in deception, who produced one thing and
called it another; that was fraud, this was just providing a
service for nice folk who liked milk. I was not one to ever
break the law, or so I thought. I paid my taxes, mostly, never
ran a red light, never drove too fast and in general have no
ability to lie.

And then one day it all changed. In the southern part of
Washington State just minutes from the Washington-Oregon
border, was a small farm that was selling raw milk on a small
scale, just like I was. This farm had set up a "cow-share program," whereby their customers technically owned shares of
the cows. Although it is illegal to sell milk without a license,
it is legal to drink the milk that your own personal cow produces. And so small farms attempt to get around the licens-

ing of dairies by "selling" a percentage of their cows to their customers. Each customer pays for the hay and grain and boarding of their percentage ownership of their cow and in return is given a share of the milk produced by that cow. The system is logical and creative, if nothing else. Unfortunately for the dairies, the state of Washington does not accept cow-sharing as a legitimate method of circumventing the licensing procedures.

Still, all would have been fine had the milk been healthy. Sadly, this farm sent out gallons of raw cow's milk tainted with $E. coli$ 0157:H7. The result was more than a dozen children sickened from the milk, five children hospitalized and two children in need of continued health care.

The news rumbled through the farm world quickly. The state moved in, shutting down the farm, and explicitly documenting the health violations. The farm was charged with selling milk without a license and additionally was threatened with federal prosecution. Because the farm's customers lived in the state of Oregon and drove across the river to Washington State to buy the milk, and because the farm owners were aware of it, the farm owners were threatened with a federal crime.

The day that I heard about the $E. coli$ outbreak, I pulled the plug on the milk cooler in my farm stand, and refused to sell milk to any of my customers until I could be licensed by the state. I contacted the state Department of Agriculture the next morning and began the steps needed to obtain a Grade "A" license for the selling of raw milk.

Six months later I had constructed a dairy fit to be licensed by the state of Washington for the sale of fluid raw milk for human consumption. Contrary to my original perception of the Department of Agriculture, they were quite cooperative. Their attitude is that it is better to keep track of raw dairies, inspect the facilities and test the milk, than to create a culture where raw milk is sold outside of the law, inspection and testing.

Although selling raw milk within the restrictions of the Department of Agriculture was at times frustrating, I slept a bit easier at night. The fear of small white government cars with exempt license plates pulling up in my driveway and slapping me with a cease-and-desist order vanished.

I do miss one part of my old way of selling milk outside of the law. Originally the milk from the cows, up to five gallons at a time, was cooled in large plastic containers. The milk was simply placed in conventional refrigerators until the next morning. I never checked the temperature hours after the milk was put in the cooler, partly out of ignorance, or partly out of not wanting to know.

Milk has certain characteristics that are not immediately apparent. Although milk is liquid much like water, it takes a considerable amount of time to cool. In order to comply with the state's requirements, the milk must be chilled to below forty degrees within two hours of the cow being milked. This is the most difficult requirement to meet.

Bacteria, both good and bad, reproduce in milk. Milk is an ideal breeding ground. It is fluid, it is warm—ninety-eight degrees—when it comes out of the cow, and it is full of sugar that is the perfect food for bacteria. These factors are what make milk so risky. If milk lacked any of these three criteria, then it would be far safer. Carrots, for example, are solid, not fluid. Pathogens cannot colonize a whole carrot within days, much less hours. If milk was cold out of the cow, bacteria could still take over the full volume, but at a far slower speed.

If milk is quickly chilled, then the bacteria have a shorter period of time to regenerate through the volume of milk. It is therefore imperative to chill the milk within the two-hour window, as required by the state. When I originally placed the large five-gallon containers filled with warm, ninety-eight-degree milk into the cooler, the milk took around twelve hours to cool to forty-degrees. The bacteria had many hours to regenerate throughout the milk, colonizing it completely.

If the bacteria were pathogenic this would have been a disaster. The hazardous agents, instead of being present in the milk in very small volumes, would have reproduced to the point that every glass of milk could have had a sufficient volume to get the consumer sick. Luckily, this never happened.

What did happen, though, was much more interesting. The bacteria present in the milk reproduced over and over again throughout the night as the milk slowly cooled down. By morning there were millions upon millions of bacteria in the milk. These bacteria are not harmful to humans; we can consume them without a problem, as the acids in our stomach subdue them.

At the same time the bacteria were invading this lovely milk, the cream in the milk was also rising to the top. By morning, part of the cream was at the top; by the next day, even more; and by the third day it had all settled on the top. The result of three days of cream rising to the top of five gallons of Jersey milk after slowly cooling it over many hours was the most exceptional cream imaginable. It was *crème fraîche*.

I could easily have floated a quarter on the top of the thick, thick yellow cream and it would not have fallen to the bottom of the milk. I could scoop the cream out with a large ladle and it would not drip, not run, but rather hold up like ice cream, full scoop on the ladle. The flavor was grassy, nutty and a bit sour, full of complexities unheard-of in the cream from a commercial dairy. The sourness comes from the lactose that has been eaten by the bacteria and converted into lactic acid. This thickness in the crème fraîche is literally the bacteria;

the cream has been cultured by the bacteria, thickening the cream in the process.

I miss crème fraîche. I miss the super-thick cream, the deep yellow color, the hint of sourness that gives it depth of flavor. Occasionally I pull a few gallons before it goes to the super-fast chiller and hold it back, let it slowly cool down naturally and allow the bacteria to take over in order to make myself a bit of crème fraîche.

Now that the milk is chilled within the allotted two-hour time frame, the bacteria do not have the opportunity to fully culture the milk. The temperature of the milk quickly plummets in the first hour from ninety-eight degrees to fifty or sixty degrees and the rate of reproduction slows to a near halt; by the end of two hours, very little bacteria have regenerated. There is certainly still cream that will rise to the top, but it will be thin, nothing like the crème fraîche of the old days.

Crème fraîche is for sale today in the marketplace, but it is not the super-rich cream with the deep yellow color and a hint of sourness that I know as real crème fraîche. An industrial process separates the cream from the milk mechanically, then pasteurizes the cream to rid it of any bacteria and then raises the temperature to a point where added cultures can survive and thrive. Once the cultures have regenerated throughout the cream, it is quickly cooled. The resulting product looks very much like crème fraîche, but the depth of flavor is missing.

Almost every drop of milk sold in America today is pasteurized and has been since the 1930s. Pasteurization is the outgrowth of a troubled milk industry from the mid-nineteenth century on the East Coast. A couple of factors caused the production of especially poor-quality milk and led to pasteurization.

The first shift was the realization by dairymen and whiskey distillers that they could profit from each other. At the beginning of the nineteenth century distillers had popped up around the big cities to supply recent immigrants with cheap whiskey. These factories used grain, fermented it to make alcohol and then needed to get rid of large volumes of the spent grain mash. They quickly learned that cows would eat this slop of wet, sweet grain and would produce milk from it.

Dairies realized that if they moved their cows to the cities and fed their cows this cheap slop, they could realize a higher profit than if they kept their cows on pasture. Their customers were the recent immigrants in the big urban centers of the East Coast.

Eventually there came to be a great deal of these slop or swill dairies, keeping cows alive for a short period of time on the waste of distilleries. As you can imagine, this is not the diet a cow would prefer, and it produced hugely inferior milk, eventually killing the cows in a ghastly fashion.

As the goals were to maximize profits exclusively, the conditions in these dairies were deplorable. These unsanitary and unscrupulous dairies contributed to the rise of tuberculosis, typhoid fever, scarlet fever, diphtheria and diarrhea in the cities. High mortality rates among infants were indicative of the poor diets and living conditions of the urban poor. Milk from swill dairies was part of this poor diet.

At the same time as the rise of the swill dairies, farms outside of the city continued producing milk and delivered in into the cities, although at a higher cost. The milk of these farms was of far greater quality and more likely to be free of disease.

The states, the federal government and local activists began to take notice of this problem and stepped in. The technology existed to render the poor-quality milk safe through heating. Louis Pasteur had established methods of heating wine to destroy all bacteria by 1862. This same practice, later to be labeled *pasteurization*, could be used to make unsafe milk drinkable.

As children in the cities grew ill from tainted milk from swill dairies, the countryside dairies began to set standards for their milk. Dairies began to be "certified"—their practices found to be of a quality level deemed adequate by the government.

Regulators were not looking to pasteurize all milk, only that which was of low quality. The certified dairies were considered a safe alternative to the pasteurized milk and continued throughout this period.

Dairies were not immune to the pressures of industrialization and population growth in the United States. Farms were becoming big business. The expense of pasteurization equipment led the large producers to push for universal mandatory pasteurization, in order to capture a larger share of the market. Interstate movement of milk would also have been impossible without standardization of the milk supply. The certified dairies lost out even though their milk was considered to be of fine quality. And a shift occurred culturally: the nation as a whole, and especially public health professionals, came to believe that pasteurizing milk was the only way to produce a safe, drinkable product. The original supporters of pasteurization had no intention of requiring pasteurizing of all the milk, only the dangerous, poor-quality milk produced at swill dairies. But thanks to this obscure agricultural history of the middle nineteenth century and early twentieth century, today almost all of the milk in the national milk supply is pasteurized.

Milk is a commodity that is transported throughout the United States. Fluid milk and especially powdered milk are routinely trucked across state lines from where they are produced to where they are needed most. Because of this interstate commerce, the federal government controls milk, along with most other food products.

The production of milk is governed by the United States Department of Agriculture (USDA). The specific document that addresses it is the Pasteurized Milk Ordinance (PMO). Even with my little five-cow raw dairy, I have a copy of the PMO in the milk room and am governed by it. The federal government gives the states the right to decide whether to allow raw milk within their state. Because all states do not agree on the issue of raw milk, it cannot be shipped across state lines.

Twenty-eight states allow the sale of raw milk in some form and with some restrictions. The remainder of the states ban its sale, although raw milk sold as animal food can circumvent these state laws.

The argument for pasteurization is simple: heating the milk destroys all of the bacteria in the milk, both pathogenic and not, making it safer for human consumption. If milk is not pasteurized, there is always a chance of pathogens sickening consumers. It is a compelling argument, without question.

I agree that pasteurization is the safer route to take for milk. Anyone who does not have the immune system to bounce back from bad milk should not drink raw milk, specifically the very young, the elderly, pregnant women and those with compromised immune systems. For healthy adults, I think it is another matter. The state's policies do not account for the beneficial elements of the milk, namely enzymes that are destroyed by pasteurization.

Raw milk is a perfect example of the tricky role the state plays in food regulation. Raw milk is both healthy and potentially hazardous to your health. It is very much like all foods in that regard. Ground beef can potentially harbor life-threatening coliforms, and spinach and tomatoes can as well. Bean sprouts, chicken eggs and salad greens all have their potential pathogens. In their purest forms, these foods are perfect: whole foods, close to the source, unprocessed and they're what our bodies need for existence. And yet, all can be deadly or sickening if poorly produced or processed.

I want to believe that if the state just stayed out of all food production, life would be grand. No regulation, no oversight, just good folks living off the land. Possibly in 1750 that all would have worked, but at the beginning of the twenty-first century, it is unrealistic.

Large businesses control most of the food production in this nation. These multinational corporations—Cargill, Tyson, ConAgra—are publicly held and driven by profit, not necessarily by a sense of "goodness." The goal of my small business is also to be profitable. I do not want to imply that large business does not care about the consumer, but rather that because I interact with my customers individually and know them personally, my level of interest in their health is greater.

We do need government oversight to maintain a sense of order, to guarantee that the food that is sold meets a basic bar. All Americans want to know that when they pick up a package of ground beef in the supermarket it is safe for human consumption: this is the proper role of government regulation.

A culture of government oversight has developed from such regulation. The state decides what is immediately harmful in raw, whole and processed foods. Pathogens, coliforms and harmful bacteria are expected to be eliminated from market goods. Overall, the state is successful in that pursuit.

Highly processed foods generally pass all government standards for basic safety. They aren't generally of a high value from a health standpoint, but you won't die from them. Some foods that are great for you, yet also could be hazardous, are removed from the market. If we have to destroy much of the potential goodness in a food in order to make sure that it is not harmful, as a society we accept this trade-off. Raw milk is a great example of this.

I look to Lord Northbourne in his book *Look to the Land* for a great perspective on health and food. In 1940 he wrote:

> *Hygiene is all very well, but it is no substitute for health. We have got into the habit of thinking that health can come from the mere avoidance of germs or dirt, while we neglect the foundations of health and so get more and more into a state in which we cannot withstand bacteria or dirt, and so we get more and more terrified of them. As always, negative policy directed solely to the avoidance of evil is useless in the absence of constructive work for good [page 42].*

Raw milk's principle threat is a specific coliform—usually referred to as 157. Although other food-borne illnesses can be carried through milk—tuberculosis, Johne's disease, Q fever, campherbacter—157 is what you hear about in the media. Honestly, I am not quite sure why—my gut tells me that it is a litigation issue. In downtown Seattle, just minutes from my farm, is the nation's largest *E. coli* law firm. Their stock-in-trade is in personal injury work, specifically *E. coli*–based. They right the wrongs of unscrupulous food growers, processors and sellers who sicken their clients.

I highly doubt that there is a law firm in this country devoted to personal injury work based on campherbacter. My guess is that *E. coli* is tremendously more profitable. It primarily affects children, it is rare, but still occurs frequently enough to keep it in the news, and it originates in manure—

no one can argue that manure should be in food. All of this plays well with a jury.

This is the basic nature of 157: coliforms are ever-present in the intestines of cows. They are part of the fluids that break down food. They can be shed in manure and all can potentially end up in food. Our own stomach acids have the ability to kill most any coliforms that are present in our food. But 157 is different in that human stomachs cannot kill it.

In the case of milk, the method of contamination is fairly simple. The explanation I have heard from public health officials is that, as the udders of a cow are located at the rear end of the animal, they will always be dirty from defecation. Sadly, this tells me that those who regulate food do not have much primary contact with food.

It is true that the udders and the teats are located in the posterior of the cow. It is also true that any manure left on the teats could very well get into the milk while the cow is being milked. The teats and the udder, however, are not soiled by the act of the manure exiting the cow. Anyone who has spent time with cows would be well aware that cows are quite proficient at defecating: the manure lands rather precisely behind them on the ground; it does not strike their body. Rather, the teats are soiled when the cows lie down on ground where there is manure. Cows are rather particular about certain aspects of their lives, but they will lounge in manure. The udders of a cow could be located in just about anyplace on their body and they would still have the potential of landing in manure.

The relative acid level of human and bovine stomachs is similar. Over our human development we have acquired the ability to eat the food around us without killing ourselves in the process. It is the slow evolution of our bodies and our foodstuffs that keeps us healthy. Recently cows have been raised differently and our bodies have not had the time to react. Or, in fact, they are reacting: 157 can kill us.

Throughout the history of domesticated cattle, cows were fed grasses. As they are ruminants, they are most suited to the consumption of grasses. Cows will gain weight on grass, but not as quickly as when they are fed grain. As grains are simply the mature seeds of grass, this still isn't far from cows' preferred diet, but an extreme percentage of grain is unlike what their rumens are used to.

Cows gain more weight on grains than by eating grasses. The fat in the muscle, known as marbling, is the basis of the USDA grading system. Meat is graded in this country at all USDA-inspected slaughterhouses primarily on one criteria— the quantity of marbling. The more grain a cow eats, the more marbling that will appear in the meat and the higher the grade. The higher the grade, the higher the price that the beef can be sold for and the higher the profit for the cattleman.

Thus, cows are fed more and more grain and less and less grass. Grain, specifically corn, is more expensive than grass, but land is more expensive than either. Grass is fed to cows in the form of pasture. Large expanses of land are necessary in order to feed hundreds of cows. Corn can be grown much more efficiently and then fed to cows held on small bits of land: feedlots.

Also, because cows gain weight faster on grains than grass, they produce more quickly and with a higher profit than when left for years on pasture. All of these factors have pushed cattlemen to keep hundreds of cows on small feedlots, feeding them with corn and little or no grass. Corn also has been subsidized by the federal government, making it a bargain to the cattlemen.

On a corn-heavy diet, the stomach fluids of a cow needed more acid to digest the grain than if they had simply digested grass. The acid levels rose to respond to the new diet of corn and other grains. When the acid levels increased, the coliforms present in the digestive tracts of these cows raised their tolerance for acid.

Unfortunately, the human digestive system did not keep up with this increased resistance to acid on the part of bovine coliforms. The acids in our stomachs do not have the ability to neutralize the bovine coliforms, specifically 157. They are therefore pathogenic coliforms to us.

I mentioned to a lawyer recently that I didn't want to fight the state on the issue of raw milk because the state always has the trump card: food safety. Regardless of the issue at stake, the state can always say that the regulations they impose are for public safety. It is difficult to argue that a small number of sick children is acceptable. His response was that there is the concept of acceptable risk—risk that justifies the potential benefit—and therefore I should argue that raw milk should be available despite its potential risk.

Yes, you can eat all the processed foods in the supermarket, cook your ground beef at a ridiculously high temperature, avoid fresh vegetables such as spinach and tomatoes, never eat in a restaurant, and you will most likely never catch any food-borne illnesses that will endanger your health.

But what a life it would be. Beef tartar, fresh spinach, eating great street food in less-than-perfect situations and drinking fresh, sweet, fatty raw milk: those are the great joys that make eating and living great.

I have had discussions with people involved with public health during the course of running my raw dairy. Most discussions have quickly become arguments. We approach the issue in completely different ways. Originally I thought that they were stubborn, until I realized and acknowledged that I was equally stubborn, if not more so.

The conclusion I have reached is not that farmers are good and health regulations are bad, or vice versa. The difference is in basic attitudes toward food. I feel that food is intrinsically good. Food is from the earth. It provides nutrition for us to live. It is the source of all life, it has the power to make us healthy, to provide us with a full life. Although there are cases where food can do harm, it is the result of processing, of man's manipulation of food. As I milk my cows mechanically, chill the milk and then bottle it, I am one of those processors. Poor processing can unquestionably cause harm to those drinking raw milk.

The regulators for public health have a different perspective, or so I believe. Their view is that food is intrinsically dangerous. It is the role of food processors to transform raw food products into safe items for human consumption. It is the state's role to monitor these food processors to maintain safe processing standards.

My quick view into this perspective came at the beginning of my Grade "A" licensing process. I had applied for a license for fluid raw milk, raw cream and raw butter. The first two were approved, the third was not. As I love raw butter and knew that my customers would as well, I wanted to produce and sell it. When the state denied my request I pushed them for an explanation. I received, weeks later, a lengthy statement concerning why raw butter is not legal in the state of Washington.

The basic argument is that by definition on the federal level butter is "made from pasteurized cream." Because I wanted to use raw cream as the primary ingredient, my product did not fit the federal definition. Incensed, I went looking for the definition of butter.

Thankfully the Internet made this task much easier than in earlier years. If I had had to leave the island, go down to the federal building in downtown Seattle and rifle through pages of documents, it would have taken weeks. But with the Internet, sitting at my kitchen table I could easily read what I needed. I went to the USDA and the Food and Drug Administration (FDA) Web sites. I had no idea what the FDA did, but I got a sense of it quickly.

The FDA is an agency of the Department of Health and Human Services. Its primary function is the regulation of many food and drug products in this country. A chunk of the material that the FDA produces is a mammoth list of definitions. Every possible food item is defined in excruciating detail by the FDA. Once I got this far, I was certain the definition of butter would pop up in a second. Butter is a very basic food that we have consumed for decades if not centuries. I could return to the Washington State Department of Agriculture (WSDA) and prove that they were incorrect. I would soon be a raw butter seller.

I was grossly mistaken. The definitions don't define butter, or a banana, or a walnut. This federal compendium addresses issues more along the lines of how you can legally make a product containing no cream whatsoever and call it butter, how many poisons can be left in a food product that is intended as safe for human consumption, etc.

Online I came across great statements like this:

Preservatives including but not limited to the following within these maximum amounts in percent by weight of the finished food: Sorbic acid, benzoic acid and their sodium, potassium, and calcium salts, individually, 0.1 percent, or in combination, 0.2 percent, expressed as the acids; calcium disodium EDTA, 0.0075 percent; propyl, octyl, and dodecyl gallates, BHT, BHA, ascorbyl palmitate, ascorbyl stearate, all individually or in combination, 0.02 percent; stearyl citrate, 0.15 percent; isopropyl citrate mixture, 0.02 percent.

At one point I thought I was in the wrong section and actually made a phone call to check. Surprisingly I quickly got a person on the phone. A very charming woman somewhere in Maryland helped me through it all. She called me "honey" after every sentence and thought it was hysterical that I was looking for the definition of butter. I doubt she had ever gotten such a phone call.

As I read through these definitions I began to get a sense of food in America. As we walk the aisles of the supermarket, we see boxes and cans and bags of "food." All are regulated, inspected and approved. A major issue for food processors is what they can call the product and what can legally be in the product. Our food language has a few terms that are powerful: butter, cookies, flour, tomato sauce, mustard and so on. We culturally have an idea of what those terms mean. Sadly, the definitions of those items do not correspond with our traditional images. Tomato sauce according to the FDA is wholly different than what my grandmother cooked on Sunday afternoons.

I returned to the letter from the WSDA and concluded the most important part of their letter to me concerning my desire to sell raw butter was the last line, where they stated that they reserved the right to protect the public health in any way that they felt appropriate. I gave in and decided to sell only raw milk and cream and not push the raw butter issue.

After four and a half years of selling raw milk to the public, at times outside of the law, at times following the law, I decided to cease selling raw milk. In the end, I concluded that I would never win the argument about raw milk itself. While selling raw milk, I worried both about getting children sick and about being sued. I never have gotten anyone sick from drinking my raw milk, thankfully, but there was always the chance. I am not sure how I would react. I produce food because I love food, love to have people eat great food. Getting someone sick is simply not part of the vision.

I also had a sense of fatigue from selling raw milk. It wore me out. Not the actual work of milking cows, bottling the milk and selling it, but rather the attention I gave to both the state and to my customers. When the WSDA changed the law to add Q fever as a potential hazard of raw milk and requiring additional testing of my cows, I found myself on the phone with the state veterinarian's office, screaming expletives at the unimpressed state worker. I was convinced there was a conspiracy in the offices in the state capital, bureaucrats plotting ways to put me out of business. I was of course wrong, but the personal toll it was taking on me was larger than the joy of seeing my cows amble down the north road, coming down from the upper pasture to the barn in the morning, their hips swaying this way and that as they plodded along.

Unexpectedly, I also was worn down by customers: the nice folks who wanted to buy good, clean milk. Many were convinced that raw milk would save them from all the ills of their bodies: asthma, cancer, arthritis. This was too great a burden to place on a simple liquid. My belief was always that raw milk is a great food for healthy adults. When customers informed me that they fed the milk to their weeks-old infants, I would shudder. Their trust in the product, their trust in me, was based on my friendliness toward them, not on the intrinsic quality of my milk.

Many products on the shelves of the supermarket are potentially hazardous: liquor, cigarettes, raw beef, raw chicken. Although there is little doubt that drinking too much alcohol is potentially very dangerous, it is still for sale in every state in the union, albeit with restrictions. Culturally we as a nation have a connection to the dangers of alcohol. Many have direct experience with alcoholism, and the national understanding is that alcohol is dangerous, especially in the case of driving while intoxicated.

I doubt that raw milk elicits those same emotions and connections. I have explained what raw milk is to people on many occasions throughout the past four years. I have yet to encounter a person who has been made ill by raw milk or who knows someone who has.

And yet, I can walk into a restaurant a few blocks from my farm, sidle up to the bar and order a shot of whiskey. I can order a second shot, a third shot and most likely a fourth. I drink little, so I am guessing that after that I would fall off of my barstool, but I know people in this small town and I doubt they would cut me off. The bottle of whiskey would bear a warning label, which I might have noticed had I purchased it in a store. If I were drinking whiskey by the shot, however, no such warning would come near me. The state trusts me to make my own decisions as an adult.

Now, if I were to ask that barkeep for a glass of raw milk, I would be immediately turned down. The state, at least this state, restricts the sale of raw milk to the consumer, and requires that the milk be sold only in a container sealed at the dairy. A warning label is affixed to that jug of milk, much like the alcohol. The state, as reflected in its regulations, believes that adults are not capable of judging the dangers of raw milk without seeing that label. Only the purchaser of the raw milk can open and drink that milk, from the original container with the warning label on it. A restaurant cannot serve a single glass of raw milk to an adult customer.

Raw milk strikes a nerve with the public health community. There are two distinct sides in the debate: those in public health who are adamant that raw milk is intrinsically dangerous and has no business being in the food supply; and raw milk advocates who are adamant that raw milk is intrinsically good and pure and it is their right to drink it. I have always fallen in the middle, believing that raw milk is a fine product, but with tremendous limitations.

Ultimately, my decision to stop selling raw milk was not simply based on my beliefs about food, but on the harsh realities of liability. I value this farm tremendously. I have worked on it for the past twenty years and have no interest in losing it in a lawsuit over bad milk. Even if I were to win a lawsuit, the stress and toil wouldn't be worth it.

After choosing to pull the plug on my raw milk operation, I had cows, a barn, a dairy and open pasture. I had everything I needed to produce outstanding raw milk, but I had become soured on the process of actually selling said raw milk. My restaurant sale payments were dwindling, and soon the buyer defaulted on the loan. I cashed the last check and estimated that I could operate the farm for six months with what I had left. My back was against the wall, but I was no longer scared. I had become used to rolling with the punches—it's an essential skill for a small farmer.

I didn't want to give up my cows, but I couldn't go on milking them every day if I wasn't going to use the milk for something. If I was going to use the milk for something, it had to be something I could sell at a profit. So I decided to press on with my dairy adventure and become a cheese maker. Although raw milk is tasty and healthy, it is also essentially limited in its depth. Great cows' milk is sweet, grassy and thick, no question, but an aged cheese from excellent milk has many layers of flavors and tastes.

Alas, the milk produced here for cheese making is now pasteurized. Presently a combination pasteurizer/cheese vat fabricated in the Netherlands sits in the dairy building. The milk is heated to 145 degrees to kill any potential pathogens in the milk before the milk is made into lovely fresh cheeses.

I believe people should have the option to purchase the food that they would like. I find it unfortunate that people have a desire to drink raw milk and yet are not allowed to in many parts of the nation. I can thank the critics of raw milk, however, since the legal challenges sent me on a course toward cheese making, a vocation I find highly enjoyable, and one which I believe will eventually bring this farm a significant income. I've only been making and selling cheese for a short time, so it's too soon to evaluate my progress from a perspective of financial viability, but I can say without reservation that I believe in this endeavor. I believe I will succeed in cheese making, and make money doing so.

And so this farm evolves, changes and carries on. I enjoy the ride. If I had originally intended Kurtwood Farms to be a producer of farmstead cheeses, I would have had no idea of its enormity. It would have been an overwhelming process— finding the land, clearing the land, planting pastures, establishing a herd of cows, learning to raise cows and milk them, building a dairy and then learning to make cheese. But when I only have the next phase in front of me I can tackle it. In another few years I expect this business to be more refined, to have evolved further. I do not know the direction the changes will take, but I look forward to them.

Nine

Vegetables

Growing vegetables has taught me a lot about farming. And a lot about myself. When I brought Matt on, the farm was a simple hobby farm, though I was loath to admit it. I grew some tasty food, but it wasn't a business. With Matt's help I pushed this farm from a hobby to a business. A failing business, but a business nonetheless. That first season quickly turned me against growing vegetables under plastic. I didn't want to join the race to grow the earliest tomato for the farmers' market. In my view, rushing to market came at a great expense, both financially and also to my sense of what was right. I just didn't like all the plastic.

I enjoyed the simple act of putting a seed in the ground and watching it germinate and grow until it could be harvested. It was pure and good, and the end result was an exceptional vegetable. I couldn't give that up.

As I had boxes of seeds left over from the vegetable enterprise, and had gained a decent amount of knowledge, plus the fields were set up—tilled, amended and fenced—I continued to grow vegetables, but on a smaller scale. I wish that I could say that this was a sudden epiphany, that one day I woke up and reduced the scale of this vegetable farm. Rather, I slowly came to my senses. The year after Matt left, I still grew vegetables for the farmers' market, but stopped running a CSA. I still grew tomato starts, more than I needed for my farm, but

I only sold them to the local hardware store, no longer to the chain of grocery stores in Seattle.

I still thought I could make it as a vegetable grower, even though I really didn't enjoy working on a large scale. It wasn't fun, it wasn't rewarding, it was a slog at times. And then, a few years ago, I came up with a solution. By this point, I had met many people who cared about good food: customers on the island and in the city and many cooks and restaurant owners I had sold food to in the city. They wanted to come to the farm, to see how food was made and to be a part of a local farm. I decided that rather than just give them a quick Saturday afternoon tour, I would capitalize on their interest. I would prepare a full dinner for them and charge them for it. I'd serve dinner in the main kitchen building of the farm, prepared with the vegetables, the meats, the cheeses, the honey, the herbs and the fruits from this small plot of land, paired with great wines. My many food-yielding "hobby projects" finally had a purpose: to stock the kitchen for simple but delicious weekly meals. And I would get a hundred bucks or so per head, which I could funnel into producing more high-quality food.

Hosting dinners is something that I would have loved whether I was charging admission or not; it brought me back to my early days at the bakery. There is an honesty and integrity in cooking food and serving it directly. That this endeavor could support my farm was icing on the cake. Weekly dinners combined with my fledgling cheese business are what support this farm today. Almost all of the food I produce—as detailed in the following chapters on vegetables, fowl and pigs, as well as the previous chapters on honey, fruit and dairy—goes into the seasonal dishes I serve every Sunday. Throwing the dinners has given me a reason to produce all the wonderful food that, to be fair, I wanted to produce anyway. Everyone wins, especially me.

Once I had decided to throw dinners, I knew I needed a name. When the windows of the kitchen building needed a fresh coat of paint, I hired Bill, a former hippie who had moved to the island in 1974. He often told me stories of life here on the island in that era, as he methodically painted. After painting, he left me a small can of remaining white paint, labeled in deliberate script *Cookhouse* to denote what building that paint was for. I knew immediately that I had a name—Sunday dinners at Kurtwood Farms would be called Cookhouse. I imagined an old cattle ranch, with a long wooden table, cowboys lined up eating full plates of hearty food grown on the ranch. The dinners have been a hit, and I have no intention of stopping them, at least until my cheese-making business takes off to a point where it demands my full attention and brings in a commensurate income.

The menus of the Cookhouse dinners only serve to reinforce the distinct qualities of the individual seasons on Vashon. It is autumn as I write this, mid-October. Summer has been long and fruitful. I am excited to see the sun setting earlier, the rains wetting the pastures after months of dry weather and a chill in the morning air. Of course, in another three weeks I will give anything to get summer back, to feel the warmth of the sun on my face as I walk the pastures. But today I welcome the rains and cool weather.

It was a great summer: the pastures grew well, the gardens filled with produce, the fruit trees burdened themselves with heavy fruit. These past two weeks large quantities of food have come into the kitchen: a wheelbarrow filled with potatoes, crates and crates of apples, trays filled with pears. At this time of year, I sit back and grin. A big silly grin. All this stuff came from the earth? After all these seasons, it's all still a wondrous mystery to me.

My greatest joy at this time of year comes from pumpkins. The pumpkins I grow are actually a variety of winter squashes, but *pumpkin* sounds more fun than the dull and descriptive *winter squash*. Every May, I walk out to the garden bed and plant squash seeds. The little paper envelopes that the seeds come in have photos of the eventual squash and five or six packets of different varietals fit nicely in my jacket pocket. I love to rip open the top of a new seed packet, see the seeds sitting in the bottom. All is possible at this point; all is good.

Into the freshly tilled earth the seeds are poked down a few inches, a bit of water goes over them if I have time and then they are left alone. They pop out in a few days if the weather is good, a couple weeks later if spring is tardy. Then through June and early July they press on until they hit their stride and go all-out. By August, vines cover an entire end of the garden plot. When the second or third week of October comes along, I drive the John Deere tractor out to the garden, open the gates and drive back to the pumpkin patch. I always think there will be just one or two pumpkins. I try not to look for them ahead of time, but occasionally I sneak a peek.

And then I lower the bucket on the front of the tractor, turn off the motor and wade into the plants, my heavy cowboy boots pushing aside the tangle of vines, looking for a place for my feet to land. The large verdant leaves cover the hidden pumpkins, only visible by the bright orange colors that explode as fall advances. I cut the stem and free the pumpkin, walk it to the tractor and stack it in the bucket. In a few minutes the bucket is full. On a good year I will fill the bucket five times. One year I drove the large Ford pickup to the garden and filled the truck bed high with pumpkins, but that was an exceptional year.

The big black steel bucket on the front of the tractor, held up by the hydraulics, is full of pumpkins. Even though I don't need to, I raise the bucket high above the tractor and make a triumphant march back to the kitchen, smiling through the whole drive.

I can never get over this. I walked out with seed packets in my pocket in May and in October I need the hydraulic arm of the tractor to haul the finished bounty back to the kitchen. How does this happen? I do water them a lot over the course of the season, of course. Many gallons of water head out to the pumpkin patch, but I always think that most of it rolls off the soil, soaks in or evaporates. How much of that water could really end up in the roots?

Potatoes are even stranger to me. For some reason the fact that pumpkins are grown aboveground makes their growth partially plausible. The sun, the air, the vines, they must be responsible in some way for making pumpkins—but potatoes? They are underground. The tuber harvest was close to a thousand pounds this past year. What are they made of? The soil is still there. I doubt that any is missing. The potato plants are dead and gone, but they are never all that big anyway. I water the potatoes the same as the squash, but that water also just seems to seep deep down into the soil. What are those thousand pounds made of?

I could go to a botany textbook, probably a pretty basic textbook at that, and get the answer, but I don't want to know the answer in that way. I leave it as just the wonderful part of growing vegetables. In no way am I a religious man, but there are miracles: Potatoes grow in the ground and they are tasty. Pumpkins come from little seeds in a few weeks. Cows eat grass and produce milk.

I want to take credit for most of the food produced here. I planted the seed. I milked the cows. I fed the lambs. In reality there is something greater at work. Not sure exactly what it is, but it is a force far greater than myself.

I am fortunate to live in the part of the country that I do. The Pacific Northwest is very temperate and here on the island we are buffeted by the marine air; it is never too hot, nor too cold. The result is a near year-round growing season. I feel fortunate to have been raised in this region and I have chosen to remain here because of this easy-livin' climate. Although it freezes here every year, in no way does the weather resemble Vermont or Illinois or most any other northern part of the country.

Although I grew up helping in the family garden as a child, the greatest adjustment I made from cultivating vegetables on a home scale to growing for a small farmers' market was in the method of starting plants. I had always been taught to direct-seed the vegetables in the rows in the garden. The soil is tilled up once it is dry enough, and long straight rows are set with lengths of string anchored at either end of the garden with a small stake. Then a hoe dragged down the line opens up the freshly tilled brown soil just enough to create a valley in which the small seeds will land.

The seeds are gently dropped in the furrow, the soil gently placed back over the seeds and with a bit of good weather the seeds will sprout in a few days. It is a great system, but except for a few vegetables—primarily carrots and radishes—it is never used to grow vegetables in volume. I do continue to seed those pumpkins, but only for nostalgia and because of the joy it brings me.

The more efficient method of growing vegetables is to germinate them in the greenhouse and then to plant them out when they have sprouted and gained an ample start on life. The advantages are many, the disadvantages just a few. Here at the farm, we have a small glass greenhouse to hold all of the plant starts.

When the vegetables are started indoors, heat can be

added to guarantee good germination of the seeds. If there are any problems with sprouting, they are easily apparent and replacements can quickly be started. When I leave seeds in the open garden they must wait for the soil temperature to rise adequately to sprout. It might happen quickly, but it could just as likely take quite a few days for the ambient temperature to rise high enough for the seeds to germinate. Greenhouses have the great advantage of easy temperature control. Even if it is snowing outside, flats of onions, leeks and scallions can begin to grow on heat mats in the greenhouse, the soil a toasty sixty degrees. When the weather is right for the plants to go in the ground, the slender wisps of the onions will be eight weeks old. If I had to wait to seed those onion seeds in the ground, those eight weeks of growth would be lost. The growing season may be long in this part of the world, but it's not endless; time matters.

Although I cannot say that I am the most efficient grower, nor am I particularly organized, it is beneficial to use the garden space for growing vegetables and not for germinating seeds. In the two weeks that it might take beets to emerge from the cool spring soil, that real estate could be used for other crops. In those two weeks the last vegetables can grow a bit more, ripen a bit more, compost can break down a bit more. Every little bit helps.

Efficiency is all well and good, but I also enjoy sitting in the greenhouse in spring as it gets warm out, but before it's quite T-shirt weather. In the warmth of the greenhouse I can pretend that it is May even if it is a few weeks and a few degrees in the future. Filling flats with clean fluffy seeding soil, going through the packets of seeds and filling the individual cells in the flats with a seed or two, writing the variety on a slim white plastic tag: it makes me smile. The dirt is clean and dry, the air is warm from the sun hitting the glass, the seeds are all very uniform and tidy, no weeds have found their way in; mud has no place in the tight world of the greenhouse.

A common sight in most small farms around here, and most small farms in this country, are hoop houses. Matt and I built one when we first started growing vegetables, to house tomatoes and peppers. They are poor-man's greenhouses, built cheaply and quickly, and are relatively portable. Made of PVC pipe bent into a semicircle and anchored into the ground, the hoops are lined up as long as the greenhouse is needed—fifty, eighty, a hundred feet long. The hoops are then covered with clear plastic sheeting that is attached to the individual PVC hoops. Hoop houses create low-cost spaces for growing vegetables that need a slightly higher temperature and protection from the wind and rain. On an even slightly warm day, the interior temperature in the hoop house will rise dramatically. The challenge of these hoop houses is keeping them cool. The plastic on the sides needs to be raised up to allow warm air to escape and drop the temperature down.

As these are covered structures, rainfall does not enter to water the plants inside. Long plastic irrigation tubes are run down the length of the hoop house, hitting all of the plants. In order to keep the weeds from taking over the precious plants, plastic landscape cloth often lines the bottom of the hoop house. Holes are cut into the landscape cloth and the plants are inserted.

Hoop houses are staggeringly efficient: they can be put together in a day once the parts are mustered, and can be moved if needed without too much effort. The cost is low considering their size and the quantity of food that can be grown in them. They lengthen the growing season for warm-weather crops such as tomatoes, peppers and melons and guarantee their success even during a cool summer. Without the added heat, these heat-loving plants would often not ripen well in the northwestern climate. Although rain is thought of generally as an asset to plants, it can be damaging to tomato plants, causing blight. When tomatoes are grown in a hoop house, the possibility of blight is eliminated.

A hoop house is warm inside, safe from the wind and the plastic covering is opaque, creating a diffuse glow of white light inside. In early spring, the newly planted tomatoes have not yet started their growth spurt of summer; they are still small and tidy. The floor of the hoop house is clean new plastic landscape cloth, the dampness of the winter months long since dried from the spring heat.

Midafternoons are the ideal time on the farm for a nap. The afternoon animal chores have not yet started, lunch is finished and the morning projects have been completed. I often nap on the floor of the hoop house; it is a private, warm, hidden spot. Where skinny-dipping is a logical extension of swimming, napping without the discomfort of muddy work clothes is a logical extension of farm napping. One warm afternoon, I decided to strip down before my afternoon doze in one of the hoop houses.

The hoop houses were located in the farthest field. Each paddock surrounding the field is gated and chained closed. The hoop house plastic is opaque and completely private. And yet, a customer looking for milk, intent on finding me, managed to walk to the upper pastures, trek through the pastures, through the gates, through the paddocks, past the cows. Looking to find some milk from the farm for her family, she made it all the way to the hoop houses.

She was a lovely mother of two beautiful young daughters, and I doubt that Lisa had expected to pull back the plastic and find a naked man asleep in the rows of small, verdant tomato plants. As I proceeded to quickly and discreetly cover myself, she made conversation. Either through nervousness or, with luck, having no idea what was going on, she chatted on endlessly, about her great interest in food, her love of tomato plants and her expectations of the summer growing season. I countered her conversation with my own banter, avoiding her eyes, yet knowing that she would never mention my weeding outfit.

Although I love napping in the hoop houses, I have intrinsic issues with them. I often wonder what the customers' perception of a farm is when they are making a purchase at a farmers' market. Prior to ever seeing a vegetable farm, I had a vision of vegetables growing in the field. Long rows of tomatoes and beans and beets, under the sun, farmers walking the rows, picking tomatoes into lovely wicker baskets. The reality is, at least in this part of the country, a lot of vegetables are grown under plastic.

Should we care that our produce is grown with the added protection of plastic sheeting? No, not really. The public is looking for tomatoes over a longer season than is possible in the northern latitudes. I have no reason to believe that the food is contaminated or changed in any way from the use of the plastic in the hoop houses. The cows are housed in the winter in a barn with cedar shakes on the roof. I expect the shakes will last twenty-five, maybe thirty years and then be removed and replaced with new roofing. Old cedar shakes can be burned or even left to rot in the forest and returned to the earth.

The plastic used in vegetable growing just gives me a lump in my gut. Something feels wrong. It looks wrong, and the shoppers at the farmers' markets are unaware of hoop houses' existence unless they travel out to the farms that they support.

The day when I walked back to the old vegetable garden after three destructive winter seasons to take down the first old hoop house is still fresh in my mind. The wind had damaged the structure beyond repair. Winter had been cruel.

I headed out to the garden, my tools with me: socket wrench, pliers, cordless drill. Little by little, through the morning drizzle of a late winter day, I took apart the PVC pipes, sorting out the puzzle that the orderly hoop house had become. The nice lines of the original hoops were now twisted pieces of cracked, brittle plastic. By noon, I had separated the hoops from the plastic sheeting; the nuts and bolts and screws that had held them all together were now in my soggy coat pocket.

After lunch in the warm kitchen, I changed into mud boots and a rain outfit of rubber overalls and hooded rubber jacket, all the snaps closed tight against the weather as the drizzle turned to showers. I spent the afternoon trudging back and forth from the back garden to the house, dragging the broken PVC pipes to my waiting pickup truck, and drove the load to the garbage dump. When the field was cleared of the white shards of sheared plastic, I set my sights on the plastic sheeting. Ripped and torn, battered by the winds, the plastic sheeting was now spread over much of the back field. I attempted to ball it up as best I could, and the ball was as big as my full-sized Ford truck.

I grabbed as much as possible and began the long drag back to the house, through the gates of the field, past the orchards, down through the muddy pastures and up past the kitchen. Along the way errant ends of the ripped sheet would snag on a corner of the fence or a stick protruding from the ground, ripping it further.

When I finally made it down to the truck, I attempted to find the corners of the long rectangle and hoist them up into the bed of the truck. The plastic was unwieldy and uncooperative. After working through the afternoon, I finally packed all of the plastic onto the truck. The sides of the truck were smeared with mud—my overalls, my jacket, my boots as well. As I drove down the driveway, out of the farm and down to the garbage dump I tried to remember the day, years before, when Matt and I had installed the hoop house.

It was a sunny spring day in April. The PVC was straight and clean, fresh from the hardware store, the plastic tight in its box from the greenhouse supplier. The field had been freshly tilled, light brown; clean, no weeds.

We measured out the hoop house, pounded in the stakes and bent the PVC in graceful semicircles. In the space of a couple of hours we had a row of hoops all in a line. And then we opened the cardboard box and pulled out the roll of plastic. We unrolled it the length of the hoop house on the dry, fluffy dirt. Then Matt and I went along the long length of plastic, found the many layers sandwiched together and opened up the sheeting, unfolding it to its full width.

With great fanfare we then each grabbed hold of a corner of the plastic lying on the ground and began to lift it up and over the waiting hoops. The plastic slid gently across the top of the hoops and back down the other side to the ground in just a few moments. We continued on down the length of the hoops until we reached the far end of the hoop house. Suddenly what had in the beginning been a series of erect sticks in the ground was a form, a covered space, a greenhouse.

As we got to the end hoop, the wind picked up just a bit in the back field and the plastic was gently lifted, but with great loft and power. We held it fast, but the sight for a moment was tremendous—like a giant butterfly, a glider rising from the earth, alive. The sun was shining and the opaque white plastic glowed.

We attached the plastic to the hoops, securing it against the wind, and immediately the interior warmed on that sunny spring day. We had been successful in capturing the heat that would be needed to keep the tomatoes and peppers thriving in the less-than-predictable Pacific Northwest summers.

It is those great spring days that I remember when I think of vegetable-growing, not the muddy winter days of cleaning up. It is springtime that is the golden time of year on a farm: everything is possible. The tomatoes will all ripen, no bugs will eat the salad greens, the soil will be weed-free, the dogs will never race through the garden knocking over the peas, all will be good. The vegetables in my garden will look just like the seed packet photos.

Reality will arrive a few weeks later. Late killing frosts, bugs that eat prized vegetable plants, drought, bad soil—all will have their run later through the year; but spring is about hope.

It reminds me of the school year as a child. Even if my fourth-grade teacher Mr. Pand didn't like me, or I didn't like him, the next September I would start fresh with Mrs. Palmer in fifth grade. She would know nothing of those dull days of winter, sitting in the classroom listening to Mr. Pand drone on. Each new school year was a fresh start, all was forgiven. Even with false threats of a "permanent record," each year was new, the slate wiped clean.

So too it is in the vegetable garden. The muddy days are forgotten, the errors and missteps in the past, in the spring all is green and fresh and possible.

Ten

Fowl

As I added new ventures to the farm, poultry seemed like a worthy experiment. Sure, poultry would never be a primary cash crop, but it's hard to imagine a proper farm without chickens pecking about, providing eggs and meat for the kitchen. Chickens have become permanent residents, year-round egg producers that become stewing hens after their prime has passed. I started my career in the food business as a pastry cook, and a love of baked goods has remained with me all these years later. With a summer garden full of ripe, full-flavored strawberries, raspberries, blackberries and currants, there was no question that I would need eggs to pair with farmhouse butter for pies and tarts. Geese and ducks have a supporting role: arriving in the late spring, spending the summer fattening up on the spoils of the season and then being slaughtered in the fall and preserved for winter eating.

Chicken, geese and ducks are essentially similar. They come from an egg, grow up, feather out, fatten up and make for a tasty roast bird or hang out longer and lay lovely eggs. If you can master and understand one bird, the rest pretty much follow suit. Geese, for example, are much bigger, certainly smarter, meaner and messier, but are not fundamentally different than laying hens.

Fowl are hardy enough to travel huge distances when they are not even a day old, which means that top-quality, interest-

ing, varied birds can be hatched in Iowa and be at my farm
the next morning, still very much alive. Hatcheries breed
chickens, ducks, geese, guinea fowl, peafowl, and ship them
overnight all over the country. Day-old birds are fairly inexpensive, even by airmail. A couple of dollars each, maybe six
dollars for a day-old gosling, quite a bargain compared to a
top-quality calf that might be hundreds of dollars plus pricey
transportation.

Each winter I page through the catalogue from the hatchery.
There is an entire section of bantams—miniature chickens—
that I find a bit too cute. Why would someone want a miniature chicken? The full-sized bird simply isn't that big to
begin with. I turn to the rare breeds section and imagine my
farm with fancy peacocks, flashing their feathers at guests.
They too get vetoed. I take a quick pass at the French varieties: Salmon Faverolles, Crèvecoeurs, Mottled Houdans. It
would certainly be a good look—the Houdans prancing by the
French-timber-frame barn—but perhaps a bit too precious.

In the end my parsimony prevails. I order the cheapest
chickens in the catalogue: either the brown egg-layer combination or the rainbow collection. With either of these selections, a motley crew of birds ships. I like their un-purebred
nature; they are "under-chickens," if you will. I make the call;
the day-old birds are scheduled for delivery.

On the appointed day, early in the morning the local post
office calls to say that they have arrived and asks me to
quickly get to the post office to pick them up. Actually it is
false to say that the post office clerk asks me to arrive quickly.
In reality I hear the phone ring, hear my answering machine
click on and listen as the clerk gives me the message. I hide
under the down comforter as long as possible. I do like chick
day, however. The phone rings exactly at six a.m., which I
am guessing is the official United States Post Office early call

time. It is usually winter and cold. I get myself together and drive off to town. I am often up early, but I rarely drive off the farm at that hour, and never before milking the cows and feeding the other animals. Chick arrival day is different and in some small way exciting. The dogs hop into the truck, I scrape the windows of the morning ice with an old credit card and we shiver in the cold pickup as the cab warms up in the short ride to town. In the old days I would just walk in the back door of the post office and chat with the mail carriers sorting mail into the little metal bins. In this post-9/11, post-anthrax world, I am left on the back loading dock to buzz in, large secure doors keeping me from the warm, well-lit interior of the post office. I still feel oddly special, though. The regular post office customers use only the front door and only come during business hours.

They grab my box of chicks; the chirping through the small holes in the box is always a welcome sound. Hopefully they will all be full of life when I open the box back at the house. Although there was a time when the dogs would have gone crazy at the notion of small birds in a tight little box chirping audibly, after many years my dogs are nonchalant. Having to share the front seat of the pickup is a greater annoyance than what is going on in the box.

As the chicks were ordered weeks prior, I have hopefully gotten ready for their delivery. Baby chicks are fully alive and not needing of motherly attention, but they are fragile at this point in their lives. They are not covered in feathers of any kind but rather a light fuzz that has little if any warming qualities. The greatest worry is that the chicks will die from the cold.

A box needs to be readied to raise the chicks in for the six weeks needed for them to grow enough feathers to withstand the cold. On day one, they are terribly vulnerable to every predator or temperature fluctuation. Heat must be added immediately to the box—the brooder—to keep them alive, usually by means of an overhead heat lamp.

I always look into the brooder coop and watch these day-old, two-day-old, three-day-old chicks and wonder about their existence. They have never met their parents; have actually never even seen an adult chicken. They were hatched in a large incubator in Iowa and now they are sitting in my barn a few days later. When they arrived from the post office, I picked them up one by one and dipped their beaks into the water trough. Without this little bit of assistance, they might never learn to drink water and would quickly die. With the exception of this bit of a head start on life skills, these chicks divine the skills necessary to be chickens on their own. Looking down at them pecking at the ground, sipping water, chasing the others around the tight, warm coop, I wistfully conclude that they are just fine. They don't appear to have any problems in life. There is no nurture, it is all nature. They never even see a mother hen. I fear a *Lord of the Flies* scenario—that I will lift the lid of the brooder coop and there will be Piggy, the fat chick, and Ralph, the bolder head chick, running the coop. As there is occasionally a dead chick found in the morning at one of the far corners of the coop, I imagine murderous anarchy among the birds, but the reality is more likely that the smallest of the flock strayed too far from the warmth of the lamp during the coldest part of the evening and died of exposure. They don't need a mother, but they do need a heat lamp.

Chickens, I am convinced, have had a great public relations firm working on their behalf ever since we domesticated them for eggs and meat. The popular vision of the chicken as chipper, kind, tidy and social, plus eager to graciously donate eggs, is nearly the opposite of reality.

In comparison to other farm livestock—cows, sheep, pigs—

chickens are by far the cruelest and most antisocial. Not too tidy either. Their cleanliness, or lack thereof, pales, though, in comparison to their greatest personality fault: cannibalism. I wish I could say that this was a rare occurrence, but no, it is a common trait.

The wonderful fowl term *pecking order* has become a part of our human lexicon and actually refers to chickens' barbarous sense of order. Those on the top of the social heap keep their standing by pecking. Not pecking at the ground, but rather at each other; frequently to the death.

When introducing one bird, or a whole flock, to another previously established flock, the result is often the total destruction of the new members, and possibly of the entire population at large. The flock that grows together from day-old chicks establishes their hierarchy early on. All the birds know their place and stick to it. Occasionally you hear an odd squawking that sounds like someone is trying to move up, but it is short-lived and order is restored, usually without blood.

When the order is tremendously upended by adding other mature birds, then the pecking order asserts itself. To find several birds pecked to death at the bottom of the coop the next morning is not unheard-of. This can go on for days. Chickens are said to get a taste for blood and refuse to let it go.

Commercial chicken farms have a couple of methods to combat this tendency. One is to keep the birds living in a red-lit coop. The blood-colored light makes the birds unable to see the blood of their fellow chickens and if there is a deathly fight, the other birds don't notice. Never having tried this, I find it very hard to believe, although I love the idea: chickens seeing life through rose-colored glasses.

The other method is to debeak the birds. The birds' beaks are cut back with an electric debeaker—a quick, sharp knife than blunts the beak. The birds cannot peck each other and their wrestling for dominance becomes noisy and disruptive but not deadly.

This is often cited as a case of animal cruelty. I must admit that it isn't a picnic for the birds, but on the cruelty meter it ranks low. Pig farmers do a similar act when they cut the tails off pigs so that their fellow pen mates don't bite their tails due to the tension over cramped pigpens.

Debeaking and tail-cutting are both acts against animals that I have trouble endorsing. Here at my farm neither occurs, but I can see the result of my failure to use the commercial controls. I have pulled many birds out of the coop over the years, massively bloodied and most certainly dead.

Chickens also face risks outside the coop. The weak link in the design of the chicken is their great love of sleep. During the daylight hours, chickens are full of life, extremely difficult to catch and quite observant. They jaunt around the yard, through the pasture, ever nervous—jerking this way and that. There is no way to surprise them; they are nervous to a fault. It keeps them alive while the sun shines. Then the raccoons come out.

At dusk, chickens head back to their coop. Like feathered zombies, they waddle back to the small door that leads into their home, unaware of the threats of the night. Their sense of security is wholly false.

Chickens sleep, or roost, on horizontal bars generally made of wood, their small talons gripping the stick, cheek by jowl with their coop mates. As night sets in, they physically shut down, their senses dulled by the lack of light. Where they were impossible to catch an hour earlier, it is now possible to walk into the coop and pick one up with no resistance; they are clumps of clay, cooing, feathered clumps, but clumps nonetheless.

This knowledge is useful for catching birds that otherwise

might be difficult to subdue. Sadly, raccoons are in on the secret. By night raccoons take advantage of chickens' vulnerability and sneak into the coop. Wily and intelligent, they are often successful at opening doors, avoiding electric fences and reaching through wire barriers. And the next night? They'll do it again. Their self-preservation is based on realizing the most food possible.

The telltale signs of a compromised chicken coop vary. The stealthiest coons remove their prey and leave no evidence. Each morning one member of the flock is missing. As chickens look alike and move constantly, ascertaining that the flock has been diminished from, say, thirty-six members to thirty-five is tricky. Even thirty-three or thirty-four birds pecking about at the ground can look similar to thirty-six. Each night the thief will enter the coop and remove one tasty bird. When one morning my favorite bird—the tall ruby-red-feathered cock with the sharp ebony talons and the commanding personality—is missing, it all becomes clear. Short of camping out in the coop, the raccoons are hard to thwart, even though you know they're coming. By the end of the next fortnight, most of the flock will have been abducted, the last few birds looking forlorn and confused as they stand alone in the once-full house.

Raccoons have no shame; self-preservation is everything. In addition to their superior intelligence over most animals, raccoons also have a most humanlike hand. Not a true opposable thumb, but close. This paw, this claw, this hand, has the ability to reach into tight spaces to extricate a chicken from its confines. The half-awake chicken is pulled through the opening by the raccoon, squawking and losing feathers along the way. Sometimes the paw can grab the bird, but can't remove it from the coop. The gruesome result is the discovery of a footless bird in the morning, stunned but frequently alive hours later.

A quick primer in avian and mammalian biology: Females, chicken or human, ovulate on a cycle. A human female will produce eggs and expel them no matter if they are fertilized or not. If they are fertilized, they will divide and become a baby, but if they are not fertilized, they will continue on as an egg. In a chicken, the same is true. The chicken produces eggs and expels them. If they are fertilized, the eggs can produce chicks, but if they are not fertilized, there are still eggs.

On the farmyard level, a flock of chickens has no need for a rooster. Without a rooster the eggs will not be fertilized, yet eggs will still be produced. A rooster adds a certain charm with his morning wake-up call, but his role is most limited.

With a single rooster, no rooster at all or a lot of roosters, hens take their time producing eggs. The official time frame is between five months and seven months from the time that the chick pecks its way out of the egg at the hatchery until the adult hen will start laying eggs. It is an interminable wait for the farmer. Months of chicks eating feed and producing nothing in return. Months of waiting and waiting for eggs. And then one day a small egg will appear. The first ovoids will be smaller than anything seen in an egg carton at the supermarket. More like a robin's egg than something you can imagine cracking and frying up for breakfast. In time, however, the first timid egg will give way to smallish eggs and then on to eggs of some repute.

Chickens will produce nearly one egg per day for years. The longer days of summer will encourage the birds to produce more; the short, dark days of winter, much less. A common trick is to add an electric light to the chicken coop in the winter months and leave it on constantly. The light will persuade the pituitary gland of the birds to think it is summertime and their laying habits will remain generous. A bit strange for the hens, I would think, but they seem to be able to sleep through the incessant light. On the cruelty scale, I feel it ranks rather low, and we do so love our eggs.

In my pursuit of producing the best-quality foods, I procured two chicken tractors. Chicken tractors are a glorious invention of the past few years. The essential idea is that instead of keeping hens in a traditional chicken coop they are kept in a movable chicken house. The traditional chicken abode is a free-standing, static building, generally built of wood, with a flock of hens, a corresponding number of nesting boxes and a few places for them to roost. As they sleep, locked in their coop to protect them from predators, they drop their manure. The combined manure of a flock of hens after a few days, weeks or months is substantial. If the farmer is on his game, he removes the chicken manure in a timely fashion. If he's a slacker, he does not. I have been both farmers. Waiting to clean out the chicken coop is similar to waiting to go to the dentist to get a tooth filled. The longer you wait, the worse the prospect becomes, and soon you can't bring yourself to do it at all.

Chicken tractors solve this issue. The chickens live in an open-bottomed box, covered well on the sides and top to protect the birds from any unwanted visitors. Inside this box are feed troughs, a water supply and nesting boxes mounted on one side for the chickens to lay their eggs in. Each day the chicken tractor is moved a few feet so that the chickens living inside are always on fresh pasture. Each day the footprint under the tractor is fertilized with the chicken droppings. The pasture never gets too much chicken manure, the chickens always have a fresh bit of grass to peck around on and the farmer doesn't end up wading ankle-deep into very old chicken droppings.

The chicken tractor is a superb system. The chickens are essentially free-range. They get to peck about as if they were out on an open pasture, and yet are safe from hawks watching them from above, and raccoons trailing them at night. They get to eat fresh green grass on a daily basis year-round, contributing to a healthy diet. I feed them high-quality organic grain every morning after moving the chicken tractor, but with the tractor excess grain never builds up and attracts rats.

The only limitation that I can see is that chicken tractors are intended for a fairly small operation. I have two here, each five feet wide, twelve feet long, two feet high and containing ten to twenty chickens. I certainly collect enough eggs each morning to supply the Cookhouse dinners. My two dogs get to enjoy fresh eggs each morning as well. If I were to attempt to keep hundreds of laying hens here with the goal of selling dozens of pastured farm eggs, I would have a traffic jam of shiny aluminum chicken tractors vying for space on the limited flat pasture.

It is a welcome chore each morning, after the cows are milked and fed, and the pigs fed as well, to move the chickens to their new patch of grass, feed them and gather the waiting fresh eggs in the tidy nesting boxes. I have no regrets about tearing down the outmoded wooden chicken coops, with their floors thick with manure, errant feathers and bits of straw.

Hens lay eggs daily in their most productive period. But there comes a point when the hens are simply not profitable. The quantity of eggs that they produce does not equal the feed that they consume. They cease to be an asset to the farm and cross over to the liability column. Their final gift, however, comes in their great worth as stewing hens. Hens wear their years in their flesh; young chickens may be tender, but their flavor comes with age.

When these hens emeritus are slaughtered, they yield an added bonus: eggs. As their imminent demise is unknown to them, the hens continue producing eggs. When the hens are slaughtered, those eggs are still inside them. What is absolutely fascinating is the quantity and quality of such eggs. The birth canal, if you will, is filled with a week's worth of eggs in varied stages of creation. Closest to the vent is essentially a full-sized egg, with shell. The shell is terribly thin and easily broken during slaughter, but still a shell nonetheless. The next up the line has no shell at all, although the smaller yolk is surrounded by the white, sans shell: truly amazing to hold. It is the whole, raw egg without a shell, the surface of the white holding it all in. Just the hint of shell binds the white. Farther up the path are a series of yolks, each progressively smaller until the final one is the size of a pearl. Each can easily be taken from the body of the plucked and gutted hen. And then there appears the challenge. These yolks are beautiful to behold, but what to do with them?

I have tried them out myself here at the farm kitchen, and the cooks that pass through have given them a shot, but little comes of the yolks. The most innovative use was by a friend who layered them in coarse salt to draw their moisture out. After a few days, the yolks had been adequately desiccated to use, but their taste was still not particularly interesting.

Chickens, as well as ducks and geese, have two great uses: as meat birds or as layers. Although each bird serves both functions, endless breeding has produced birds that are superior either at egg-laying or at meat production.

I find the meat birds are a sad lot. The most common breed is the Cornish X, or cross. As the mantra of raising chickens for meat commercially is "Time is money," these birds have been bred to put on weight as quickly as possible. In a matter of six or eight weeks they are fully grown. To watch a day-old chick become a three-pound bird in less than two months is startling. Further, these Cornish birds have been bred to produce a great deal of breast meat at the expense of the rest of their frames. The result is often birds that are so chest-heavy that they have trouble standing erect.

In my experience, it is very difficult to grow a bird as rapidly as the hatchery catalogues claim is possible. Perhaps I'm cheap on the grain, but my hens take twelve weeks, sixteen weeks to fully fill out to cooking size, which is fine by me. It seems more humane, more gracious. As I raise maybe two dozen of these birds at a time, the extra time and additional feed is inconsequential. When the large growers are raising ten thousand birds at a time, an extra day of feed has tremendous financial implications.

Slaughtering chickens is not a party. Slaughtering pigs, sheep, calves is not a pleasure either, but the sheer size of them and the number of people involved gives those activities weight, gravitas and a purpose. Plucking chickens is more tedious and dirty than anything else. There is no gravitas involved.

The meat chicks are delivered day-old to the farm in boxes of two dozen from the hatchery, just like chicks destined to be layers. With luck, most of the birds live through the transport and the first couple weeks of life in their brooder. Slaughtering two dozen birds at once is a task I would avoid; a few at a time makes much more sense. The justification is that the birds will be at different stages, different sizes for a variety of culinary uses. The first three or four will be very young, very tender and respond well to a quick sauté. A few weeks later, a bit bigger, a bit fuller: roast birds. A month later, big solid roasting birds will emerge from the coop. When the last few chickens are sent to slaughter, braised chicken is in order, full of flavor befitting their age.

To begin the preparations, a large pot of water is put on to heat, preferably on a portable outdoor burner. The water is heated to 140 degrees to release the feathers. Too hot and the skin will cook; too cool and the feathers will stay put no matter how hard you tug.

The chickens are removed; ideally those chosen are pulled earlier and set aside in a separate cage. One by one, I grab the birds, flip them upside down and hold them by their feet. This position will calm them, at least calm them a bit. Attached to a large tree near the heating water is a killing cone. Constructed of galvanized tin, it is of ample size at the top to hold a chicken tightly; the bottom is a small hole adequate for the head of the chicken to drop through. When the bird is placed in the cone, the head and a bit of neck show, the legs sticking straight up. Although the chicken is in a compromised position, it still has the physical ability to flip itself out of the cone, and will try to do so.

Holding the head in one hand to stretch the neck, I quickly cut the throat of the chicken with a very sharp knife. Blood will spurt out immediately if the cut is proper. The goal is to quickly bleed out the bird. Cutting the head off completely is a possibility, guaranteeing that the bird dies instantly. With the brain unattached to the body, the chicken as we know it is dead. A steady hand is needed to keep the chicken in the cone, because its body will continue to try to right itself for a few seconds. While I've never let a bird run around with its head chopped off, the body does certainly continue with motor functions, so the adage appears to be rooted in a real natural phenomenon.

I hold on to the legs of the chicken. Partly to keep the bird secure, but also because it fascinates me. The talons of a chicken, especially a big old rooster, are tremendous. Scaly, fierce, with a sharp claw on some roosters, they bring to mind the old fantasy books. I think of such sharp-clawed chickens as characters in a C. S. Lewis story, J. R. R. Tolkien beasts, not of this world. As the head is cut, the feet will come alive, full of vigor. And then, moments later, as the muscles relax, they flex out, once, twice, maybe three times, and then go limp. Holding on to these feet as you feel the life drain out is a powerful experience. I can't say that I like it, that I enjoy it, but that I respect it.

Once the bird has finished in the cone, it is transferred to the hot water. The goal is to cook the feathers adequately to release their hold on the bird. An adult chicken is covered in feathers, feathers designed to fluff up and keep the cold out, the water out. They are not prone to get wet, so a thorough dunking to adequately wet the bird is called for. Birds also float, so dunking with a stick is encouraged. Maybe thirty seconds underwater, a quick test of a feather, and then the bird is pulled from the water; longer dunking may be needed if the feathers do not release.

This is the beginning of the less-than-glamorous part of raising chickens. The birds, especially those meat birds whose oversized breasts drag on the floor of the chicken coop, are less than clean. Many birds will be caked with manure. With a dunking in a pot full of hot water, the manure will be released, fouling the water, fouling the air. There is nothing charming or quaint to say about this.

If the feathers are adequately loosened by the hot water, then the chicken can be hung for plucking. Plucking a bird on the flat I find difficult; hanging works best. I tie a rope around one foot and hang the bird from a nice height. The ground beneath is covered in paper. Some feathers are easy and simple to pluck, others most difficult. Legs, breasts,

thighs and back are mostly a breeze; the tail is a bit challenging but gives in with a tug. The wings are different. The
powerful wings have large, formidable feathers that are well
anchored. As the wings themselves carry little meat on them,
I skip them entirely. The ratio of work to reward is simply
not there.

The large feathers come off first, then the smaller and then
smaller still, until the bird is essentially bald, except the wing
feathers hanging down rather forlornly. A second or third
dunking may be necessary to get to the bald bird stage.

Chickens are relatively easy to pluck—a joy, you might
even say, compared to geese. Geese have feathers the size
of ballpoint pens and the feathers stick in as if they were
glued. Ducks are easier than geese, although a bit more of a
challenge than chickens. I have often thought I would save
the duck or goose feathers for use in house pillows, but with
the feathers collecting beneath the dead bird, near steaming
water stinking of excrement, it simply doesn't feel like a Mar-
tha Stewart moment.

One by one the bald birds are brought into the kitchen for
further cleaning. If the plucking was tedious, the gutting is
downright distasteful, although thankfully quick. In a nod to
our personalities, I generally have Jorge kill and pluck the
birds; he is the most thoughtful and takes his time with a
task. I reserve the gutting and cleaning for myself; I like tasks
that are quick, even if dirty.

Gutting a chicken, or a duck or goose, for that matter, is
essentially the same as gutting a cow or a pig. The goal is to
remove all the entrails, leaving none in the cavity, saving the
best parts and keeping the manure in the intestines where it
belongs and not on the meat.

The first cut is to encircle the bung of the chicken to remove
the intestines in whole. Once the bung is released, then a

larger cut will open up the cavity adequately for your hand to
enter. The intestines will immediately fall out with a bit of a
tug. They will be attached to the gizzard, although the tender
guts will generally tear before releasing the stubborn gizzard.
The guts are immediately dropped in a bucket to be sent to
the pigs at the end of this task.

The guts that we seek to preserve are the hearts, gizzards
and livers. All else is uninteresting and unnecessary. The livers of a bird are out of scale with the size of the animal and
also quite tender. Large, a silky caramel color, the liver is gently pulled out of the cavity. It most likely will tear in the process, but no matter. The bile sac is a small bag of chartreuse
liquid that is unfortunately tethered to the liver. The liquid is
bitter and most undesirable. While the outer skin of the sac is
tender and easily ruptured, with a bit of delicate knife work
the livers can be extracted for later culinary use.

The gizzards are the most phenomenal part of a bird. There
are few parts of animals that I can gush about, but chicken
gizzards are one of those. Like a great beefsteak, but steak
seems so very predictable compared to a chicken gizzard.

The gizzard of a mature bird is approximately two and a
half inches long, and as much as two inches across—similar
in shape to a kidney but flattened a bit. The gizzard is hard
and feels like a hard rubber ball, with little give. It feels out
of place in the guts of a bird. With dramatic white and dark
brown crenellations along the flattened side, up close gizzards
give off the impression of an abstract painting.

When I have finished cleaning the outside of the gizzard
and hold it in my hand, I marvel at it. I take a knife and cut
in along the center of the outer edge—the longer side of the
kidney-shaped organ. I always use an older knife, as it will be
immediately dulled. The gizzard is filled with small rocks and
gravel and as the knife cuts it, it slides against those pebbles.

When the gizzard has almost been cut in half—butterflied, if you will—then it can be splayed open to show all its glory.

I take the now-opened organ to the sink and begin to rinse out the rocks and bits that were held in the sealed gizzard. The birds use these rocks to grind their food before it passes to the stomach for digestion. A crude system, perhaps, but it appears to work for them.

When the gizzard is laid out flat, it is a tremendous thing. The colors are the colors of an earthy palette: deep reds, almost blue tones, dark browns. The interior texture is crinkled thick leather, unlike the slick firm rubber of its exterior. It is far too beautiful to be hidden in the gut of a chicken, grinding grain.

Once the livers, gizzard and heart are removed, cleaned and cooled down for later use, the wings are quickly chopped off, still retaining their stubborn feathers; the pigs will chomp on them minutes later. After a final rinse, the last bits of errant guts are pulled from the cavity and the bird is cooled down in the refrigerator.

The kitchen counter will be covered with bits of guts, slime and the odd broken bile sac. Only a thorough scrubbing and bleaching will get me ready to think about roast chicken.

In my early years of growing food, I met Suzy, the owner of the local feed store. I would go in to buy dog food and quiz her on how to raise chickens. One Sunday afternoon I suggested to Suzy that I wanted to raise chickens so that I could go out into the yard, grab a bird, clean it and roast it up for dinner. "Wouldn't that just be a lovely thing?" I mused. She quickly set me straight. She raised birds for meat, and had for years. Once a year she and her husband slaughtered four dozen birds, plucked and cleaned them all. The birds were then wrapped and frozen for Sunday dinners later. She let me know that after spending the day cleaning chickens I would have no interest in eating one that night. I felt terribly green, and was rather embarrassed. Although today it wouldn't bother me to clean and cook in the same afternoon, the meat is far more tender if left to settle for at least twenty-four hours in the cooler, if not longer.

When the memory of chicken guts has receded, the birds can be cooked up. A great roasted bird is the perfect farm dinner. It is simple, of the earth and satisfying. When the golden, crispy bird comes out of the roasting oven, all of the plucking and cleaning is forgotten; only the rich, moist chicken matters.

For chickens, nothing beats roasting. For ducks, a simple confit is perfect. French in origin, the basic technique of confit is to preserve meat by slowly cooking it in its own fat. The goal is to keep the meat usable through the difficult winter months after the animals have been slaughtered in the late fall. Beyond simple preservation, the confit technique results in absolutely delicious meat.

Ducks follow the seasons. They are born in the spring when the chills of winter have lapsed, and the grass has begun to grow in the warmth of spring. Through the summer they fatten on grass, and in the fall on the ripening grain. As the season cools, the ducks begin to fatten, to gain an insulating layer to protect themselves through the long cold winters. We take advantage of nature by bringing in ducks from the hatchery in the early spring, raising them through the spring and summer and then slaughtering them in the late fall. By October they have grown to mature size and have a respectable amount of rich fat.

When the ducks are gutted and plucked and chilled, they are ready to butcher. A chilled duck is a marvel: firm from the hard fat, full of muscle and easy to cut. First the rosy breasts are removed from the rib cage and set aside. Then the legs

and thighs are removed. Two delectable morsels of meat, each
the size and shape of an oyster, lie on either side of the back,
and they must be included.

All that's left is a carcass. Any fat that can be harvested
from the carcass can be taken at this time. The vast majority will lie around the vent where the guts were removed.
Large clumps of hard yellow fat should be found ready for the
claiming. Those bits of fat are collected and melted slowly in
a heavy-bottomed sauce pan with a bit of water on the bottom
to prevent sticking.

The remaining picked carcasses still contain lovely fat.
Halve them and place on a large sheet tray in a hot oven. Let
brown till a nice caramel. Not so that they are burnt skeletons,
but gently roasted and still having a bit of moisture to them.
Pull the tray from the oven gently; the tray should be filled
with more rendered duck fat. Tilt the tray so that one corner
is lowered into the saucepan on top of the stove with the first
bit of fat-rendering going on. Drain the tray completely.

Toss the carcasses in a stockpot, cover with cool water and
a bit of aromatic herbs. Bring to a slow simmer and make a bit
of stock. When the stock has simmered for two or three hours,
drain and chill. On the surface will be another bit of fat. The
fat that has collected on the stock can be added to the duck fat
that was rendered earlier.

While the stock is simmering and the fat rendering, season
the legs and thighs. The classic seasoning is salt, bay and
fresh thyme. The classic technique is to lay the legs/thighs
fat-side down, meat-side up on a large nonmetal tray. Liberally sprinkle the meat with coarse salt, and then I was always
taught to lay fresh bay leaves and large sprigs of thyme on
top of the duck. I never really understood this and thought it
more perfunctory than realistic. I remember coming up with
the idea of taking the thyme and fresh bay leaves and grind-

ing them in a spice mill with the coarse salt. The result is a beautiful chartreuse salt: vibrant, full of flavor and more likely to be absorbed by the duck. I thought I had truly come up with something new until I later saw it in a Thomas Keller cookbook. Even though I'm not the father of green salt, I still use it to good effect regularly. Cover the duck, leave in the refrigerator overnight to season and return to the stock-simmering and the fat-rendering.

Twenty-four hours later the ducks are seasoned, the stock has been strained and the fat rendered. Pull the leg and thigh pieces from the cooler, brush the salt off completely and towel-dry. Place them all in an ample, heavy-lidded casserole dish and pour enough of the duck fat to cover completely. Reserve whatever fat is remaining, if any.

Slowly heat the casserole on the top of the range until it begins to very slowly simmer. Keep the flame low enough and steady enough to maintain that delicate simmer for hours, until the duck is fork-tender and close, but not quite, to falling off the bone. Then allow to cool to room temperature.

Transfer the duck legs and thighs into a small stoneware crock that can hold them. Melt the duck fat if it has begin to solidify, strain out any bits and pour it over the duck legs to completely cover. The goal is to seal out the air entirely, preserving the duck in its own fat. The duck will have rendered more fat during its cooking, so there should be adequate fat to work with. Place the crock, with a heavy lid to discourage nibbling, in the cellar for safekeeping. With luck it will be forgotten until the depths of winter.

When the duck is desired, bring the crock up into room temperature, or possibly onto the back of the range. When the fat has softened adequately, reach in and grab the meat. Melt the remaining fat, strain and save in the cooler for future projects; the fat will get saltier with each use, but can be reused.

A great way to use the preserved duck is in a salad: sweet greens, a bit of bitter lettuce, thinly sliced winter pears, honey, apple cider vinegar and the precious strips of duck confit.

A lovely thing happened in the process of finding a working model for the farm. I tried growing different foods here: vegetables, fruits, goats, cows, ducks and chickens. Although the goal was to find a way to keep the farm operating without returning to the city to work, I discovered that my eventual farm would not just raise one crop, but rather produce a variety of different foods alongside what would become the primary product—cheese.

The food that I created here—the duck confit, the roasted chickens, the roasted leg of lamb, the aged cheese—was good. Really good. Controlling more and more aspects of the food made the quality higher. Slaughtering the chickens myself, although certainly not my favorite task, assured me that the chickens would be tasty, and also prepared me for slaughtering larger animals—sheep, goats and eventually pigs and cows. The more I enjoyed the food from this farm, the more animals I wanted to raise, and to raise well.

Eleven

Pigs

Pigs are the centerpiece of many a traditional farm. Rivaled only perhaps by cows as the symbol of the farm, pigs are perfect farm animals for a small operation. They consume all of the waste a farm and its kitchen can produce, and when slaughtered, all of their parts can be utilized for feeding the farmer throughout the year. We could not design a more perfect system for transforming the wastes of the farm: old milk and soured cream, vegetables at the end of the growing season, the apple pressings from making cider and the wastes from slaughtering chickens, lambs and calves, are transformed into beautiful hams, bacon and pork chops.

These porcine creatures have real personality: they are smart, attentive, aggressive, stubborn and charming. I have been furious with pigs when trying to move them, and find them insanely lovable at other times. On a beautiful day when the pigs are lying in the sun, their large bellies splayed out, they are wondrous, and it is then that I forget the agonizing days when they have escaped or flipped their water troughs over again and again.

Pigs are unique in that you can sense that they are looking at you and thinking. The cows, the sheep, even my most beloved dogs, certainly look me in the eye, but there really isn't anything there. The house dogs are hoping that they will go for a ride, the cows looking for more hay, the sheep don't even have such an ability. Pig eyes, however, show something more.

I generally try to steer away from anthropomorphizing farm animals. When people describe a mother sheep as "just like my sister the way she takes care of her kids" or some such rattling, I assume they have very little experience with sheep. They want animals to be family members, not beasts that will be slaughtered in time for the family barbecue. I make an exception in naming my cows, but recognize that they are animals first, not humans or friends. Pigs I never name; they are only here for their eventual role as meat.

Pigs make me wonder, though: is there a soul lurking beneath that bristly hide? I tend to think that yes, they are certainly more intelligent than a sheep or a cow, but no, they are not capable of anything more complex than trying to get more food and water and shelter from me. One possibility is that their eyes are just more evolved. The actual eye, the shape and the cornea and the eyelash looks very much like a human's eye. The eye of a cow is larger than ours, rounded and without depth. I look into that eye and see nothing more than a blank stare coming back from the cow. I look into the eye of a pig and perceive a person dressed up in a pig suit staring at me.

I wanted pigs at my farm more than any other animal. I yearned to make prosciutto out of the legs of my own pigs. Eventually I did, but it took more time than I had anticipated. I had trouble finding pigs. This was only a decade ago, and yet it might as well have been a hundred years in the past; little had changed in pig availability over those many years until recently. There was really no good system for finding items like pigs before the introduction of Craigslist.com. As a method for people in small rural communities to buy and sell farm equipment and animals, Craigslist is unsurpassed. It is

immediate, free and reaches out to many people efficiently. I
used to have to go to a feed store and read what were in effect
weeks-old postcards announcing baby pigs for sale posted on
the bulletin board. By the time I found the notice and called
the farm, the pigs were most likely long gone. Craigslist has
changed all that. I can now quickly find specific breeds of pigs
or sheep or cows that are for sale and know a few hours later
if they are still available. Old farming equipment, such as
tractor parts, is equally well served. I wouldn't be surprised if
small farming in America will have a renaissance because of
this simple technological advancement. A Web site that was
never intended by its designers to aid in the sale of disc har-
rows and baby Toulouse geese has greatly improved small
agriculture in America.

Even before the advent of Craigslist I did manage to pro-
cure baby pigs. They were found at a feed store an hour or so
north of the city. I happened to wander in to buy a watering
trough or something for my sheep and saw a sign for piglets.
I inquired and there were some available that day. I never
really knew why they were available right then, but I took
it as a bit of fate and bought three baby pigs already weaned
from their mothers and therefore known as *weaners*.

As it turned out, finding them was the easy part. Pigs are
unbelievably strong for their size. They are just bundles of
muscle. Even at seven or eight weeks of age, they are very
difficult to catch and hold. The feed store put them in a simple
cardboard box and duct-taped them closed. I casually put them
in the back of my truck and we headed down the highway for
the hour-long drive to the ferry dock and then the boat ride
to the island and on to the farm. Fortunately, I didn't travel
solo, as my friend Marc agreed to join me on what I had sold
him as a lovely country drive. Once we got onto the freeway
and I began to accelerate into traffic, I looked in the rearview

mirror and realized that the pigs were beginning to break free of their flimsy confines and their little pink snouts could be seen peeking through the folds of the cardboard box.

I pulled the truck over quickly on the shoulder of the busy interstate and found that the only solution was to bring the cardboard carton with the three young and frisky piglets into the front of the pickup truck and have Marc keep his hand on the lid for the trek back to the farm. Marc tried to look annoyed throughout the long ride back to the island, but I think that the piglets, with their small pink snouts poking through the cardboard flaps, eventually cut through to his sense of humor.

A pig's life here at my farm follows a traditional seasonal calendar. I raise a few hogs every year. Buy them in the spring, fatten them up over the summer and slaughter them in the winter. Animals consume food and convert it to protein, gaining weight in the process. If a portion of the calories they eat goes to keeping them warm, then those calories don't go toward weight gain. Therefore, raising any animal in the spring and summer is more productive than in the colder months. In the summer months and early fall there is also an abundance of waste in the garden. All the overripe produce, cabbage leaves, broccoli stems and so on go to the pigs to eat. In the darkness of the winter months, food is an expense and must be brought in to feed the pigs.

In addition to the garden waste, the pigs eat food waste. Some comes from the kitchen at the farm and some from restaurant kitchens in the community. Every week Jorge drives around to the restaurants and collects food from their kitchens. The technical terms for the waste are *pre-plate* and *post-plate*. As you can imagine, waste is divided into two groups, waste from prepping the food before it gets to a customer and the waste that is left on the plate by the consumer. The county health department feels that pre-plate food is safe for pigs, but that post-plate is not. I respect the health department's vision, and limit what the pigs are fed to food waste that comes directly from the kitchen.

Jorge gets food from restaurants that are not organic and do not necessarily buy the best-quality food, but it fills up the hogs and they grow quickly. You can't argue with free. To buy bags of commercially prepared organic hog feed, I would need to drive my truck off the island to a large feed store in the county south of the island. Spending half a day making the drive, then paying for the feed and then disposing of the plastic sacks that the feed is sold in seems worse from an environmental perspective. The waste food from the restaurants is just a few minutes from the farm. There are lots of greasy french fries, lots of carrot peelings from commercially grown carrots and old soup with mysterious ingredients. Feeding the animals with buckets of lesser-quality food keeps that slop from the island landfill and stops me from driving off the island every month for feed. If it fattens my hogs and I don't have to write a check for it, I'm happy to take it off a restaurant's hands.

At the end of the long center worktables in the farm kitchen are three buckets. You might call them the garbage cans. The first holds all refuse made of paper, things that are burnable. Right outside the kitchen door is the wood-fired oven. All those bits of junk mail, envelopes from bills, paper sacks that the coffee beans are packaged in—all those bits of paper are burned to start a weekly fire in the oven.

The second bucket is a larger container with a lid. In it all food wastes are dumped. The contents of this bucket are emptied almost every day, headed to the pigs, nature's best composters. They eat everything. They prosper by it, loading on pounds from food waste.

The third bucket is for garbage in the most traditional sense of the word. Items that will be dragged to the dump. I like calling it a dump. For years it was just that. Here on the island, garbage was driven to a large tract of land and dumped into a hole, a large hole, in the ground. Over time, the hole filled with garbage and then for a few years you would simply throw your stuff onto the ground from the back of your car. At the end of the life span of this garbage dump, the refuse of the island's inhabitants was pushed up into a mighty hill by large bulldozers, creating a knoll of baby toys, broken lawn mowers, raincoats, shower curtains, and the other detritus of our existence.

The garbage dump is now called the "transfer station." Garbage is transferred—which reminds me of changing colleges, of being given a new job in a new fresh city, of riding a different bus route. The island has a service that drives around weekly and picks up our garbage cans filled with our unwanted items and treks them over to the transfer station for us, just like in a proper city. The cans are left by the side of the road in the morning and are emptied by evening. Transferred.

I have never participated in this service. Mostly from my inherent cheapness, but also because I want to be more engaged in the farm garbage. I save up my garbage and when it is quite a large mass of sacks and boxes and bags, I load it all into my truck and drive it across the island to the transfer station. The back of the small pickup truck is filled, a tarp covering the potentially loose bits, a rope tying down the tarp to the sides of the truck. It is then that I can see what I am responsible for, what I have created. When I unload each bag from the truck into the deep concrete canyon, I am made aware of how much garbage I have asked to be transferred.

That image is in my head when I see the new toaster at the

store. Shiny and new, packed in a box, surrounded by Styrofoam blocks. This toaster will change my life; make my toast quicker, more evenly browned, more pleasing to me. And then I fast-forward to the time a month, a year, a decade in the future when I am pitching that toaster, older and less shiny, into the belly of the transfer station. Toasting my bread in the morning on the rack of the oven suddenly seems good enough.

Although very little refuse ends up in the third bucket—the one headed for the transfer station—plenty ends up in the second bucket—the one headed for the pigs. The diet of pigs is oddly controversial. The question is whether they are carnivores or herbivores. If I go to my shelf and pull out ten books on raising pigs, five will tell me never to feed them meat and five will say feed them everything including meat. I am confused. So I have gone the omnivore route. My hogs eat meat as well as vegetables.

I've searched for the term—and never found it—that describes the quality in animals (including humans) that causes us to find our own species' flesh abhorrent and inedible. That reticence keeps us healthy, keeps diseases isolated and rarely, if ever, fails. Pigs will not eat raw pork except in dire circumstances. They know that it is bad and avoid it. Raw beef or chicken or lamb, no problem, but pork they will leave. Once it is cooked, it is just meat, but raw is a problem.

I did make this mistake early on in keeping pigs. One of the waste products that need to be dealt with on a farm is the detritus from slaughtering animals. Although most everything is used, a few things still remain: spleens and pancreases, intestines and stomachs and lungs. None are particularly tasty, some are downright awful and all require a great deal of work to clean and prepare for an eventual poor gastronomic result. Burying these bits is certainly a possibility but there is a lot of protein in the guts of an animal. The farm has paid for that protein either in the form of actual cash for feed or from crops grown on the farm that were fed to the animals—pasture, corn, milk. If that protein is buried deep in the ground so that dogs cannot dig it up, then the value of that protein is lost; it cannot be utilized by the farm. It is a loss. If it is composted or fed back to other animals, then that protein capital can be captured. We have all learned from the mad cow problems of the past decade that animals have been routinely fed back to animals and that it causes problems. The problems arise when the same species is fed back to other members of that species—for example, chicken guts turned into chicken feed.

So the safest option is to feed lamb and cow and chicken guts to the pigs, but never pig guts. The best part is that if you forget, as I did once years ago, and dump pig guts into the pigpen, they will run over to it and sniff it and push it around and then walk away. You then have a mess of pig guts to deal with. I would not recommend it.

There is a trend lately to feed pigs specific diets with the goal of affecting the quality and taste of the eventual meat, especially the hams. The Iberian pigs of Spain are fed acorns from the surrounding oak trees and are thought to be the reason that the jamón ibérico is so tasty. I find this all so very silly. If you have a great many oak trees growing and the ground beneath them is littered with acorns, then running pigs in the orchard is a great solution. The pigs are well fed, you don't have to exert any effort to take the feed to the pigs and the resulting hams are tasty and unique. If you have a hog farm, need to feed your pigs and you are having acorns, hazelnuts, or chestnuts shipped in from elsewhere, it is folly. The costs, both in terms of effort and time and money to ship the feed in, might be recouped from the eventual selling of a high-end ham, but the result is tainted: a forced product, not one that is the result of a natural synergy.

I am limited, at my farm, in the number of hogs that I can raise per year by the amount of feed I have. I grow a small amount of corn, use all the kitchen waste and garden waste I can for feed and bring in local restaurant food waste. I do keep some grain on hand for days when I need all the milk from the dairy, when there are no kitchen extras and the local restaurants are slow. Pigs, like most of us, expect to be fed each and every day, and prefer at least twice per day. A bag of grain is a useful thing to calm the porcine stomachs on a slow day.

Here at the farm, the hogs live in a small grove of cherry trees that grew from the fallen cherries of a former orchard. I call it Pig Forest. It is dark and cool even during the hottest weeks and has plenty of nooks and crannies for the pigs to root around in and explore. Probably a quarter acre in size, it has housed hogs for the past four years. Surrounding Pig Forest is a simple fencing system. A small wire, eight inches off the ground, runs around the perimeter. Held in place by fence posts, it is electrified by a fence charger located at the barn.

Pigs abhor electrical current, which makes them easy to confine. A fence charger sends a pulsating charge through the thin electrical wire every second. It is a charge that is high on voltage and low on amperage. The charger is grounded with a deep metal stake at the barn. When an animal, with its feet on the ground, touches the wire, it completes the loop and it receives the shock. If you were to touch it, you would certainly feel it, but it is hard to classify it as pain. A shock, nothing more. Pigs avoid such a shock at all costs. Once they learn that the wire contains a current, they will not break through it, even though they are strong enough to easily break the wire.

Pigs use their snouts to test the world around them. Pig snouts are generally moist and free of hair, so when they approach the hot wire they inspect it with a smooth, wet, flat surface, which is perfect for conducting current. If they were to pick up their hoof and tap the wire, they would probably not feel a thing.

Pigs love to eat. Actually, all animals love food, but pigs especially love food and learn very quickly where they are fed and when they are fed. If they are fed in the same spot, they will make sure they will be there the next morning, the next afternoon or even all day, in hope of another meal. If they were to get beyond the confines of Pig Forest, they would most likely return by the next feeding for a bucket of pig slop.

Pigs are great escapers, none more so than the first and last boar I've owned. After a couple of years on the farm, Junior, a name he aquired from previous owners, was rather rotund, slow to move and quite set in his ways. Junior discovered a place in the fence where the electric wire in no way crossed his path; he could walk under it and avoid the shock. If he had simply climbed under the wire and headed for greener pastures, I would have immediately noticed. Junior would leave just after his morning feeding, presumably just after I returned to the house. He would travel quite a ways, crossing three other properties to a lovely pasture with a small creek running through it. When the afternoon arrived, he would venture back, walk under the fence and take a nap, awaiting my arrival for his afternoon feeding.

This went on for at least a few weeks. Although the owners of the bucolic pasture rather quickly noticed a four-hundred-pound boar in their midst, they had no idea what to do about it. He appeared to be far more menacing that he was in reality. He also had no tags, no brand, no moniker that would give them an idea of his home base.

I raise pigs in a suburb where the primary crop is children, not farm animals. There are few pigs in these parts, and consequently I had, unbeknownst to me, a reputation for errant farm animals. Years later, when I meet someone from the neighboring properties, they often mention that my pigs, my sheep, my cows, my goats have traversed their land at some point. Although I have generally forgotten, they have not. Some find it charming, say that this reassures them that they live in an agricultural community. Others find it downright annoying and take pleasure in reminding me whenever we meet. "Oh, yes, you are the man with the pigs. . . . In 1996 they got loose and walked all over my lawn, don't you remember? Should I remind you? All over my lawn."

Thankfully this part of the country does not have the tradition of pig reeves. In New England, small towns appoint a resident to be the reeve, the one responsible for tracking down errant pigs, and for enforcing local laws against pigs running amok in neighbors' gardens. I would have run afoul of the reeve on many occasions.

The pigs test the wire often, squealing with a sound that greatly exceeds their discomfort. They are vocal beasts and can certainly be classified as drama queens. My neighbors must have the idea that I am torturing pigs on a daily basis. Nothing could be further from the truth. In reality I have given them so much food that they are climbing on top of each other to get the best bits. They push each other so that one slides into the hot wire and gives an extremely vocal response. As I don't worry about them being hurt, I simply take these sounds as confirmation that the hot fence is on and working adequately.

Pigs are rambunctious and take their eating seriously. They are not dainty eaters. When the food hits the ground, all the pigs attempt to get to the center of the pile of food. As we all learned in high school physics, only one bit of matter can occupy one space. The same holds true with pigs. If one pig makes it to the top of the pile of food, all the rest will immediately attempt to topple his domination, and one will be successful. Once that lucky pig has his time on top, others will bring him down and so on. In a few short moments the food will be eaten.

At this point, bits of food remain: the odd kernel of corn, crust of bread, corner of cheese. The pigs are thorough; they want it all and they will find it. And this is where it gets interesting. Pigs are insanely qualified to root. Their snout is a rigid bit of cartilage with great strength, and they have a tremendous sense of smell. They use this snout to unearth, to burrow, to upend anything in their way. When they have found the morsel that their keen nose alerted them to, they eat it. Seems rather straightforward, except that this often happens within the soil. As they are constantly rooting through their paddock, the soil is often deep and friable.

Their snout may be delicate, but their mouth appears crude and awkward. What they appear to be doing is eating great quantities of dirt, and in the wetter months, mud. I watch this daily. Are they eating the dirt? Are they filtering out the dirt? Do they digest the dirt and then it passes through them? My conclusion, although not proven, is that their tongues are actually as developed as their snouts. A pig can pick that individual kernel of corn up from within a great sea of mud and draw it into its mouth.

The pigs here often frustrate me. I don't understand why they don't have enough smarts to take care of their food. The most common scenario involves them walking through their food, trampling the food with their hooves in order to keep other beasts from eating it. True, their competitors don't get the food, but they don't either; it is completely soiled by the time they are finished with it. After this little scenario plays out, they look up at me, hoping for more food.

In addition to a great deal of food, water is also an essential ingredient in pigs' diet. Presently we use plastic troughs to hold their liquid nourishments. Pigs have great strength and ability with their snouts and hooves to move, upend, destroy, flip, break and smash anything in their pen. A water trough is no exception.

One system to avoid the problem is to move the water from a large trough that the pigs can walk through, to a trickle system. The hardware involves a stainless steel nipple that attaches to a post. The nipple is hooked up to a water line that delivers water. When a pig is thirsty, it pushes its snout against the protruding edge of the fitting and water dribbles into its throat. Luckily, pigs have the brainpower to quickly figure this out and adapt to it.

The pigs don't knock their water troughs over if they are getting their water from a metal nipple fitting. Should be a good thing: less wasted water, cleaner drinking water for the pigs, more water when they need it. The downside rests in a trait of pigs: They do not have the ability to perspire. They do not sweat and do not pant like a dog would. They utilize water and mud to cool themselves.

When the temperature rises, pigs knock over the water buckets, spilling water in their pen. Then they flop down into it, covering their bodies in mud and water and dirt. The first summer in a new pen, this might be a small bit of water, but after a few weeks and certainly after a few years, the action of large hogs flopping in the ground creates divots in the soil. Over and over the pigs settle the mud and water until it becomes impossible for the water to drain. Small pools of muddy water develop around the pig yard.

I have had these divots in past pig yards and then tried to

change the area back into garden or pasture. With a plow on the back of the tractor it is difficult to rip through the holes. Mud packed over and over and then baked dry through the hot summer months creates a durable, rigid surface. When I look out at the old garden, there still appear to be dents in the landscape left over from past pigs that have long since moved on.

Old water frequently remains in the dents without any new water coming to freshen it. The result after a few weeks in the warmth of the summer is a fetid, verdant pool of water— water that pigs have lain in and eaten and probably urinated in. Quite smelly.

This leads me to make a note in defense of the pig. Pigs are essentially clean. Probably the cleanest barnyard animal, plus they don't smell. The fetid water in the hollows around them stinks; pigs do not.

One thing that differentiates pigs from chickens or sheep or cows is a basic behavioral trait. Pigs will not defecate where they live or eat. It is rather basic, but puts pigs on a rung above the others animals who have not learned this important bit of class. Pigs will find an area separate from their living and eating area to manure. In the world of animal evolution, this is big. It makes for a healthier existence for the pigs. Worms that may live in the digestive tract of the animal can pass through via the manure and would be less likely to be reingested by that pig or another. Sheep especially are susceptible to reinfecting themselves with worms by grazing near where they defecate. Cows have the undignified tendency to graze and manure simultaneously. This does spread the manure through the pasture, bringing necessary nutrients to it, but the cows may end up sleeping in the manure piles. For a beef cow, not necessarily a troublesome thing; but for a dairy cow that needs a very clean udder, it can be a disastrous problem. Pigs do not sleep near their feces. I appreciate that. They leave their manure in the field but not where they sleep or eat.

I picked up my original vision for raising pigs from an old book on small farming. The book described a symbiotic pig setup, which I have sought to emulate. The basic idea is that you have two adjacent pens. Not small pens but large, a half acre, an acre apiece. Both are well fenced and connected to each other. In one, pigs are raised through the year, where they manure the soil and add a great deal of nitrogen to it, raising its fertility.

In the other paddock, corn is planted midyear, to mature in the late fall. Instead of harvesting the corn by hand, the farmer lets the pigs into the cornfield and allows them to eat one row at a time. Portable electric fences keep them where they are wanted; each day the fence is moved over a row. The pigs will eat the corn plus the husk and the stalk. As they graze on the rows of corn, they trample the stalks and root up any remaining corn.

Because the pigs have been removed from the original pad-dock, it will have a chance to rest through the winter and spring months before it will be planted with corn in late May or early June. The pigs spend the winter cleaning the corn-field, eating every little bit of food available, and in doing so spread their manure on the field to nourish the next year's corn.

It is a great little plan. It is symbiotic; a bit of a perpetual motion machine on a farm scale. The pigs go back and forth each year, rooting up the soil, refreshing the nutrients in the soil and producing pork. The great part about it is that a lot of the labor of raising animals is removed. There is no need to harvest the corn, store it and then feed it to the pigs each day. The pigs do the work. They also do some, if not all, of the till-ing of the soil and the spreading of manure. The much more standard method would be to keep the pigs confined, collect the manure and then distribute it onto the fields. Not a fun task, and one that is legitimate work. This system eliminates those tasks and yet accomplishes the same goal.

I tried it out. I fenced a large flat field, divided it in half and set about finding a few pigs to work on it. My calculations were a bit off. Originally I had four pigs on this one-acre field. The land was bad. Really bad. In places, especially where the pigs were to begin their alternate paddock lifestyle, the soil was especially poor. The first winter, soon after clearing the land, I walked across the field in my rubber boots and started to sink. I had walked across a section that was primarily sand, saturated with rainwater. I began to sink into the soil, and eventually came to rest with my knees just above the surface, my feet deep in the quicksand. The soil had no ability to support me; it was not soil. With my poor soil, the three pigs made little dent in raising the fertility of the entire acre. The chance of growing corn on this land in the near future was limited.

And so began my pig raising. I brought in the three young weaner pigs from the feed store up north. I let them out of their flimsy cardboard box and they began their life on this lifeless paddock. Twice a day I brought in buckets of food for them and kept them with ample water.

Little by little they changed from those cute piglets, to actual pigs, to large hogs ready for slaughter. There is a basic idea of pig raising that I have never challenged so I must assume is correct. Hogs raised to market in this country are slaughtered at 220 pounds. The wisdom is that that is the upper limit of muscle growth; beyond that pigs only gain fat. Whether this is true or not I don't know, but most pigs are slaughtered at that weight. Your basic supermarket pork chops come from 220-pound pigs. You will recognize the ham or the loin or the tenderloin or the bacon from that size of pig.

The question that quickly comes to mind when raising pigs is, how do I know when I have a 220-pound pig? Pig farmers of old devised a great invention: a pig tape. I ordered one up from a farm supply catalogue and was totally intrigued when it arrived in the mail. They look just like your mother's cloth measure in her sewing basket: about three feet long, a half inch wide and flexible, with an assortment of measurements written along its length. Instead of inches for hemming skirts, however, the hog tape has the weights of pigs inscribed. There are also a few additions and subtractions listed for longer pigs, shorter pigs and so on. The challenge is to have the hog stay still long enough to wrap this tape around its midsection and then to try and read off the appropriate poundage. I did it once, years ago, and have convinced myself that now I know the basic sizes of hogs. With the tape draped around my neck like a Seventh Avenue tailor, I emptied the largest bucket of food in the pig paddock. I chose the calmest pig I had and came up behind her. As she greedily consumed the food in front of her, I bent over, wrapping my arms around her rotund midsection and pulling the flimsy paper tape around her fattened torso, all the while trying to read the numbers I now realized were far too small to read on the fly. I'm not sure I got it exactly right, but I didn't feel like trying again. Since then, I usually just estimate by sight.

I find the standard market weight to be a bit pale anyway. I like fat, I want more fat and it makes for tastier, moister pork, in my opinion.

After setting up this corn-pork relationship and raising a

couple of young weaners, I took a bit of a wrong turn. A path that I needed to follow, but not one that I would recommend. I decided to breed one of the young female pigs.

It sounded like such a great idea. One boar, one sow and in a few months I would have ten young weaners, maybe fifteen. I could sell most all of the weaners to others on the island, make a few bucks and keep the best two weaners for myself. Great idea, right?

Pork is relatively cheap compared to lamb and beef. Pigs can convert feed to muscle quickly and efficiently. The twenty-pound weaner on April first can be butchered at 220 pounds by Halloween of that same year. If I were a big factory farmer I could rattle off their "feed conversion index," but I find that quite creepy. Pigs are animals, not protein machines.

The ability of pigs to reproduce quickly adds to their financial benefit and the eventual low cost of pork. The gestation period of a pig is three months, three weeks, three days. A litter of pigs is generally around ten, but fifteen would not be unusual. As the gestation period is so short, it is possible for a sow to have two litters per year.

For these reasons you can go from a breeding pair of pigs to conceivably twenty pigs in the space of twelve months. This was quite intriguing from a business standpoint. Weaner pigs sell for a fair price and the demand for quality pigs is always high.

I also reasoned that I could drive my boar around to other farms on the island and leave him with neighboring sows to breed them. The standard relationship is that the owner of the boar gets his pick of the litter or cash for the stud fee. This idea of breeding pigs just seemed better and better. When the boar is at the neighbor's farm, it is fed by the sow's owners, reducing the costs of keeping it. The idea is to keep the boar in motion from farm to farm, except when he is needed at home. I was hooked.

And so quickly I had a sow and a boar: Junior. And then life got more complicated. The sow was quickly bred. So far, so good. She was kept in the hog half of the paddock; the corn was yet to be planted on the opposite side. The boar ended up taking up residence on the not-yet-corn-growing side.

And in less than four months, the day finally arrived for her to farrow. Actually I had lost track of the time when she was due, so I was a bit surprised one morning to find her with the hours-old piglets suckling on her side. There were not a dozen, nor even ten, but six. My business model was quickly evaporating, but I was still hopeful and excited. Baby pigs are most endearing. I was especially fascinated by the looks of the pigs. Because a litter of pigs is so large relative to other mammals, you get to see many offspring all at once. A cow having one calf at best per year doesn't give you any sense of the span of genetic traits that is possible. With six, eight, ten progeny in front of you, the full spectrum is covered. Both the boar and the sow were dark brown, almost black. Of the six piglets, no two looked the same. A couple were all black. A couple were spotted in a variety of ways with black and white and two others had great white banding around their midsections on a black ground. Breeding for a specific look could take place quickly. Breeding for specific physical traits as well.

If we go back to drawings of pigs a couple of hundred years ago, we see fat, rounded, squat pigs. They appear to nearly drag their bellies on the ground and yet are very short in length. The hog of today has completely different dimensions—lean and long. The best description I have heard is that a modern pig is "as long as a school bus."

Breeding for specific traits reflects our use of pork and our cultural attitude toward it. Up until the middle of the twentieth century, lard was the primary fat used for cooking in this country. As large quantities of cooking fat were needed on a daily basis, pigs needed to produce a large volume to stock the larders of the American kitchens. Since that time, we have collectively switched to vegetable oils as the primary cooking fat. Pig lard has been replaced. As there is very little need for pig fat, pigs are bred and grown to produce very little of it.

If you walk through the meat aisle of the supermarket today, most of what is in the trays of pork are pork chops and bacon. Certainly the odd pork roast shows up, a few "country-style ribs," but for the most part, pork chops rule. The goal of the contemporary hog grower is a lot of bacon and a lot of pork chops. The result is breeding pigs for length: the longer the hog, the more bacon, the thicker the pork chops.

At this point I had a sow, her fairly small litter of pigs and a boar next door eating away.

I proceeded to start hiring out Junior. I found a couple of guys who had a sow that they needed bred. I borrowed a horse trailer from a friend and dropped Junior off across the island. At this point he was fairly manageable and still not too large. He was still young, still easy to lead with a bucket of food and still interested in entering a horse trailer. It would be the last time.

Unloading the boar was painless. He was curious where he was headed and happy to be out of the tight horse trailer. He was introduced to the sow and then I got a quick lesson in the intricacies of hog breeding.

Pigs gain weight fairly quickly and never stop. It's what they do. My boar was a spry young man, full of life, but not terribly tall or large at this point. His potential suitor was a mature woman of some girth and stature. Although he had an interest in the ladies, her size was a difficult obstacle for him to overcome.

The owners of the farm wanted to keep my boar around for a while; they felt he hadn't done the job he'd come to do. Since

they were feeding him, I thought it was great. Finally, three
months later, I returned to pick him up. I now knew why their
sow was so large; they were most generous with the feed. My
young spry Junior was now an obese sloth. He also seemed to
have lost any curiosity concerning entering the horse trailer.

A very long afternoon and many buckets of grain later, we
had him reloaded into the trailer. My business plan was in
tatters.

Junior never did sire any offspring from that long visit to
the neighbor's piggery. I can't say for certain why, but most
likely it was a problem of sizing. Pigs are not static animals,
they are dynamic; they gain weight and size daily. Hundred-
pound boars can physically breed hundred-pound sows, but
don't have the stature to breed four-hundred-pound sows.
Same is true if the weights are reversed. I realized that I
would have to match the boar to his intended.

Junior arrived home that day and was returned to his
former partner, the ideal sow. Being the same age, he was
similar in size even with his overfeeding, but his strength was
dramatically more than hers and sadly he broke her leg soon
after arriving. She would be put down later that week, never
to breed again. Pig breeding seemed rather more complicated
that week, but I still had Junior.

A few months later I bought another young sow and began
again. As it turned out, my original sow was a tremendous
mother; she took care of her piglets, and only one died of the
entire litter. Visualize the birthing of pigs: the sow is certainly 250 pounds, and could easily reach 500. Her hooves
are small and pointed, and the baby pigs weigh at most three
pounds when they are born. The result is sows crushing their
baby pigs, often by simply lying on top of them and stepping
on them.

Commercial pig breeders have devised a solution to this

problem: a farrowing crate. This contraption is a means to keep the sow completely vertical before, during and after she births her piglets. She is given very little room to move about and does not have the ability to lie down and squash her young. These crates continue to be used, so I must assume that they are successful.

As with most things in life, moderation is everything. Keeping a sow in a farrowing crate of some kind for the week that she gives birth might be reasonable. Three months I would consider animal cruelty.

I kept my sow outside with a bit of a shelter provided to allow her to get out of the rain if the weather went bad. She made a nest of leaves and ferns in the woods and proceeded to almost bury herself in this large mound of greenery. As she was building this nest I knew that she was soon to farrow; I had also kept better track of the breeding date this time.

When the day came, it was amazing. One by one the small piglets emerged from her and entered the world. I so wanted to take charge of the situation and help them along; bring them closer to her teats, bring them back to the nest when they blindly wandered off. I forced myself not to interfere.

The next morning was not so jolly. Even with the large fluffy nest of woodland ferns and salal branches, the mother had crushed several of her young to death. Three lived through that first week and were raised up for meat. More shocking than the deaths themselves was the mother sow's reaction. Those that she had mistakenly killed, she eventually ate. Or so I must infer. They were gone hours later, and although it is conceivable that a raccoon might have enjoyed a small piglet, the sow never would have allowed anything near her. Her protective strength kept me at bay for weeks; there is no chance anything else could have gotten near enough to her to remove one of her piglets.

Which is crueler—the farrowing crate to protect the young, or letting nature take its course with all its inherent cruelty? I have since seen an acceptable pigpen that is the best of both worlds. The sow is confined in a relatively small indoor pen of maybe ten feet by five feet, with areas in the corners where only the piglets can escape. The sow, being tremendously larger, is stopped by a strong metal bar that blocks the corners. The piglets can easily slip underneath to safety if need be.

My days of pig breeding ended there. The piglets born that day were raised up for meat, the sow and boar soon slaughtered. Buying weaner pigs each spring and slaughtering them for meat ten months later works well. Breeding pigs did give me an insight into their unique nature, but overall it was an experience I'm happy not to repeat.

Twelve

The Slaughter

I grew up in the city, buying meat in the grocery store that was sold in foam trays, shrink-wrapped in plastic and bearing little if any resemblance to an actual animal. I was content with that, as most people are. It is easy and normal and expected. No butcher shops remain in the city where we can see sides of beef, no farms are nearby to trigger thoughts about where meat comes from. We have collectively removed animals (save for housepets) from our lives, and yet we consume vast amounts of animal protein. Yet I never had a problem with it.

Once I had moved from the city and started the farm, animals were an obvious next step. Sheep arrived first, cast-offs from other farmer wannabes unaware that sheep are quite boring, not to mention the significant work involved in making tasty lamb. Pigs followed, as the idea of delicious pork was a great motivator. Getting my first pigs and setting them up at the farm was a challenge, but slaughtering those pigs was totally unknown territory for me.

For a few years I would call a local custom slaughterhouse. These slaughterhouses are licensed by the state, but not by the federal government. Their license gives them the right to slaughter animals for private use only, not for commerce; you are not allowed to sell the meat that they slaughter and butcher. These are guys who drive a large step-van out to local farms, shoot the animal in the field, gut it and skin it and then hang it in the back of the van for transport back to their butchering facilities. The mobile units have some great advantages: the killing is done in the field so that the animals never get agitated, the butcher takes the by-products from the kill and removes them from the farm. It is also perfectly acceptable to point out the animal to the butcher and then go off to work, picking up the meat from his butcher shop days later. I like to think of the mobile slaughter system as training wheels for performing animal butchery yourself. You get to bike down the street wobbling back and forth with no chance of falling and yet you learn a few things.

The first few times I couldn't watch the actual kill, but would come out of the house once the gun had gone off. I would actually make some kind of excuse to the butcher like, "Gosh, I have to catch the teakettle before it burns dry," or some such nonsense. As I look back, he had probably heard it all before. Once the shot went off I would emerge from the kitchen as if that teakettle were now under control and head over to where my sheep or pig now lay dead. At that point I could watch the butcher bleed and gut the animal. The first cut was always the most difficult to watch, but after that it was more fascinating than anything. I would stand there and observe everything the butcher did. He had years of experience and was exceptionally quick and precise. Without question it was better than any book for learning the basics of slaughter.

And then tragedy struck: my first sow, a very large, lovely female hog, ended up with a broken leg. The vet was called and informed me that she could not be helped, but that the hog was not sick and therefore the meat was good. There I was, standing in the field with the vet, realizing I had to solve this problem, but the mobile butcher was busy for weeks and could not come out to the farm.

I think this is known as trial by fire. I had a hog I felt compassion for, who needed to be slaughtered immediately. I had seen it done a few times when the butcher had slaughtered this very sow's grown-up offspring, but had never done it myself. As best as I could, I stepped up to the plate. My neighbor Larry is a man twenty years my senior who grew up on this island and who has acquired many of the skills I was looking for in my new life here. From chatting with him over the fence I knew he was a hunter and I was confident that he would have a gun and have no qualms about shooting an animal. I enlisted his help to shoot the pig and slit her throat.

And then Larry left.

There I was at the end of the afternoon with a dead pig in the field, bled out but needing to be butchered. As I had spent the best part of the short winter day pacing around the farm trying to figure out a way to solve my pig problem, by the time I finally chatted with Larry and got the sow slaughtered, darkness had fallen on the farm. By the light of the small headlights on my tractor, I loaded her in the tractor's bucket, drove her down the hill to the driveway in front of the house and laid her on the open tailgate of my truck. I grabbed what knives I had and began to attempt to repeat what I had watched the butcher with thirty years' experience do many times. All the while, the diesel motor of the tractor was running to keep the lights shining on my work, the otherwise quiet winter night filled with the slow rumble of the engine.

The meat was oddly cut, not professional in any way, but the pig was eventually broken down enough to get the pieces into the coolers. I think this is the best way to learn—on your own, with some knowledge under your belt, but with no safety net.

Although the sow with the broken leg was a great start to my career as a butcher, I didn't actually slaughter the animal, my neighbor did. Butchering is a complicated skill, but involves the same basic skills as cutting up steaks bought at a grocery store; killing an animal is much different. It is the taking of a life, deliberately and intentionally. You know that that sheep that is walking around the pastures at this moment will be dead minutes later, by your own hand. In late fall a few years back, Matt and I had decided that the time had come to kill a couple of goats for a holiday barbecue without the assistance of the mobile butcher. We discussed it and were confident that it was appropriate and that we were capable. Actually, we discussed it for weeks. Endlessly. In hindsight, I am struck by the tremendous luxury of being able to discuss the killing of an animal for food for weeks. Only recently in human history has that been possible—hunger would quickly have made the decision for us.

As there were two goats, we each would kill one and then help each other skin and gut. Goats and sheep are killed by slitting their throats; hogs are shot with a rifle. I'd had the cooks at my restaurant in the city sharpen knives for me and we each proceeded to slit the throats of the goats, bleeding them out.

We both discovered in those quick seconds that although we had spent many hours talking about our roles in killing animals for meat, the actual kill was not terribly difficult. Anticlimactic, if you will.

I still think about the taking of life beforehand, thank the animal for its life and proceed with a professional detachment. I never talk to anyone while the gun is in my hand. I want no one to chat with me then. Others may be chatting behind me, but I can't hear. My only concern is a successful kill: the animal having no idea what is coming and dying instantly, and no one hurt in the process.

I have learned to have a few guys around for the slaughter,

particularly with pigs, though with creatures as lightweight as lambs it's hardly necessary. Without people around it is a sad moment. A larger crew makes it more socially acceptable: if all of us think this is a good idea, then of course it is. With just you and the beast there in the field, it is an open question.

A question that has bothered me for some time is whether children should be present at the kill or at the cutting up of the pig. Early on I suggested that my friend Dan bring his young son D.J. Being a responsible, if a bit high-strung parent, he shrieked and assured me that D.J. would have nightmares for years if he witnessed such an act. I tried to reason, with no success, that children had been present historically at such porcine preparations and that they seemed to live through it. He didn't buy my argument at all and his son was absent, as was he, for the slaughter. Jorge's sons often come out to pig slaughters and are generally bored by the whole affair.

My thought has been that if the parent is upset by killing animals, the child will pick up on it and assume that killing is bad. If there is an attitude of normalcy to preparing food, then the child will pick that up as well. I can see where parents would not want to risk scaring their beloved children, but it is that nervousness that indicates their apprehension with the entire process. They are more comfortable buying a pork chop in a Styrofoam tray at the local supermarket.

Although Matt does not work on this farm any longer, he often brings his daughter to the pig slaughters here. She is two now and has witnessed a few goats and pigs, plus plenty of chickens, come to their end. He feels that this is a gift he can give her: the ability to see the animals, raise them, slaughter them and then eat them. We adults who grew up in the city can never obtain an early exposure to a true connection between food and animals.

For pigs we muster at least three guys for a slaughter.

Although I get many requests to join in, I prefer to have a select few guys who know what they are doing and have the temperament I like: professional, yet fun; solemn, yet never dour. Certain jokes are fine, others inappropriate. Respect for guns and knives is essential. A few outsiders have joined us, but the small circle remains. Others are rarely invited back to help a second time.

Slaughtering is always done in the cool months: October through March. Without nighttime temperatures below forty degrees, cooling the meat down is difficult if not impossible. Freezing temperatures are ideal, but rare.

We start after the morning chores are finished. The animals are all fed and watered, the cows milked and the milking equipment cleaned and put away. The day begins as every day begins at the farm. The morning chores have usually been completed before anyone else arrives. I like to have my chores done so that no one will interrupt and throw off the sequence. Chatting and catching up with friends is put on hold until the chores are done.

The pigs will not be fed on the morning of the slaughter. They will have to wait for their breakfast until we all head up to the pig yard that morning. The pig to be slaughtered will be kept with the others so as not to induce any stress into its life. The pigs came to the farm months ago and have never been moved from where they spend their entire lives. Trucking them to a slaughterhouse in my opinion would cause them too much stress, running the risks of damaging the meat and making them suffer unnecessarily.

The morning crew gathers near the kitchen, kicking their heels to stay warm, smoking cigarettes in front of the wood-fired oven. While I finish the early chores, coffee is brewed, toast is made and bacon and eggs are fried. A hearty breakfast is the best start.

Although the core crew is always the same, often a new guy has joined us. Whether new or old, there is still an uneasy tension in the air. Nervousness is assumed, but not showing nerves is essential. Chat about food, restaurants, chefs and girlfriends fills the void.

When the crew is fed, the necessary tools are brought together: sharp knives, gun and ammunition, water hose and bowls for blood and offal. A quick toast to the pig with shots of bourbon ends the morning and begins the slaughter.

Ritual and repetition are crucial at this point. Everyone knows what to do and what will happen. Anyone new knows well enough to follow along, yet not get too close. The first few times were more difficult as we were trying out different methods and procedures.

The jobs are preassigned, briefly discussed and tend to match personality and task:

Trigger-man, always myself. The one who will pull the trigger and kill the animal. A bad shot is a disaster; a good shot essential.

Knife-boy, the one who will slit the throat of the pig, quickly, precisely and confidently. The blood must be pumped out of the pig quickly while the heart is still beating. The window of opportunity is the minute following death. Sloppy cutting destroys the jowls that will later be used for guanciale. The best for the job are always great restaurant line cooks: stress junkies who can jump in immediately and make a precise cut without panicking. Knife-boy will begin the morning by spreading out his tools, soaking the sharpening stone in water, dragging his knife precisely across it back and forth. He will spend the morning honing his knife, checking it often, fearful that it has dulled in the minutes since he last checked it.

Blood-boy, the one who will jump in after the throat has

been cut and catch the blood coming from the slit throat into a large bowl. The blood will be stirred by his hand as it comes into the bowl, his fingers catching the coagulants to be pulled out of the full bowl. Obviously good hygiene is important, no squeamishness at all and a great love of the eventual product: blood sausage.

Bung-boy, the least glamorous job; the one who will tie off the anus with a string, keeping the manure safely in the intestines.

Others assist but don't get a cool nickname. One will help hold the moving hog still so that the blood can freely flow to the bowl. Another will hold the head steady for the same goal.

The whole process takes a very few minutes. The walk to the Pig Forest takes longer. The pigs will be given a bucket of grain, the selected hog will come into the ideal position and the gun will go off. The throat will be slit, the blood collected. Visitors watching usually comment that they thought it would take longer. The sound of the gunshot announces to all that the pig is dead.

The sound of a gunshot is shockingly loud. I am always amazed that neighbors have not called the sheriff to investigate what is occurring on the other side of the dense brush that surrounds the farm, separating it from the more suburban lawns on the other side. The law has never arrived, convincing me that I do live in an area that has a bit of rural grit left in it. Never in the city could a gun go off without causing some alarm.

The gun used for the killing of calves and pigs is a .30-30. Honestly, I do not know what that means. When I say it to people who grew up with guns, they all immediately remark that it sounds a bit large for hogs and calves. I concur that, yes, it is large, but does the job well. I truly have no idea;

the animal falls quickly and dies immediately but the connection between the gauge of the gun and the ease of death escapes me.

My friend Matthew lent me the rifle years ago. He started by teaching me how to shoot with a .420. It was the most beautiful gun I had ever seen. In fact, it was the only gun I had ever seen. Having grown up in the tranquillity of Seattle, I had never seen or discussed guns.

The liberal middle-class predisposition against guns is the norm here in the coastal edge of the country. The NRA is considered a sad, lower-class, red-state institution and there is rarely room in the discussion to consider guns for hunting.

When I was in the process of looking for the appropriate weapon to kill a pig, I stopped in a gun shop off-island that I had driven by for many years but had never entered. Why would I have entered a gun shop? With me that day was one of my farm interns, a terribly idealistic young liberal farmer-to-be. I carried my cultural reservations with me, but marched in, viewing it as an adventure. And I needed a gun.

I began walking around the store, trying to look like I did this all the time, but really I was clueless as to how the store was arranged or what I was supposed to do. A few minutes into my vague browsing, I turned to my young intern Evan to ask him what he thought. He was standing in the middle of the store, frozen, not finding this in the least bit amusing. He could barely speak; there was a tension that couldn't be broken. I told him he should wait in the truck and that I would be out soon. You would think that I had thrown him into the middle of the Republican National Convention.

I continued with my shopping, hoping to find a gun to buy, as the weather was soon to break and the pigs were getting bigger every day. Quickly I discovered that gun shops, or at least this one gun shop, have a basic system. You go up to the long glass counters, chat vaguely about the guns in the case or on the back wall behind the case, then the salesman pulls a weapon out for you and places it on the case in front of you. You then pick it up and point it at something other than the salesman or another customer, look through the sight and then make a comment—"Yes, very nice" or " Hmm, seems a bit tight."

I did this a few times, trying not to look like a complete neophyte. When Matthew had brought over the small shotgun to the farm a couple of years earlier, we shot cans in the back pasture. I was not much of a shot, but I got the idea of putting the butt up to my shoulder, squinting one eye and pulling the trigger with my index finger. I doubt that I fooled anyone behind the counter with my crude ways and so I just told the salesman what I wanted. "I need to kill a pig and I need a gun to do it. What should I buy?" He suggested—rather oddly, I thought at the time—to just smack the pig over the head with a two-by-four and then slit its throat. I reassured him that I wanted a gun and could he suggest one. After much chatting about this one and that one, I realized I had left Evan in my truck, exited gracefully and committed to carrying on my search for a gun later.

I now admire guns deeply. I like the wood on the butt—smooth and somewhat exotic. The varnish is often thick, yet not chipped or yellowed. The metal has a depth to it. Blue-black, slick and hard; cold. The process to make a gun must be very exacting. Even being on a factory line, producing rifle after rifle after rifle, the worker must still respect the product—it is a gun, made to kill, not just a knickknack to tell the time or hold flowers or cut paper. The same is true after the gun is made and shipped and sold. No one leaves a gun out in the rain to get rusty and dirty. People love to shine them and clean them and polish them. Guns get attention; they get respect. Few things, actual things, get respect throughout a lifetime.

In a family album is a photograph of my father in 1939 standing with his friends on a log spanning a creek in northern British Columbia on a hunting trip. In his hand is a large rifle. I have often peered at that small photograph, wondering where that rifle is now. It has to be somewhere, it would not have been thrown away with the trash one day during housecleaning. To have that gun, to hold that gun, my father's gun, would connect me to my father. Guns bridge the generations.

Matthew would later lend me a larger gun—the .30-30—to slaughter pigs. It has served me well. Slaughter day on the farm is often foggy, and generally quiet and muddy. By this time of year it has been raining enough to soak the ground through. We all have mud boots on and dirty work coats. Those who are part of this are trusted friends, and I have no trouble nowadays telling people who are only casually interested that they are not welcome—this is serious business.

As soon as the gunshot breaks the silence, the activities begin in rapid sequence. As the shooter, I will return to the kitchen to put the rifle back and lock it up until its next use. I then start the tractor to warm the engine. The knife-boy will jump in quickly to cut the jugular veins of the pig, as another friend or two hop on the pig to steady it. The knife will usually be a scimitar, bearing a long, curved razor-sharp blade, a potentially dangerous tool with a bucking animal on hand.

The hide of a pig is thick but not especially hairy. A very sharp knife can easily pierce the skin. The jugular veins are located on either side of the larynx, and both need to be cut through to allow the blood to exit quickly. The animal is already dead at this point. A large bullet has exploded in the pig's brain. The heart, however, will continue to beat for some moments. It is this residual action of the heart that will cleanse the meat of blood.

Throughout the animal run blood-filled veins and arteries. If this liquid were allowed to remain in the body, a large and efficient highway would be available for bacteria. The blood also spoils faster than the meat. We want all the blood to leave the body as fast and as completely as possible. Hence the need to immediately slit the throat while the heart is still beating.

It is a quick job—the knife-boy's—but a difficult one. The adrenaline will carry you through it, but you never know until you are right there if you can perform. I have seen guys freeze when the pig goes down, unable to jump in and do the job at hand. Most rise to the occasion and can control themselves enough to do an accurate and thorough job.

Once the throat is slit and a guy or two still are steadying the pig, the blood-boy steps up to the stage. He will place the large stainless bowl beneath the throat of the pig and try to catch as much of the blood as possible while it spurts out of the arteries. With luck he can capture three quarts of blood from a large pig. Once the heart has relaxed, the blood flow will cease and the pig will lie still. The blood-boy then will stir the blood with his fingers. Any coagulants will stick to his fingers as he passes them through the warm blood. A few quick shakes of his hand, and the coagulants will fall to the ground.

At this point of the morning experience, one thing will become oddly clear. It is always a bit of a shock to anyone witnessing it for the first time. When we first arrive at the pig yard, I pour a bucket of grain in a long line onto the ground to bring the pigs—all of the pigs—into a line side by side, where I want them, so we will have a good shot at the chosen pig.

When the pig in questions falls, you expect the other pigs to run in fear or at least slowly leave the scene. As humans we really want these beasts to have human qualities—to be sad, to be fearful, to be concerned about their fellow pig friend. Nothing could be further from the truth. The other pigs, if anything, seem more energized than concerned. There is now more food for them, less competition for the grain that is in front of them. They will push their now-dead "friend" out of the way in order to get the grain that lies beneath its head. There is no mourning apparent at this point. As we tend to slaughter the largest pig, who most likely is the most aggressive and biggest eater, its death appears to be a relief to the others.

The pig now lies in Pig Forest; its heart has stopped, the blood has ceased and the crew has calmed. The excitement of the morning has ended and now the real work will begin. I have by this point driven the tractor up from the barn and up to the pig yard. Together we will roll the pig into the bucket of the tractor and lift it, to be transported back down the hill to the kitchen. The crew will follow the tractor, opening and closing the gates as the cortege progresses.

Less than ten minutes have gone by and the most drama of the day has passed.

While the bread was toasting and the eggs fried for breakfast, every large stockpot in the kitchen was filled with water and put on the range to boil. Gallons of boiling water will be used to scald and scrape the hide of the pig.

Customarily a pig is dipped in near-boiling water before it is scraped, in order to facilitate removing the bristles on its hide. Any slaughterhouse would do it this way; the pig is hung on a chain and lowered into a vat of hot water for long enough to loosen the bristles. As you can imagine, this takes a very large kettle, a proficient hoist and a lot of precautions to ensure against boiling water overfilling the top of the pot as a huge hog is lowered into it. We have never devised a way to get an animal of such size into a pot or a way to heat the water safely under it.

Instead we have devised a simpler and safer system. We boil the water in stockpots on the range, bring the water out to the pig and pour it onto the hide little by little. First the pig is placed on a concrete slab so that it is clean and stable and as hygienic as possible. Then the hot water is poured over it quart by quart to loosen the bristles. When the hair starts to give, we begin to scrape. Using knives and a round bell scraper, the bristles are removed little by little. More heated water is poured around the different areas of the carcass. It is a slow and tedious task, but a necessary one. Off flavors will remain if the hair stays on the pig. We want to keep much of the hide in place for curing the pork. The thick nature of the pig hide will help to protect the eventual hams and bacon from flies.

The most difficult areas are the ears and feet. They are small and shaped in such a way that makes maneuvering the knife difficult. Further cleanup takes place when they are cut off of the body and can be dealt with on a tabletop instead of attached to the hog.

The dousing of the animal with hot water and the scraping will continue until it is completed—maybe an hour—with the hog being flipped over halfway through to finish the other side. Eventually a bald pig will remain.

The tractor is started again and the pig rolled back into the cleaned tractor bucket to be moved to the hoist. The task next is to open the pig and remove all of the guts, leaving only the meat and bones of the pig. We want to get the temperature of the meat down as quickly as possible, and removing the guts is the most important part of that goal. The meat needs to be cool to keep any bacteria from spoiling it. The guts pose the greatest threat of bacteria entering the meat, as they contain the stomach filled with half-digested food and the intestines' remaining manure. They must be rapidly and efficiently removed.

The first step in keeping the meat safe is to tie off the bung of the animal. While the pig lies in the bucket of the tractor horizontally, with no tension on the animal, the bung-boy steps up with a piece of string in his hand and a very sharp boning knife. The string is looped and tied into an open cinch knot. We want to seal that tract off so that any remaining manure cannot exit, in the process releasing the intestines, so that they can be easily removed when we gut the animal.

The bung-boy cuts around the anus with his boning knife. The cut must be complete, deep and accurate. The goal is to have the intestines free of the body and yet not punctured by the knife. The knife will pass through the outer hide and then through the fat and muscle at the back of the pelvis until it hits the gut cavity of the pig. We want the muscle and fat and hide cut but the intestines intact. Once the anus has been encircled, the string with the cinch knot will be looped around the intestines and tightened, sealing off the tube. A knot will be made to ensure it stays tight. At this point the bung-boy's job is done and he can go back to the kitchen to enjoy the rest of the morning's breakfast.

The pig is now ready to be hung and gutted. A gambrel is used to raise it for gutting. A thick stainless steel bar with a hook in the middle and two raised ends, the gambrel will connect the back feet of the pig with a cable overhead. The raised ends will keep the feet from sliding off and the cable will attach to the gambrel at the center hook. When I first began doing this, an old threaded rod with bolts on the ends seemed like it would suffice, but slippery, fatty, cold pig feet slipping on a metal rod showed me otherwise. A sturdy gambrel that can hold the weight of the hog is essential.

Slits are cut in the back legs of the pig. The tendons on the trotters will carry the full weight of the hog and therefore it is important that the cuts be careful. If the tendons are cut, they could tear, allowing the pig to crash to the ground in a most ungraceful manner. There are two potential spots for cutting into on the trotter—one near the hoof and one higher up on the lower leg. I had always used the higher tendon but recently switched to the lower on the advice of a cook. He explained that the chance of damaging the ham was too great with the higher cut and that the lower tendon could still carry the weight without the possibility of a cut allowing bacteria into the future ham.

Once the gambrel is attached to the pig, the cable is hoisted with a block and tackle and the pig slowly rises into the air. The goal is to have the head reach to just above the ground. The throat of the pig has been slit, but blood still remains clotted in the throat and there is the potential of bacteria if the head lies on the ground. We need easy access to the belly to cut it open and remove the guts; if the pig is too high it will be difficult to reach.

The belly of the pig is comprised of the outer thick hide—now with its hair scraped off—the fat and then the muscle. After those layers the inner cavity is mostly open; the internal organs are anchored but almost float in the cavity. We need to cut through the belly without damaging the inner organs, especially the stomach. The smell of a stomach's contents alone is incentive enough, but the health risk is also very real.

A sharp, small boning knife works the best. The blade is short, curved and easily manipulated. The first cut is made at the center of the belly, between the legs, three inches down

from the top. A few shallow cuts work well to get a sense of
the thickness of the belly at this point and on an animal of
this weight. There could be a great deal of fat or it could be
a leaner pig with mostly muscle. After a number of short,
shallow cuts, the knife will break through into the gut cavity.
Often the best tell of this is a release of pressure and the smell
of the organs filling the air. This is a very unique smell, but
not a putrid one. I can't say that I love it, but it brings back
memories of pig slaughters past, and the friends who pitched
in at each.

The knife can now be brought down to slice through the
belly from legs to the beginning of the sternum. Once the cut
is a few inches long, you can push your hand in to the guts,
pushing them back, separating the belly from the guts. With
one hand the organs are held in, while the other hand guides
the knife down the belly. If the knife is turned so that the
sharp edge of the blade is toward you and the dull side is
toward the guts, then there is less chance of puncturing the
stomach and intestines.

The pig is now hanging upside down, the belly and part of
the chest are being opened up and the guts are free to move
even though they are still attached to the back wall of the cavity. The guts will begin to fall out of the center of the pig. The
large and small intestines and the stomach are large, heavy,
slippery and tend to move. A deft balancing act must be performed to finish the cutting with one hand and hold back the
emerging guts with the other.

Once the cut is completed, the guts can be removed. The
cleaned bucket of the tractor is placed in front of the pig to
catch the guts and a number of stainless steel bowls are readied to hold the valuable organs. If the bung was completely
released earlier it will be easier to begin pulling out the intes-

tines. If not, cut around the lower intestine at the anus from the outside and the inside of the pig until it moves freely.

The guts will begin to move. We want them to fall into the tractor bucket without touching the ground. A load of pig's guts is a slippery, warm, wet, heavy, disconnected bundle. Imagine trying to carry a dozen half-full wetted water balloons. To make this task even more challenging, we want to keep some of the parts of this first set of guts. Surrounding the stomach is one of the most beautiful parts of nature—the caul fat. It is a large membrane—maybe twenty inches square but of an irregular shape, with a thick fatty edge and a thin gossamer center. Large veins of fat run through the center in a lacy pattern. If it was only beautiful I would still want to save it, but it also has an important culinary use.

Caul fat is just that: fat. What makes it unique and useful is that it is very thin, a large flat piece of even-thickness fat with a beautiful web pattern. The classic method is to cut it into four-inch squares used to wrap small pork patties. As a sealed disk, the patties can be cooked. The caul holds the sausage meat together, gives it a beautiful design and keeps it from drying out with the melting fat as it is cooked. The French call these *crépinettes* and they are divine.

Another great use for the large sheet of caul fat is to prepare a long slender pork roast and instead of tying it with string to keep its shape, wrap it with the caul, rolling it around once or twice depending on the size. During roasting, the caul will moisten the meat, keep the roast intact and hold seasonings against the meat.

After a few minutes, the guts will have been pulled from the carcass and dumped into the bucket of the tractor. The useful bits of offal are headed to the kitchen to be chilled and cleaned. The tractor will move the heavy, unwieldy mass of internal organs away from the work area and off to the compost to be covered with dirt to begin its breakdown into goodness for the soil. In an amazingly short period of time, the guts will compost away, nothing to be found in the soil. Bones will take considerably longer, but they too will eventually dissolve back into earth. Although this compost is excellent, it is only spread on the fruit trees and never onto the vegetable gardens for fear of any potential pathogens that may remain in the compost from the animal guts.

The carcass is now rinsed off completely, ridding the meat of any trace of blood or residual guts. With a bit of strength and a sharp knife, the head can be removed by cutting between two of the vertebrae at the neck. Once the head has been removed and the neck opened up, water can flow over the insides and down and out onto the ground. The water will also help cool the warm meat to a safer temperature.

If a large walk-in refrigerator is available, mechanical refrigeration can assist in the meat-cooling. The challenge is having the tools necessary to mobilize the hog. The weight of animals fascinates me. Farm animals, whether cows or pigs or lambs, look very lithe and light when they are walking around on their own. When the beasts are dead, their bodies flat on the ground, their weight appears to double from just moments earlier when they were upright. I always think I can pick up a lamb with one hand, and yet I struggle to load its bulk into the tractor.

At this point in the day, the guts have been buried, the offal is in the cooler, the meat is hanging outside cooling down and it is lunchtime. Almost as if pigs had planned it, there is a lovely little piece of meat that is great for lunch and easy to access: the hanger steak. The French call it the *onglet*, but I like the term *hanger* much better.

It is the only cut of which there is only one per animal. Animals are, thankfully, symmetrical. Each animal has a couple of legs, a kidney on each side, two rows of chops and so on, except the hanger. As the name implies, it is the muscle that connects the guts to the back of the cavity; to the spine. On a pig it is maybe six inches long depending on the size of the hog—it's also found on cows and sheep. A couple inches round, with a long muscle structure running the length of the cut, the hanger is quite easy to access with a quick cut during the gutting of a pig.

The hanger is easily cleaned of any fat and trimmed down to tidy it up. We cook and serve it like this: Roll it in chilies and salt and pepper, grill to medium rare, turning the meat so that all the sides get nicely charred and then let it rest a few moments. With a sharp knife the hanger is sliced very thinly against the grain. A few warmed tortillas, some chopped cabbage from the field, a bit of salsa, and a nice taco awaits. It is one of the few times when driving off the farm to the store for a couple of limes seems like a good idea.

The day is half over, the hanger tacos were great, finished off with a couple of cans of ice-cold Tecate. The pig is still hanging and will continue to cool off till the next morning. Attention can be given to the organs that were pulled out and cooled in the cooler while lunch was made.

I find the offal craze a bit odd, to be truthful. Fergus Henderson, in his book *Nose to Tail Eating*, makes a fine case for many of these underused bits, but I just can't warm to them. There is a reason these parts are made into dog food.

I've also got two dogs to feed. They are my companions; they are a part of this farm. They need to be fed and there is no way I would feed them store-bought dog food. Alongside my epiphany that I should eat well and not consume poor-quality food products, I came to a similar realization about my dogs. They must be well fed.

There is a basic hierarchy here for all food. The very best, highest-quality products are sold. The perfect tomato, the freshest cheese, the ideal lamb chops, all go to customers. The second tier, still high-quality but not necessarily perfect, I consume with my friends at the table of Kurtwood Farms. The fact that I forgo the best things for myself will keep my therapist and I busy for many years, but I am a businessman first and foremost. After customers have been served and I have been fed, my dogs get what they need. They eat the spleens, pancreases, kidneys, ends of the cheese, overly crispy bacon slices, the bone after the leg of lamb has been roasted and so on. The next tier of food is what the dogs pass on, these things go to the pigs: stale bread, trimmings from fruits and vegetables. My dogs tend to go for the milk, meat and potatoes; they have very little interest in anything else. They are far from vegetarians.

Without much thought I boil the spleens and pancreases and odd bits. I don't really know why, but it makes me feel better about the whole experience. Cutting up raw spleen and handing it over to my dear pups seems just wrong to me. A quick boil of the offal, time for it to cool off, and my dogs are the happiest two beasts on the farm.

I do, however, enjoy pork liver pâté.

A pig liver is rather large and unwieldy. The first task, as with the chickens, is to remove the bile sac. In the center of the pig's liver is a small bag about the size of a walnut. In it is a liquid the most amazing shade of green. Almost fluorescent, it seems terribly unnatural in the context of the interior of an animal. For all its beauty, however, it is truly vile. Bitter, the bile sac can also taint the meat, so it must be removed. Attached to the liver by a thin seam that runs along its backside, the bag is rather fragile and yet at the same time difficult to cut off. The best method is to sacrifice some of the liver and cut around the bile sac with a bit of liver attached. To attempt to trim the sac off tightly will result in failure. Once the bile is removed, I puree the pig's liver with a bit of pork fat, cream and seasonings and gently cook it into a smooth, silky pâté. What was once a large unwieldy slab of liver is transformed into a refined gastronomic delight.

The hog is hanging, the tacos are finished cooking. The first day of the pig butchering is finished. I often sit back at this point, still nibbling on the pork tacos, and think about how this pig was walking around a few hours ago. The transformation from live animal to sustenance is rapid. It reminds me of when my first dog died. A dear companion, Zetti ran into the road one night, was hit by a car and died immediately. I found her a few minutes later after she didn't return quickly to the house. The dog that had sat next to me looking me in the eyes was now sprawled on the asphalt on the side of the road in front of the farm. I had never been this close to something that had died. I wanted the long death scene from movies, but as I learned, death is often instantaneous. The transformation from soulful being to lifeless muscles is quick and one-directional.

I think of the pigs the same way. They lead their pig lives until the shot goes off and then they are meat. There is no middle ground, no intermediate stage that they pass through as they ready themselves for their final role. Once you reach your hand into the warm gut to pull entrails out of an animal that was alive an hour earlier, this is abundantly clear.

After evening chores of day one, the pig is checked out. The evening chill has brought the temperature of the pig down to a respectable forty degrees. The meat is firm, the fat not jiggly and the whole thing begins to feel more like a culinary project than a slaughter.

Though I run a tight ship when it comes to slaughter day, sometimes surprises are inevitable. One perfect winter morning, snow on the ground but dry and crisply cold, we slaughtered a pig and hung it to chill for the night. As it happened, the temperature had plummeted during the night and frozen the pig solid. Not a bad thing, except we had to wait two days for it to thaw enough for butchering. I loved wading out into the snow to gaze upon it, hard as a rock, with the low winter sun glistening on the pork fat, not a fly in sight. We called it the *pigsicle*.

Thirteen

Butchering

When the day is over and the hog is hanging from the gambrel outside the kitchen window, I would prefer to be finished. It has been a long, full day slaughtering the pig, feeding all the helpers and cleaning up the place, in addition to the standard chores of the farm. But more effort is needed to transform this hanging animal to the eventual bacons, hams and pork chops that we desire. The cool evening air will have cooled the carcass down, firming the meat and fat. Cutting up an animal, any animal, is essentially the same. Sheep, pigs and cows all have four legs, ribs, shoulders, loins running down the length and so on. Learning how to break down an animal is easiest with a lamb. Lamb is rigid, small and lightweight, without the heavy fat of a pig. A lamb is easy to pick up and move around on a wooden table, as opposed to a large cow that is nearly impossible to maneuver without a great deal of help.

This book is not meant to be a forum for describing the method of breaking down an animal in detail. But the basic ideas are fascinating in their own right. Interestingly, there is no right way to cut meat. Americans have classic cuts, the French slightly different, the English as well and so on. We want our meat to look like the pork chops in the grocery store meat case; the bacon to look like the sliced pork in the slick plastic envelope at the supermarket. But it doesn't have to be that way.

The goal of specific meat cuts is to isolate pieces of meat that will cook well and consistently. If we had a fatty piece connected to a lean piece and we sautéed it, the result would be steak that was half juicy and rather raw and half dried out and quite overcooked. We want to maximize our pig to its fullest and best use. Theoretically, one option would be to remove all of the meat from the bones and grind it up for sausage. Certainly a passable option, but a lot of great pork chops would head to the grinder.

The other concept that surrounds meat cutting is that it is a zero-sum game. You can't have everything you want in one animal. Capturing one cut means that you are letting go of other cuts. For example, the loin of the pig is the large central muscle that runs down the main torso of the animal. It is the most tender piece of any animal. In a cow it would be the filet mignon. In a pig it is customarily kept in the center of a pork chop, surrounded by the bones of the ribs and the spine. The center is the pork loin. If the loin is not sliced rib by rib into pork chops but rather is removed whole from the bones, it becomes the pork loin, which in its cured form is Canadian bacon. A choice always has to be made between numerous potential butchering plans. Rib bones left on the pork chops means that the pork ribs themselves will be a bit shorter.

As the pig is butchered, bits of trim will begin to pile up. Hunger will pile up among the butchers at the same time. A solution is in short order. "Fatty toasties" fill that bill. One of the cooks made this for me the first time he helped butcher a pig here.

A recipe is really not needed, just the general idea. Take a large loaf of great hearty country bread. Slice thinly and toast in the oven. Keep it warm. And use a whole loaf, not just a couple of slices.

In a large steel sauté pan, throw in fatty chunks and meaty

chunks from the butchering of the pig. Knowing that fatty toasties will be part of lunch, a side bowl for saving such scraps is always good. Gently render all of the fat on the stove, with the meaty bits cooking up at the same time. Some thinly sliced chilies, saved from the fall harvest, add some zing; throw those in the sauté as well. Maybe even a bit of garlic, but just a small amount; we want this to be about the pork. When all is rendered and fried, there should be far more liquid fat that you can imagine consuming. A half a cup, three-quarters of a cup, maybe a full cup—that kind of quantity.

Take the toasted bread from the oven, pile it on a large platter. No need to arrange in some prissy way: pile it up. Pour over it the contents of the sauté. The fat will run over the toast, soaking into the bread. The meat will alight on the tops of the toast, the chilies as well. Salt as needed, pepper is good too. Eat it up greedily. Tomorrow's lunch will be salad, don't worry, just enjoy today.

Familiarity with a couple of basic cuts is in order, though: the legs and the bellies. Both are uniquely useful in a butchered pig. They are the two cuts that made me want to raise pigs.

"Belly of the pig" is a funny phrase. I have heard people confuse the *stomach* with the *belly*. The words sound like they are referring to the same thing. The stomach is an organ. In it the food that the pig consumes is digested. I would just as soon leave the stomach to the compost pile. The belly is the outer layer of muscle and fat at the bottom of the pig's torso. The belly is split down the center when the animal is gutted. An inch and a half thick on a two-hundred-pound pig, twice that on a four-hundred-pounder.

In this inch or two or three is a nice skin with very little hair, lots of tasty fat and layers of meat in the middle streaking through the fat. The uses of this delicious cut are generally bacon, pancetta and "pork belly." The first two have been popular for decades, while pork belly is a culinary phenomenon of the last ten years. I have no recollection of ever seeing it on a menu up until the mid-1990s, and yet it is on virtually every respectable restaurant's menu today. I'll leave the pork belly to restaurants; bacon is what I love.

The basic concept of curing meat is to use salt to remove enough of the moisture of the meat beyond the point where it is moist enough to grow bacteria. Salt desiccates the meat and draws out the moisture. In drying out the meat, salt also firms it up and adds flavor. In the case of bacon, the meat will also be smoked to add additional flavor and protect the meat even further.

If we look to a time prior to having efficient home freezers—and that is most of human history—preserving foods was a huge concern. Animals are big. A large hog is around four hundred pounds live weight. Cows can double or triple that weight. No family can eat that much meat at once. The options are to quickly sell the meat that your family cannot eat in the week or two before it goes off, or to preserve it.

As other local foods could be scarce in the cold winter months of Europe and the northern United States, finding a way to preserve meats through the winter meant a source of protein when other foods were not available. The traditions of preserving meats were born out of this need.

The biggest challenge is stopping bacteria from reproducing in the meat and spoiling it. Bacteria need two things to reproduce: warmth and moisture. Without either of these, spoilage can be discouraged. The contemporary method of preservation of meats is generally to freeze the meat. This reduces the temperature to a point where the bacteria cannot reproduce.

Certainly freezing accomplishes the goal of keeping meats fresh, although it does little to make it more interesting and tasty. In parts of the country where electricity goes out during storms, storing hundreds of pounds of meat in the freezer is a frightening prospect.

The much older and more traditional method of preservation is to remove the moisture and not worry about the temperature. Without adequate moisture, the bacteria cannot reproduce even if the temperature is above freezing. Dehydrating meat is one option, but how many of us want to chomp on beef jerky all winter? The best method is to salt the meat to remove only part of the moisture. Salt has a valuable ability to permeate the meat and draw the liquids out while at the same time seasoning the meat. You don't generally think of salt as a desiccant. Its usual role is simply as a table seasoning, and yet if you were to place a pork chop on a plate, cover it with salt and wait a couple of hours, the pork chop would be swimming in its own juices, and the salt would have completely dissolved.

The other great challenge of preserving meats concerns flies. Big slabs of pork and beef are aromatic and flies are attracted to them. The problem is not the flies, but rather the eggs they lay on the meat. When the eggs hatch, huge numbers of maggots invade the meat, eating it as they grow. Generally the maggots will be very crafty. They will enter the meat through one hole and then hollow out the inside of the meat, eating from the inside out. Although often only a couple of maggots might be visible around the hole, hundreds may be in the center, creating a slimy, decayed interior.

Maggots are a tremendous problem on the farm. With lots of animals and lots of manure, there are always some flies around. Keeping them away from the meat is always difficult. One remedy is smoke. In addition to using salt to dry out meat to an adequate moisture level to keep bacteria from spoiling the meat, smoking the meat helps keep the flies away. The smoke dries the outside of the meat, giving the maggots less of a way of entering. The smell masks the natural scent of the meat, making it less attractive to the flies. And so bacon was born. Smoking is also used for country hams and *speck*, a German smoked dried pork.

It is very easy to find and cut up bellies for bacon. The bellies are large—maybe twenty-four inches by fourteen inches, one on each side of the pig. They cover the ribs and run down to, well, the belly of the animal. Loosening them off of the ribs is fairly straightforward. The ribs are long bones and are all at the same level; sliding a long, thin knife blade between those bones and the meat that will end up as bacon is simple. The result is two large, heavy, flexible, flat, fatty pieces of meat.

Lay them out on a large cutting table and start to even up the sides: turn this irregular-shaped piece into a big rectangle with straight edges. It will cut easily and cleanly, revealing the strata of the meat: layers of fat and flesh. When you look at the side it will quickly start looking like bacon; then you can get your bearings. It looks like the slice of bacon that we have all seen since childhood on the Sunday morning frying pan. As you move around the belly, you will quickly see sections that are more baconlike and others less so. Be judicious. Use the best for your bacon; the rest will certainly not go to waste. A mix of fat and lean is ideal. Too much fat and your slice will waste away quickly in the pan. Too much lean and the fatty flavor and moistness are lost.

Think of the container that they will be cured in. Four squares in an eight-by-eight-inch container are ideal. An inch less in dimension than that container will give adequate space all around for curing.

A square plastic food box is great. Round seems rather wasteful of salt, but could work just fine. It is always said to avoid metal, although I doubt the world would end if you did need to go in that direction. Gather a couple large boxes of good salt and make sure the bellies are nice and cold.

Recently I started adding nitrites to my bacon cure. Nervousness, mostly, I must admit. *Charcuterie* by Michael Ruhlman and Brian Polcyn, gives a great sensible and simple recipe for curing. Following his example, I mix a pound of kosher salt with a half a pound of sugar and just a couple of ounces of *pink salt*, making sure to mix the three ingredients thoroughly. I take a plastic food box, put some of the cure on the bottom, lay a slab of belly, add some more cure and so on. If I have any cure left I just pour it on the sides, add it on top. The last thing needed is another little container with a bit of salt in it.

My basic rule for the time the pork is left on salt is seven days for every inch of belly thickness. Generally the bacon will be an inch thick, so a week is standard and easy to remember. If the meat is a bit thicker, then a few more days in cure are handy. You want to have the meat salted adequately to preserve the pork but not so much that the bacon is inedible. I have experienced both. Neither is pleasurable. If the bacon had inadequate time on salt, either returning it to more cure is possible or simply cooking it quickly is an option. The pork should have a firmness to it, so the fat will feel less like the jiggly pale fat that entered the cure and more like a solid white rigid fat. Too much salt will result in a quite rigid block, cool-looking but difficult to enjoy.

Once the pork has gone through its requisite salting stage, it is removed from the cure, and any remaining salt wiped off. Dry with paper towels to remove any last bits of salty liquid. It is time to smoke the pork.

A simple smoker will suffice to further protect the precious belly slabs. Much chatter goes on about cherrywood or apple

wood or hickory. Maybe my palate is simply unable to discern
the subtle differences, but for me well-raised and -cured pork
nicely smoked is excellent no matter which wood is used.

At my farm we use an old barbecue made from a steel
drum. It has a small side chamber that is connected to the
large barrel where the racks are located. In the small chamber I place a cheap hot plate from the local hardware store,
the cord exiting from an air vent. On it I place an equally
cheap cake pan that I've long since retired from baking. The
pan is filled with chips of whatever tree I have recently felled.
There are a great deal of old apple trees here, so often I use
fruitwood, but birch makes appearances as well. Sawdust can
work just fine, I have found, but soak it well first. The goal
is to produce large amounts of consistent smoke; flames are
in no way needed or desired. Low heat and smoldering chips
work well.

Every few hours I flip and shift the bacon slabs. The
leading edges near the smoke chamber always get the best
exposure; the far edges barely get a kiss of smoke. Constant
rotations keep the exposures even. Because the hogs are
slaughtered in the late fall and winter, the smoking also
occurs in the chilliest parts of the calendar. I have no wor-
ries about leaving the pork outside in the smoker day and
night. A couple of days are sufficient, but three are even better. The trick is always to mound up the pile of wood late at
night and turn the heater to the lowest setting so the wood
can smolder through the night to keep the bacon on smoke
continuously. If the pan runs dry, it tends to burn the pan
out much quicker than one would want. Not much chance of
danger among the bacons, but I prefer to not wear out old
cake pans prematurely.

Once the bacon slabs have a leathery caramel exterior
and you are content that they have been smoked enough,

pull them, dry them off if necessary and chill them down. They should firm up a bit more in the cooler. Slice a bit off and fry it up. With luck, they will be tasty, not too salty, full of smoky porkness and a touch of sweetness.

Bacon was one of the first products that I made here. Prior to smoking bacon I had slaughtered animals and cooked up roasts, grown lots of vegetables and harvested a bit of honey, but bacon was a product. Bacon is a pretty common thing: every supermarket has a row of shiny plastic envelopes with the bacon splayed out to see; every diner has a BLT sandwich and a bacon cheeseburger. We know what bacon looks like in America; its taste and look are fairly universal. But making your own bacon does not necessarily result in the same kind of bacon.

Store-bought food products have become the norm. It is very rare to find homemade bacon, homemade butter, even a homegrown chicken. The store-bought product grown and produced by large factories has become what we strive to emulate. We want our bacon to look like the mediocre product made in a factory hundreds or thousands of miles away. An inferiority complex sets in: "Why isn't my butter like the block at the store?"

An additional dimension must be added to this dilemma. You can't make bacon or butter like factory-produced bacon and butter. Even though I am confident that mine is much tastier, healthier and better for the land, not only will it not likely resemble the store-bought entirely, it also might not cook like the commercial product.

I have found farm bacon shrinks far more than commercial bacon. It is difficult to get it to crisp up without all of the fat becoming rendered in the pan. The ideal of a seven-by-one-inch crispy bacon piece with streaks of fat and lean is difficult to achieve. Butter is similar. Butter from my lovely Jersey cows is an amazing-tasting product. It has a better color, better flavor and better pedigree. But it does not necessarily have the same consistent water content from week to week. It whips a bit differently, it melts a bit differently and it bakes a bit differently. Not poorly, but differently.

To me this is a great example of a simulacrum. The butter in the store references butter of a hundred years ago. It obviously has a direct lineage, even if it has been greatly altered. Interestingly, that authentic source is not what is referenced now, but the imitator. We all want to create industrial butter, industrial bacon, industrial pork. That is our reality. None of us, or very few of us, can reference the authentic because it has been entirely replaced with the facsimile. Maybe our grandparents can vaguely remember the bacon of their childhoods, but primarily our culture is a culture of supermarket industrial food products.

Possibly the bacon of 1840 Virginia, for example, shrank when cooked, never crisped up well and was too salty. Hormel has certainly created a product that we now know as bacon that has a very specific size, flavor profile and texture. It is what we have come to expect as bacon and what most likely was created through focus-group testing. America at the turn of the twenty-first century has a salt threshold for food. It is not based on the amount of salt needed to cure pork, but rather on what people enjoy.

 · The idea of salting pork to remove the moisture with the goal of preserving the meat has many different forms. Different cultures created distinct riffs on this basic idea; the most famous is likely prosciutto, the style credited to the Italians of Parma. Virginians developed their Smithfield hams, Germans speck and so on.

I have made hams many times with a variety of outcomes. Some were so salty as to be inedible. Trying to soak the salt out yields some success, but generally the dogs enjoyed them, we ate a lot of soup seasoned with bits of salty ham and the compost heap got a bit larger.

Some hams were quickly and distinctly damaged by flies and maggots. The entire center of the large twenty-five-pound blocks of pork would be liquefied and grotesque. Straight to the compost.

There have been, however, a few hams over the years that were exceptional. Salty, but not too salty. Sweet, yet not sugary. Fatty, yet a pleasure to leave on your tongue to melt.

The great challenge in making hams is that the time frame for producing a success is not a few hours, or a few days, but months. It isn't until the ham is pulled down from the rafters and sliced that its glory shines, or its tremendous deficits become apparent. I persevere, though, confident that with time and more experience, the success rate will rise.

A large fatty pig is essential. I have often seen precious little legs dried to the point of taxidermy, having insufficient fat to sweeten the end product and preserve the moisture of the ham. Raise a large hog. Fat is good, more is better.

The first goal is to remove the legs from the body of the pig. At this point the pig is scraped clean of hair, the guts have been removed, the meat chilled, the fat firm. The legs are easily seen; there is no doubt where they start and finish. At my farm we start with the hind legs, and the hooves will still be attached at first. The Spanish tend to leave the hooves on; I find that a bit much, and the Italians concur. The hoof does make it a bit easier to tie a rope to the ham for hanging, but it still is more animal than you need. Cut it off just beyond the joint. A Sawzall works just great; not what those saws were designed for, but cutting through bone is comparable to cutting pipe and plasterboard.

Where the leg meets the hip is the pelvis. The ball joint that connects the leg to the pelvis is where we want it to be separated. As I break down a pig, I constantly look to myself as reference: my foot, my ankle, my hip and so on. If that doesn't work, I call over one of the dogs, feeling around on their legs, trying to figure out how the bones are laid out. Once a pig is slaughtered and gutted, there is no frame of reference. It is hard to put it back together in your head. A carcass on a big table is no longer an animal, it is a piece of meat.

The goal is to remove any muscle, fat, skin, bone that is extraneous to what the ham will be in its final form. But keep in mind that any cut, slash or opening becomes a pathway for bacteria to enter and potentially ruin the final ham. One side, the skin side, is well protected. The flesh side, the side that was attached to the pelvis, is much more difficult, and this is where problems can happen. Leaving only the ball of the joint is good; some people leave a bit of the pelvis attached to seal the joint as well.

Trimming the fat and muscle on the skinless side makes for a tidier result. Be bold, don't be cheap. Bits of stray muscle or skin will not be usable months later when the ham is to be eventually consumed. If they are trimmed now, they can be rendered to lard, ground for sausage or fed to the dogs for lunch.

Keep as much of the skin on the hind end while slaughtering the pig. The skin will provide excellent protection against flies on the sections it covers.

Once the leg looks like a ham, footless, tidied up, essentially flat on the muscle side, it can be salted. Although for bacons a cure mixture is nice, pure kosher salt works quite well for curing hams. Different methods of salting abound. I prefer to place the leg in a large high-sided storage container that can hold the ham completely. Traditionally the English would use wooden boxes. I never seem to get around to building a wooden box; a plastic container will have to do.

As with bacon, put a layer of salt on the bottom, and also rub plenty of salt deep and well into the fleshy side of the pork. We want the salt to make contact, to be a part of the meat. The pork will quickly begin giving off liquid and, as this is the goal of salting and curing, it is most welcomed. I drain it off as it occurs, but a wet brine would work well too, so I don't fret if it begins to build up. Keeping the meat cool is important at this stage, as it is not presently cured. Forty degrees makes sense to me; the salt can do its work while the meat is kept safe.

The general rule I find works well is to keep the leg on salt for one day for every pound of weight that the leg weighs the day it is slaughtered. Twenty-five pound leg, twenty-five days in salt. As I am a nervous man, add a couple or three days as well. Too little, and the meat may go bad; too much, and it is bound to be preserved, but be too salty to consume. Which is worse? My thought on most things is to experiment and use the experience of trial and error. Last year's ham too salty? Pull the salt back a bit. Smell a bit off in a month? Salt it more next time.

Once the appropriate time has elapsed in salt, drain the brine from the meat. Wipe the pork down, and feel it. It should be firm; a lot of liquid will have been drawn off. The weight will be a bit less. The color will have changed as well. Where the pork going in was red and vibrant and wet, now it will be darker, more ocher and have a flat sense to it. The glossiness will have left.

The rest of the process is time. Sounds simple enough, but all can still go wrong. The goal is to keep the ham fairly cool, safe from predators and pests and in a space where the air can circulate to dry out the ham. Easier said than done. In the case of *prosciutto de Parma*, the hams are aged in the mountains with cool alpine air breezing through protected curing rooms. Since most of us do not have such conditions, we must improvise.

Because the pigs are slaughtered in the late fall early winter, it is most likely that we have three to five months before the warmth of summer approaches. By that time the ham will be well enough along to protect itself. In the winter, temperatures are lower, and with luck the fly population is much smaller or nonexistent.

I have seen folks in the city keep hams in refrigerators. It is often the best and only possibility. The temperature is cool and generally very consistent. There is no chance of a sudden warm afternoon. The cooler is completely sealed; no chance of flies getting to the ham, birds pecking it or rats nibbling on the edges. Coolers even have fans to move the air around. Moisture can be a problem, though. Some coolers simply add too much and make dehydrating the ham difficult if not impossible. Try it, though; it may be your best bet.

Here on the farm, curing is a challenge. The best hams I have made were aged in a back shed. With a great deal of ventilation, the air moved through freely. A huge elm tree to the south side provided constant coolness; even on the hottest day of summer the shed would stay cool. Because the shed was open to breezes, it was also open to flies. Many a ham has been lost to maggots gnawing internally. One solution I tried was to wrap the meat in muslin fabric, tied well. It usually worked, but still wasn't perfect.

For years I have tried deboning the hams prior to salting them. To this day I am not sure which preparation I prefer, so I will give you an overview of the deboning method.

The leg is removed from the carcass as with the more traditional ham style. Then a very sharp, short boning knife is used to remove the entire bone from the ham. I have heard of splitting open the leg, removing the bone and then sewing up the opened leg, but that is not as much of a challenge.

Little by little, working from both ends of the leg, cut the muscle from the bone. At the shin the muscle will be very thin at the surface and difficult to remove; patience and perseverance are required. Have care—the pork at this point is rather chilly, the fat slippery, the meat still rather wet. Your hand with a sharp, small knife is reaching deep into the center of this doughnut of pork. Where the pork ends and your fingers begin is sometimes in question.

Once you have the deboning halfway finished, cutting the meat off the bone from both ends, you can hold on to the leg bone and let gravity pull the remaining leg muscle down. One hand holds the bone aloft, while the other slowly cuts the remaining muscle from the bone. With luck it will all come out without damaging the cylinder of pork.

I like this method. I've done this for years. Recently I have had cooks inform me that it is simply not how it is done. I am not sure what that means, but I don't care. I think that the goal of farming and cooking is to find your own way, to learn from the traditions of Europe, but then to adapt them to your climate, to your needs, to your skills and products. If I wanted to live in Europe, I would pack my bags and move. My goal here is to live my American life on my little farm, eating great food; food with integrity, not food that is imitative of my counterparts a continent away.

Once the tunnel boning is complete, salt the meat in the same manner as ham that still has a bone. The salt will permeate well, as there is more surface area. Once the salting is complete, remove the meat from the brine in the same manner. Dry it, and tidy it up. Now the challenge is to tie

it together to make the pork look less like a doughnut and
more like an apple fritter, solid. Easier said than done. Drying the pork will close the gap in the meat, but it needs some
assistance. We don't want an air pocket in the center. We
also need a way to hang this ham from the rafters to dry.
Again, easier said than done. The pork has firmed up, but it
is still meat. Slippery, unwieldy, with no hard edges to tie
on to.

Both methods—with bone or without—will make a nice
ham. Another option is to smoke the pork as well as to cure
the pork. After the salting has cured the meat, the ham can be
smoked in the same manner as bacon. The result will be more
like a Tyrolean speck than an Italian prosciutto, but smoke is
a lovely flavor. There will also be less chance of flies nibbling
their way into the heart of the pork.

Salting and drying is the basic technique used to preserve
pork for a length of time. You can apply this technique to other
parts of the pig. Any meat can be salted and air-dried. Some
cuts of meat, however, will be tastier than others. You could
conceivably cure the ribs, but why bother? Roast them up the
first day and enjoy them. There is not a great deal of meat and
really not that much fat either. The best cuts for curing have
fat. Fat is flavor. Fat is moisture. Fat is your friend.

A couple of classic cuts to preserve with salt: the jowls turn
into a lovely guanciale; instead of curing the bellies on the
flat and making bacon, season them liberally with chilies,
roll them, tie them tightly and cure them for spicy pancetta;
large slabs of fat make for tasty lardo; the main muscle of the
shoulder transforms itself into coppa. These are classic Italian treatments. Instead of trying to duplicate these traditions,
use the idea of them as the basis for preserving your own pork
in your own traditions.

Turning lovely bits of the pig into fine slices of delectable charcuterie for the table—nothing could be more in the spirit of my farm. The ingredients are basic: pork that was well raised and a simple box of kosher salt. Nothing is wasted, all is utilized. The transformation is profound, yet simple and achievable.

Fourteen

The Present-Day Farm

Kurtwood Farms is located on an island near Seattle, surrounded by suburbs and small one-acre lots. Compared to the humble gardens of the city, a twelve-acre plot is tremendous: room for animals and row crops and a woodlot. Coming from the Midwest, however, a visitor would think this parcel tiny and un-farm-like.

The terrain of this farm is varied. The upper pasture is high on the western hill, the house and its outbuildings lie on the lower, eastern border of the plot. Between the upper pasture and the buildings are the lowest sections, below the water table much of the year. This band of land, running north to south, is perennially wet, muddy and difficult to traverse. The eastern section, where the barn, the dairy, the kitchen and the rest of the structures are clustered, is close to the neighbors. From the house I can hear the neighbors mowing their lawns, their children playing on their Slip 'n Slide, the cars coming and going down their driveways. It is the suburban quadrant.

On the upper pastures, the cows relax, the calves graze in their paddock, and the orchard trees stand in tidy rows. Standing on this verdant stretch of land uninterrupted by buildings or power lines or neighbors, I can see Mount Rainier in the distance.

This island was settled by farmers and loggers 150 years ago, but today only a handful of its twelve-thousand-plus

inhabitants make their living from the land; the vast majority commute off the island to the city for work. This piece of
land was originally part of a larger homestead, settled by a
German man who in 1881 built the log house that is the center point of the farm. Soon after the house was completed it
was sold to the Beall family, who grew this homestead into an
agricultural powerhouse on the island, erecting acres of glass
greenhouses to raise vegetables and later roses and orchids
for close to one hundred years. This farm, this land, is the
legacy of a long agricultural tradition. These hills and knolls
and small valleys supported the Beall family. The pastures
grew kale to feed their prizewinning chickens.

Today, Kurtwood Farms is a mixed farm, one with animals,
vegetables and fruits. The cheese ends up for sale and the rest
of what I produce gets served at weekly dinner events. The
more customary model in this country is a large farm with one
or maybe a few similar crops: large hog operations, corn and
soybean farms and mammoth dairy enterprises. Those farms
are based on the idea that animals, vegetables and fruits can
be produced via an assembly-line model. A production farm is
efficient and profitable. Kurtwood Farms is neither efficient
nor particularly profitable.

My vision of a farm is a throwback to an earlier era. It is,
I must admit, a time that never really existed. I have taken
bits and pieces of agricultural design over the years and used
them as I see fit. The barn is a large timber-frame structure
that looks much like any French barn of the nineteenth
century. I keep an old Oliver tractor from 1949 around simply
because I like its design, sturdy and redolent of post–World
War II industrial confidence. The tractor I use the most is the
compact John Deere, with its hydraulic steering, four-wheel
drive and three-point hitch. The kitchen garden is a study in
modernity: large, repetitive stark cement beds surrounded by

mute gray gravel and low concrete curbs. My greatest tool on the farm is most likely my cell phone, plus an iPod for keeping my sanity on long lonely tasks. The buildings reflect a taste for all things rural French, while still utilizing the great materials of Douglas fir and western red cedar, ubiquitous in Pacific Northwest forests. I have shaped this farm over the years and love it, and yet I still think it should be bigger, produce more food, be tidier.

I am a more experienced farmer now, but that does not mean that I am immune to the unpredictability, and sometimes downright cruelty, of nature. This past spring, soon after the ewes had lambed, the field was filled with a dozen ewes and close to twice that many baby lambs. A potential problem for any newborn animal is scours: known to humans as diarrhea. The youngster eats too much or too little of one thing or another and promptly gets sick. The danger is dehydration. The animal will stop eating, lose weight, weaken and most importantly stop drinking water. A quick death is often in order. I have had animals with scours over the years. With quick attention, I can get them back to health. If I don't notice it early on, their demise is generally assured.

In this case, I had caught it early. One young lamb was slowing down, sitting by herself and not eating. Her rear end showed the telltale signs of scours. She was an incredibly adorable little lamb, maybe six weeks old, already a nice woolly coat of brown and white. She looked at me with a lamb's characteristic bright eyes, all hope and optimism. The sour eyes of an old ewe were years away.

I headed for the back field with my standard help kit for young lambs: a small syringe with no needle, a bottle of Pepto-Bismol and some sugar water. I filled the syringe with bright pink medicine, and holding the small mouth of the lamb open, I squirted it into her mouth. Not sure that she liked it, but she ingested enough of it to help. I followed with ample syringe-fuls of the lightly sweetened water, trying to get her rehy-drated. Each day I would trek back out, giving her a bit more pink and as much water as she could drink, four or five times a day. After the third day I was convinced that I had saved this one. After all these years I had a sense that I knew when I had rounded the corner of survivability. Although the young lamb stayed in one place, I moved her around each day, and she could hold her head up and seemed to be gaining strength. Each time I went out to feed her she would look up at me with those innocent eyes.

On the fourth day, I trudged back to the pasture, carrying the small syringe, more water and a bit of milk for my young charge. I had fallen into a routine, checking on her every few hours, looking forward to seeing her, confident of success.

As I unchained the gate of the paddock and walked over to where I had left her the night before, she looked a little different from a distance. A bit more hunched over, but I still had hope. I had kept sheep for years; I could revive a young lamb.

As I approached the innocent young lamb I knew that things had gone terribly wrong. Yesterday in the late afternoon, as she sat still, unable to get up and move about, waiting for me to return with more water and food, one of the crows that also call this farm home had come down to the sheep field. With his prey too weak to struggle, he had proceeded to peck out her eyes. The still-alive lamb simply lay there, dying a slow death, blood dripping onto her fresh young wool.

I returned to the house, grabbed the locked rifle and a bul-let, and marched back to the paddock with a stride that befitted my anger. A moment later I was back in the paddock, wanting to scream, wanting to cry, but mostly just wanting to end her life as quickly as possible. As the shot went off, the resident crows, perched and watching from high above on the treetops surrounding the pasture, flew off with a racket. I put the gun away and traded it for a shovel from the shed. In a few minutes my young charge was buried. Nature is cruel. Farming has brought me close to the wonders and joys of nature, but also to the dirt and death that make them possible.

This past summer, the parents of a friend of mine here on the island came to visit me. I had met them briefly and knew a little bit about them, but they had never come to my farm. I agreed to the visit with a great deal of trepidation, despite their innate grace.

My friend's father, Marv, was here to celebrate his eightieth birthday. He had spent his entire life on his family's farm in Lewiston, Idaho. Although I had never seen his farm, I had heard about it many times and was in awe simply of the idea of it. Not just a farm, but also a cattle ranch, it sprawled over thousands of acres. Their family farm grows lentils, wheat and cattle, lots of cattle.

Marv came out to my humble farm to take a look. He and his wife got out of their car slowly and deliberately, looking around in a polite but confused manner. He walked to the milking parlor, through the barn, up the north road and across the upper pasture, through the orchards and down the lower pasture to the kitchen. Wearing worn cowboy boots, the ubiquitous Wrangler jeans and a large oval belt buckle shiny from years of wear, he slowly plodded across the pastures, commenting on this cow and that, his wife taking pictures, him asking me questions with the respect of a man who sees me as his equal. Marv looked over at me and asked "Do you have the problems with calving on a Jersey cow like that? We do with our cows in the early spring back on the ranch, but not later in the year . . ." his scratchy voice trailing off. Could he really have wanted my opinion on calving?

I was shocked and a bit embarrassed as he and his wife asked me how I kept this all going. *All this going?* I thought. Marv never talked about his "farm," but rather referred to the "corporation." He rarely spoke of "acres," but rather referred to land as "ground"—"This spring we bought more ground for winter wheat." To have this farmer, a man at the top of his profession, ask me about my cows—my five cows—and about my pastures—my eight acres of pastures—took me off guard. I stammered, trying to find the words, making excuses for not having more cows, more land. "I hope to buy a couple more next year. . . . Maybe eight cows would be nice." As we walked back to the house, I muttered sheepishly, " Next month I am going to clear that brush there and plant more grass . . . really I am. . . ."

It was during this brief visit on a sunny summer day that I finally got it. This farm has place. It has standing. And a great deal of high-quality food comes from this soil. It is large enough to force me to take it seriously; to recognize that I must be the steward for this land, protect the soil, improve the soil, leave these acres in better condition than when I arrived. And not worry if I have the right boots, the right jeans, the right truck.

My goal is for all the parts of this farm to work together to produce a whole greater than the sum of its parts. The classic small family farm of the past worked well because each of the different aspects complemented each other. For example: Growing vegetables requires fertilizer additions to the soil to maintain fertility. Whether it is a natural product such as compost or a chemical-based fertilizer, it still needs to be purchased and brought in if it is not produced on the farm.

The best way to produce compost is with animal manure, especially from cows. Without removing the manure from the barns and composting it for the vegetable gardens, the manure will back up and the nitrogen levels will increase to unhealthy levels. In a large industrial dairy, processing manure and getting rid of it is a huge problem. On a small-scaled farm, it is an asset.

This same logic follows in many aspects of the small enterprise. Pigs fatten by feeding them excess produce from the vegetable gardens, apple pulp from pressing apples for cider, and excess kitchen waste. Chickens eat the grain and fly larvae from the cows' manure piles, spreading the manure out so that it will decompose faster into the pasture, and then they'll lay beautiful eggs.

The ideal farm—and the one that I strive for here—has all the parts in play. A garden for vegetables, an orchard for fruit, pigs for meat and to consume waste food, cows for milk and cheese and to provide manure for the gardens, sheep for meat and to keep the grass low and chickens for eggs and to clean the pastures.

The other goal is to make the farm a closed system. I want to bring as few things into the farm as possible. The inputs, such as hay, grain, baby animals and seed, are often from other parts of the country. They are not necessarily appropriate for this climate and region. We want plants and animals to thrive, to be ideally suited to this locale. Also money must be spent to purchase the inputs. Any cash outlay brings down the bottom line of the farm at the end of the year. If feed for the animals can be grown on the farm and not trucked in with transportation costs and taxes assessed, then it is a better deal for the farm as a whole. The farm will be more profitable and the animals will eat food that is better for them. My disdain for packaging contributes to my goal of not buying feed or supplies.

I started my cheese-making business with a cheese named Dinah's Cheese in honor of the first cow that I bought. Although she was stubborn and difficult to milk, she still has a place in my heart. Dinah's Cheese is a fresh cow's milk, bloomy rind cheese, usually known as a Camembert-style cheese. I choose not to call it Camembert, however, as this isn't Normandy, and I am in no way French. My small round wheels of Dinah's Cheese, covered in a snowy white mold, came from this island, even if they are inspired by the French originals.

Every other day I make a batch of half-pound cheeses, forty-eight at a time, in the creamery. Throughout the day the milk is heated, cooled, stirred, cultured, coagulated and cut. By the early afternoon the curds are ready to be ladled into the awaiting molds. On a large stainless steel draining table the whey will drain away. Later that evening I will flip the molds once, twice, three times before I eventually go to bed, leaving the cheeses to firm up by morning. The next day I will unmold them, salt them and begin their aging process. After a total of twenty-five days they are ready to be sent to the small cheese stores, the large grocery stores and the chef-run restaurants in the city that appreciate this local cheese.

A second cheese is also in the works, a hard, aged cows'-milk cheese that will be prepared in eight-pound wheels. I have tentatively named it Francesca's Cheese, after the second cow to call this farm home. This Italian-style hard, grating cheese will age for at least ten months or, with a bit of luck and patience on my part, a full year.

Taking fresh raw cows' milk and transforming it into a

new product is both exhilarating and, so far, profitable. I have found that people are far more willing to pay a premium for an exceptionally made local product such as cheese than a really good local carrot. I can price my cheeses to compensate for the price of the land, the buildings, the upkeep of the cows and also for my own time. I did not have the ability to price my vegetables or fruit or even raw milk high enough to pay for my expenses. These goods have a perceived value based on supermarket prices. Artisan cheeses do not. In cheese making I have found a balance, something that I love doing that also has the potential to support my farm.

Whether or not this farm is profitable in an economic sense is difficult to calculate. My goal, and I would assume the goal of many other such small farmers around the country, is to sell enough food to pay the bills so that a job in the city is no longer necessary. I have pursued this objective for years and spent much too much time thinking about it, puzzling over a way to make this goal possible. I have come to a few conclusions.

Growing a commodity crop is a bad idea. Commodity crops are products that are the basis of much of the food we eat: corn, soy beans, wheat, etc. On the scale of a farm such as this, the possibility of growing wheat is pretty unlikely, but I would include items such as carrots, beets and lettuce in the same grouping. Whether it is corn or carrots, there will always be a large industrial farm somewhere in the country that grows the item on a huge scale, both cheaper and more efficiently. There is little chance of competing with these producers in a financial sense. Even though the carrot grown on my few acres is better, fresher and tastier than those produced by commodity farmers, it is unlikely that the consumer will pay three times as much for it. When I realized this I quickly got out of the vegetable-growing business. Primarily because I was not particularly good at it, but also because the numbers just never added up. I could see no possible way to pay my bills selling tomatoes, cabbages and garlic.

I tried moving up the food chain, raising more expensive food items: raw milk, meat and eggs. Although these foods brought in more money than vegetables, they are all regulated by the county, the state, the federal government or all three, and therefore require greater investment in infrastructure, permits and insurance premiums to sell them. The result is little profitability from the selling of these high-ticket but highly regulated products.

And so I have found creating value-added food products to be the best model for financial self-sufficiency here on the farm. Making cheese feels right to me. I ran a small business for nearly two decades in the city and I always had a sense of when something was working and when it wasn't from an accounting perspective. I must confess, however, that since the day I left my job in the city, I have always felt that the golden ring of profitability was just a few months, a bit more volume, the next season, one new product away. It keeps me motivated, keeps me striving to make it to the next step toward a goal of financial stability from growing food.

Right now this farm couldn't operate without the weekly cash infusion from the farm dinners. The money a dinner takes in as compared to a weekend night at my old restaurant is minuscule, but because I don't have to pay rent on the space, purchase the food or pay a staff, almost all of the proceeds contribute directly to the farm's operating budget. I would like to believe that in five years cheese making alone will be able to support the whole farm, but the last twenty years have taught me not to make grand proclamations extending five years into the future.

There is an extenuating circumstance that makes my challenge realistic, makes my goals of stability conquerable. It has allowed me to become a cheese maker on the eve of my fifth decade. I bought this land when I was still in my twenties, when the price of real estate was lower, and spent the years since then both paying off the debt and transforming this land from the low-value acreage that I had purchased, to the highly productive farmland that it is today. If I, or any beginning farmer, were to purchase a farm identical to this one today, the sales price, and therefore the debt associated with it, would be dramatically higher than the price I paid all those years ago. A new farmer would have to sell ten times the cheese I do today and throw dinners every night to pay his mortgage.

I also kept my well-paid job in the city for many years, paying down the mortgage, paying for the barn, land-clearing, fencing and pasture work. Without that income, the present-day viability of this farm never could have been achieved. As a result, do I turn a profit today? I wouldn't know exactly what to include in the expenses and earnings, but I make enough to keep the operation afloat and support myself, so in that sense I believe I do turn a profit. My bank account is not getting fat, but I never expected it would.

When I have read books on farming or attended lectures, the most important lesson I have gleaned is that not creating debt is imperative in building a sustainable small farm. Saving money beforehand to buy a small piece of undeveloped land or keeping a city job while paying down a mortgage and then farming seems to be the best, if not the only, strategy for making a small farm possible economically. A heavily mortgaged farm is always a bad idea, no matter the scale. A case could also be made for keeping a side job throughout the life of the farm. Gene Logsdon, a farmer who writes on the joys and perils of running a small farm, makes the argument that throughout American history the farmer or his wife, or both, worked off the farm to bring in needed cash. Even if this is the case, I want to believe that growing food can be profitable, inspires me to work harder, producing more and better cheese, improving the herd and raising the productivity of the pastures.

Fifteen

The Table

Daily life on my farm starts at a very civilized hour: in winter, when the sun is just about to come up; in summer, when the sun has already risen. Each of my days is bracketed by two bookends: morning chores and evening chores. In the middle lie tasks that vary from day to day and from season to season. The bookends are the same year-round.

The morning and evening chores are the same every day. The animals are fed and watered. The cows are milked, the milk is processed and the dairy is cleaned. No bookend task is negotiable. Animals always need to be fed and watered. Cows always need to be milked. I can be sloppy and rushed about additional tasks during the middle part of the day, but I have a responsibility to the health of the beasts that inhabit this farm. They are fenced in pens for the nourishment of my friends and family, so the very least I must do is to ensure their good feeding and health. When there is a party that evening that I would really like to get to, the evening chores can be very rushed and hurried, but they are never skipped.

Farms operate around the clock. Farming is not a nine-to-five occupation, but rather a full-time job in the most literal sense of the term. There isn't necessarily something to be done during the odd hours of night, but there could be. I share this property with some four dozen other beasts and if it happens that one of them needs some assistance in the middle of the night, I must be available. Cows calve at strange hours, lambs can be born in the wee hours, dogs have been known to get onto the property and wreak havoc with the sheep, raccoons make it into the chicken coop. All this chaos happens after normal business hours.

Although I expect to live for forty more years, I am a stubborn man and will most likely live out my years here. When I bought this house nearly twenty years ago, I thought, as many do, *I bought this house; now I own this house and I own this land.* You can own a house, a building, a structure, but I feel differently about the land. As I began to work on the land, clearing scrubby trees, improving the soil, I started to feel a responsibility toward it. I am protective of this parcel, possessive of it, but I am aware that I do not *own* it. No one can own land. We are all mere stewards of the land. You may own your condo, but land is different. I have an obligation to pass this farm on to someone in better condition than when I first set foot on it. I want to leave it cleaner, less polluted and more productive when it's my time to go.

I like the project of creating a farm and being a steward of the land; I am attracted to the enormity of that task. Years ago when I attended Henning's lecture and heard him speak about the history of his land, he talked of a fifty-year plan. He felt it would take that long to accomplish the goals he had set out for his farm. At the time I thought he was crazy, that I would be "done" quickly. I have now come to realize that fifty years is a good time frame. Raising the quality of the soil, bringing trees to their maturity, learning the way the land reacts to time and weather—it all takes many years.

Over ten years ago I started planting the orchard, mostly nut and fruit trees. Many have done well, some have suffered the plague of deer chewing on their leaves and some are long since dead and replaced. I cannot say, a decade later, that the orchards are mature and at their full capacity. If at the half-century mark they are still not mature I will be a bit discouraged, but at this point I am still quite hopeful, optimistic for the day when the walnut trees tower over me and in the fall I struggle to harvest all the nuts that fall to the ground.

To the north of the log house is the kitchen, guarded by two sentries of towering bay laurel: the cookhouse. A low, long building, it contains the energy of the farm. In a very literal sense, all the utilities run through this building. The range is heated by natural gas, the main boiler heats the water that runs through underground pipes heating the log house and the kitchen. The kitchen is filled with coolers and freezers humming around the clock, those coolers and freezers filled with meat and produce. On the long stainless steel counters are mixers, meat saws and meat slicers, all run on the electrical current that comes into the building from underground wires. In this building, nothing is quiet or calm. The log house is peaceful, the grandmother of the land. The kitchen is full of youth and life. At night the long rows of multipaned windows shine with the bright lights reflecting off of the worktables and eating tables. Only late at night after the day's work is finished are the lights in the kitchen shut off.

I wish I could say that I do every task here personally. I want to pick every strawberry, feed every chicken and mow the lawn with the regularity of my tidy neighbors. A few times per week Jorge comes to the farm to work. Born in Mexico on a small subsistence farm, Jorge has great experience with cows and welcomes working on my farm as a pleasurable alternative to being a cook in a hot commercial kitchen. For years he worked on the line at my former restaurant in the city, cooking hamburgers and pastas and flipping many fried eggs on busy weekends. Little by little he started to come out to the island to work on the farm. Now I could not run it without him.

Jorge treks out to the farm early in the morning, most of

the year while it is still dark. He lets himself into the kitchen, turns on the lights, fires up the dishwasher and makes a pot of coffee. Soon thereafter, at a more respectable time to get out of bed, I stumble down the stairs of the log house and head over to the kitchen. The sight of the kitchen filled with light warms my heart. It is close enough to the image of the *Leave It to Beaver* home with June Cleaver baking cookies all afternoon that I longed for as a child. With a bit of a smile, I open the kitchen doors, Jorge pours me my coffee and offers me a *concha*, a Mexican pastry shaped like a snail, and the farm day begins. Each morning, after a discussion about his three young sons and how they are doing at school, we move into a chat about American politics, Mexican politics and the intersection of the two. Jorge repeatedly chides me for my naïveté about corruption and bribes; I counter with pushing him to abandon his small-town ways now that he is in *el Norte*. Once the preliminary conversation is complete, we discuss the plans for the day: which animals need attention, how we will fix this or that problem that has arisen since he was last here, the field that I would like tilled or planted, weeded or harvested. We also talk about our mutual excitement and optimism for the near future. "Next month the grass on the upper-back-side pasture will be especially great, no question," he proclaims, confident that the work he has done there will pay off in a few weeks' time. His favorite calves he declares to be the best ever, forgetting that he said the same thing last year about that spring's calves.

The dance complete, the coffee finished and only a few crumbs of the *concha* remaining, we head out to get the morning chores completed. Once those chores are done, we will return to this vital kitchen space to wash the vegetables from the field and store the eggs gathered from the chicken coops. Running the length of the main room of the kitchen is the dinner table. Constructed of long planks of Douglas fir, it was made from wood cut down on the island a few blocks from this farm. I know where the trees were. I watched them as they were felled years ago. When the trees were milled for the replacement logs to repair the log house, the planks that were cut off of those rounds became the top of this table.

This table is at once grand and humble. It bears no resemblance to a Queen Anne table, or Sheraton, or even Duncan Phyfe. The table has long planks, adhered together to form the top, and a simple trestle base of additional Doug fir. The edge is not straight, the thickness varies and there is not a hint of square or level or true. To me, however, it is true. It reflects this land and this life.

When I originally made the table, the surface was rough from the blade of the portable mill. The planks were never put through a planer or sanded down to make them smooth. I would have preferred it, but never found the time or the equipment. From the passing of platters of food and the sliding of wineglasses, the rough edges of the wood have been worn smooth. Pork fat, butter, spilled red wine, salad dressing have all been added in layers to this surface. It has a finish. It speaks of the meals that have been eaten here, of the people who have dined here, of the conversation that has passed here.

I often reach under the table to the underside of the table planks. It is still rough, still reflects the crudeness of the mill blade with the heavy kerf. I have no interest in sanding it down. It is my way of marking time, of knowing that change has happened.

Sunday evenings are reserved for Cookhouse dinners. The meats, the cheeses, the fruits, the vegetables, the eggs, the herbs—they all come from this farm. Only a short list of ingredients—flour, sugar, salt, pepper—are brought in from the supermarket. Here are a couple typical seasonal menus from Cookhouse dinners:

FALL/WINTER

Thin, crispy pizza from the wood-fired oven with guanciale, chilies, fresh herbs

Winter squash soup from Musque de Provence squash, pureed, finished with cream, garnished with brown butter, fried sage

Hard rolls, sweet cream Jersey butter

Antipasti course: hard, aged eight-month cows'-milk cheese, membrillo / quince paste, pickled pumpkin, pork rillettes, black pepper crackers, pork copa

Fresh slaw of shaved Brussels sprouts, with apple cider vinegar, pickled red currants

Poached farm eggs, sauce Bernaise, sautéed lacinato kale

Tagliatelle noodles, butter, fava beans, cippolini onions

Pork shoulder roast, braised in milk, sliced, with boiled bay leaf potatoes

Caramel ice cream, butter shortbread cookies

SPRING/SUMMER

Thin, crispy pizza from the wood-fired oven with fresh tomato sauce, whey ricotta, fresh herbs

Light pork brodo, English peas, chervil, thyme, parsley, chives

Hard rolls, sweet cream Jersey butter

*Antipasti course: fresh cows'-milk, bloomy rind cheese,
tomato jam, pickled lemon cucumbers, pork liver pâté, black
pepper crackers*

Nantaise carrots sautéed in butter, fennel pollen, honey

*Fresh heirloom tomatoes, sliced and served with
clarified butter, salt*

*Pappardelle noodles, braised beef shank ragout,
grated hard cheese*

*Boneless pork loin, roasted in the wood oven,
thinly sliced, pan juices*

*Rose-geranium-infused custards, raspberry puree,
butter shortbread cookies*

It is a different way to cook; a different way to eat. Seasonal and always fresh, a farm dinner could be said to be the ultimate in local eating. I think of this dinner and the entire lifestyle of raising food and cooking it to be a denial of the present times. The four ingredients that are brought in are slightly processed: the flour has been milled, the white sugar processed from sugar beets, but they are minimally processed. The salt and sugar, the flour and pepper look essentially like they did one hundred years ago. I want to believe that the industrial food revolution that took place in this country after the Second World War never existed.

It is most likely that I am imitating a time period and a lifestyle that never truly existed. I will take that criticism. This is, however, how I like to eat. I need to see the animal that will eventually be my dinner. I want to pull the carrots from the soil the morning that they will be cooked for the evening

meal. The cream, the milk, the cheese, the butter that grace
the dinner table come from a cow with a name familiar to me:
Dinah, Boo, Lily.

This is my personal choice. I don't expect, or desire, to have
the entire nation return to a pre–World War II era in terms
of agriculture and food culture. I don't have the facts, but I
doubt that there is ample farmland near the cities for a serious part of the population to have their own twelve acres and
live off of the land exclusively. I cannot advocate for most of
Manhattan to be depopulated as the stockbrokers and clothing designers return to the country to raise their own cows.

My way of life, I sadly conclude, is rather elitist. I enjoy
a life and diet that few can enjoy. I don't have a recommendation for a way of growing food that would be accessible to
everyone. I can only say living off of the land, and grandly, is
possible.

I enjoy serving my dinners every Sunday; it is the family
that I wanted to create, if only for a meal per week. When
I was a kid my mother always worked. I was envious of the
other kids in the neighborhood whose mothers were home
during the day making soup, baking cookies. At this point in
my adult life, my guess is that the domestic bliss was illu-
sory; those mothers most likely didn't all love being home
all day making soup and bread. It is a great vision, however,
and one that is comforting to many. The folks who trek out
to this farm every Sunday either miss those Sunday dinners
at their grandparents', or want a Sunday dinner that they
too never had.

We serve dinner family-style at the long Doug fir table, a
bench on one side, old wooden chairs on the other. The guests
are seated cheek by jowl, the large platters of food passed
from person to person around the table.

Early on Sunday morning a cook comes out to the farm

to help prepare the evening meal. When I first started planning these dinners, I envisioned sturdy home cooks coming by the farm to make a home-cooked meal for the table. Friends' mothers in town for vacation from the Midwest, roasting chickens, steaming green beans and mashing big pots of potatoes with butter and cream: that was the menu I expected. Sadly, or at least realistically, those mothers and grandmothers never materialized. My guess is that the mothers I imagined have been dead for years. My mother, for example, spent her adult life cooking with cans of mushroom soup, Jell-O pudding and frozen vegetables. Presently the guys who cook the Sunday meals come from restaurant kitchens in the city. Their background is different from home cooking; they are trained to cook quickly and to order. Generally restaurant menus are written and printed in advance and remain the same for a number of days, a number of weeks or perhaps even for years. Quality of preparation in a restaurant kitchen comes from repetition: making the exact same dish many times a night, every night of the week. Although restaurants often prepare specials every night, and some change the menu weekly or even nightly, it is the repetition, even if only through the evening, that makes the food great. Cooking for this table is different. Ideally the menu is different every week. There is no chance to repeat a dish completely. Yes, scrambled eggs pop up often, pasta is rolled out each Sunday, hard rolls are baked from the same recipe, but the core of the meal is new, changing from season to season and week to week.

I also find that cooks—or anyone, for that matter—are very used to shopping for vegetables, meat and dairy rather than picking from the garden or bringing it in from the cellar. The farm cook's mind-set must be distinctly different.

There is a finite and varying volume of food produced here.

Every year I get a bit better at working the land, a bit more efficient, and the farm's production tends to increase, but the weather often plays a large role and crops fail. The list of foods grown here is long; you might say that our portfolio is diverse. In any given year a few things do extremely well. They may have been planted at just the right time, and gotten just the right amount of water, thus all the elements came together to produce a large volume of, say, pears. On the other hand, each year a few items fail miserably. They were planted a little too early and froze, or a little too late and dried up from the heat of the sun before they could gain roots, or perhaps I just plain forgot to take care of them. The rest—the majority of the crops—do just fine and produce an ample supply for the kitchen.

I am keenly aware of what is available at the farm every week. I spend enough time in the gardens and in the cellar to know how many carrots we have to use, how much cream, how much pork. I am aware that when the carrots run out, it is impossible to have any more until the next row has matured. If that is in the middle of June, the pantry will be replenished quickly. If it is December, the wait will be months until fresh carrots will grace this kitchen again.

When working in a restaurant, or, more simply, when cooking at home in the city, there is always the possibility of more. If you need additional carrots, buy them at the store. When you run low on onions, a simple call to the wholesaler and another case will show up the next morning. We do not have that luxury here. When the last of the onions have been consumed, they are gone.

This is the distinct difference between this kitchen and a kitchen in the city. We don't have the luxury of more. The culture of this kitchen is of abundance, but of calculated abundance. This changes the way you cook and the way you look at the seasonality of the food. When new cooks first arrive they invariably grab an apronful of onions, a handful of garlic and begin to chop and sauté to begin a sauce or start a braise. They do it because that is how they are taught. Onions are cheap and they give depth to food. Here at the farm they are always limited. I dole them out judiciously. To me they are precious and valuable.

The cook who grabs the onions—more than he needs—is thinking in the mode of the city kitchen. He hasn't looked around him or acknowledged the season. In the city kitchen there are no seasons: onions are delivered every day of the year; carrots as well, same with garlic and so on. Onions on the farm follow a path of the seasons. In the early spring, bits of small green onions can be pulled from the garden, both to aid the cook and to give the neighboring young green onions a bit more growing room. As spring turns to summer, all of the green onions will be used in those few weeks. Soon after, the leeks seeded in the depth of winter in the greenhouse and transplanted to the garden in early spring will begin to mature. They will be the aliums to follow the green onions. The heat of summer will beat down on the onions, seeded at the same time as the leeks, yet given a bit more time to bulb, rising up out of the warm dry soil, their skins beginning to dry. At the end of summer they will all be pulled and allowed a couple or three days lying on the sidewalk to finish their husking before they go to the cellar for storage. The fresh onions will be used in the kitchen first, full of the tastes of summer. When they have started to sprout and soften up, we will move to the storage onions, those that we were able to hold through the winter despite the freezing cold weather just outside the cellar door. As late winter turns to early spring, the cycle will begin again, the last few storage onions grabbed off of the bottom of the box on the bottom shelf of the cellar.

The box will be filled mostly with dry dirt, the lost dried skins of onions eaten weeks before and the odd remaining onion rolling around.

One of my favorite cooks to make a meal in my kitchen was Joseph. He got it. On one of the Sundays when he was planning on coming out to the farm to make dinner I sat waiting in the kitchen for him. As this is an island only accessed by ferryboat, I can always predict when guests will arrive. I know the ferry schedule and can calculate the time for the crossing, the unloading of the boat and the drive down the spine of the island to the farm. I have very few surprises.

Because I didn't see his car coming down the driveway to the cookhouse, I began to be worried. He knew the way, having been here many times before. A few minutes later, his car peeked through the brambles at the base of the driveway, slowly heading up the hill. As he got out of the car and explained, I felt all of my apprehensions regarding his tardiness dissolve. At the driveway down by the main road, he had seen the cherry trees that form a canopy over the drive, and realized they were in full bloom, this being a beautiful spring day. He stopped the car, hopped out and with the help of a friend who was with him proceeded to climb up and pick the cherry blossoms. When he had his empty coffee cup filled with the delicate white flowers, he could then proceed.

That evening he prepared Choiggia beets, fresh from the garden, roasted in the oven, sliced and served with pickled cherry blossoms. It was lovely, innovative and most certainly of this farm.

When I go into the produce section of the supermarket and see the rows of vegetables, I can tell which items are produced close to home. My garden is the control specimen; I know that the vegetables that are ready at my farm are those that are the most in season. Granted, better farmers could push their vegetables to ripen a few days or a couple of weeks earlier, but essentially our crops all respond to the same weather in the same general location.

In the supermarket are seasonal and local items, but also the vegetables and the fruits that have a seasonal reference on a cultural basis but not necessarily on an agricultural basis. For example, fava beans are thought of as an early spring vegetable. They appear on the menus of restaurants in April and May and in the supermarkets around the same time. Unless it is a most bizarre spring here and a quite mild winter, there is very little chance of my having a ripe fava bean in April. Yes, the plants will have sprouted and grown and possibly even bloomed by the time I see the beans in the produce aisle, but mine will ripen a month later. Shelling peas are the same. I would love a bounty of peas in late April or early May, but I am often disappointed.

I think this is the result of a uniform national culture of food despite a tremendous variety of climates over the fifty states. Making pumpkin pie on the third Thursday in November is expected no matter if you live in Hawaii or Alaska. The ripening of winter squash cannot possibly follow all of the many climate zones of this vast land.

The nature of the food media has a contribution to this as well. I am not in the business of publishing magazines, but I would reckon that parts of the June issue of *Food & Wine* are written in the dark of winter, anticipating the sunny days of summer before they actually arrive. Even the food section of the *New York Times* is written days prior to its publication. Hence the food press and the national consciousness of the growing seasons is planned and standardized; ripeness is set by publication dates, not by the weather.

The weather and the seasons control what comes into

this kitchen to be prepared for dinner. Although I occasionally plant fruits and vegetables that are not ideally suited to
this climate, I do tend to stick with those plants that thrive
here. I think of it as a survival-of-the-fittest. Two years ago
I planted four different varieties of raspberries in the beds
directly behind the kitchen: one golden, one black and two
different red raspberries were given equal real estate in the
raised bed. I had thought that with the four varieties I could
span the season well; keep raspberries on the table for a longer time period than with just one variety. I also envisioned
a bowl of multicolored raspberries when all four berries came
ripe at the same time.

I never intended this bed of berries to be an experiment,
but rather a simple way to secure good fruit. Although all four
varieties have done well, grown high, flowered and fruited,
the golden raspberry has done the best by far. The black
raspberry plants are small and fruit sparingly. The two red
raspberries persevere and I enjoy their fruit. As they are all
planted in one bed, the golden raspberries are taking it over,
spreading faster than the black raspberries can. I expect in
time to have a bramble of primarily golden raspberries, with
bits of the reds and few if any of the black raspberries. The
goldens are simply better suited to this spot and climate, this
terroir.

Similar processes play out all over the farm. This winter
one of the quince trees will be ripped out to be replaced by a
more suitable variety of fruit tree. The tomato plants that I
remember the most fondly from the heady days of summer
will be reordered and replanted in the spring. The cow that
is easily bred back and produces a beautiful calf is kept on
the roster of the herd; she that has trouble being bred will be
culled from the herd, replaced with a younger heifer.

I enjoy this constant refinement of the makeup of the farm. It keeps my interest. It is dynamic, not static. On my daily walk around the property, I pass the different fruit trees, look in on the gardens, the pastures, the orchards. I often touch the trees, feeling the branches, the leaves in my hands. It gives me a connection to the plant. When I can feel that leaf in my hand in summer I can get a sense of the health of the tree. In the dead of winter, the brittle twig tells a story as well. As I pass across the large upper pasture in the late fall, the sun is low, the cows appear to know that their days on the pasture are coming to a close, soon they will be in the barn for winter. I need to go up to each cow and chat with her, feel her hide. The flat, smooth summer coat will be filling out more; the winter coat growing in. Cows that I milk daily are always receptive to the attention, while the young heifers are still skittish, quickly jumping as I come up near them.

In this way, the farm improves. The best raspberries overtake the weaker varieties. The best cows become the basis for the future herd, the fruits trees that respond the best to this climate endure. The weak are quickly culled once their flaws are revealed.

There are food items that are a part of the nation's larder that are never seen here. The item whose absence is most noticed by dinner guests is olive oil. Over the past quarter century olive oil has moved from the exotic to the indispensable in this country. I have encountered many cooks, guests and visitors who find it absolutely incredible that there is no olive oil in this kitchen. Not simply that it is absent, but that food can be prepared without it. They are in disbelief not only that I have chosen to keep it from this kitchen, but also that vegetables can be eaten, meats prepared, pastas served without the golden oil from the warmer latitudes.

My decision to exclude olive oil from the kitchen is based

simply on location. Olives can only grow far to the south of here. Olives would never make it through a winter here. Certainly I could keep them in pots, bring them inside in the cooler months or find varieties that could tolerate the freezing weather of January, but I choose not to. It would be the same as keeping the bad apple tree in the orchard, the one that doesn't really produce because it isn't suited to this climate.

If this lack of olive oil were a great sacrifice I might feel differently, but I never miss it. We have an abundance of beautiful butter from the Jersey cows and excellent, flavorful lard from the pigs. The butter and lard are fats that come from this land.

I have no recollection, from growing up in the sixties and seventies in Seattle, of olive oil in cooking. Certainly my mother never used it in her cooking. Our fat of choice was vegetable oil: corn oil and tubs of margarine on the table. The large plastic tub labeled *Country Crock* was our substitute for butter, my mother feeling as I expect many did at the time that butter would lead to immediate heart disease. Butter was also considered too expensive, a luxury that was allowed only on holidays. Although bacon fat was drained off of the frying pan and kept in an old tuna-fish can by the side of the stove, it too was felt to be an unhealthy pleasure. I revel in the irony today that I produce many pounds of animal fat here every year. If my mother realized, she would consider it the ultimate in unhealthiness.

I am not certain why we collectively came to love olive oil. Health claims most likely contributed to its popularity; the greater ease of travel to Italy and Spain also probably helped. My personal theory is simply that we have culture envy. We have received a view into the world of warmer Italian climates and it is good. In those parts of the world the sun shines often, food is an important part of daily life and life moves at a slower pace. Tuscany was the *it* girl of the end of the twentieth century. We wanted vacations in Tuscany, we loved stories of moving to Tuscany—think *Under the Tuscan Sun;* seemingly every restaurant opened in the 1990s had a rustic look with a burnt-ocher palate, and we loved the Italian food and its centerpiece—olive oil.

Don't get me wrong, I have fallen under this spell as well. I term it the "tyranny of the Mediterranean." I think we truly want to believe, maybe actually do believe, that we live in Italy or Spain or at the very least southern California.

Our culinary traditions have an agricultural origin. The foods that we eat and the way that we eat is a direct reflection of the way people ate on the farm. Today pickles are a lovely appetizer before a meal, but for generations pickles were a way to preserve vegetables that were prolific during the late summer but were not available during the rest of the year. Most of the best parts of our culinary traditions—prosciutto, parmesan, wine, marron glacé, jams and duck confit—are simply ways to preserve meats, milk, fruits and vegetables from before the era of refrigeration.

Generally speaking, animals and crops are started in the spring, mature through the summer and are harvested in the late fall. The challenge lies in that we need to eat throughout the year, thus we need to level out the peaks and valleys of available produce and meat. Guanciale was not developed to be a cute appetizer for swanky New York restaurants, but rather was a method of saving the jowls of a pig that was slaughtered in the fall and that would rot and be eaten by maggots if not salted, cured and dried. The same goes for vegetables. Cucumbers grow prolifically in the mid- to late summer. Small starts put into the soil become prolific vines stretching around the garden, with masses of beautiful cucumbers hidden under the leaves. Making pickles becomes the order of the day.

A lot of time is spent in the kitchen here compared to shopping at a store and then cooking. Although the actual preparation of a meal is rather straightforward, making the components that go into a meal requires constant preparation. Stocks need to be made, vegetables pickled, fruits made into jams and jellies. When I have spent too long making a wheel of cheese I begin to understand why people stopped doing this and were happy to buy cheese in the stores. It takes time.

Life is rather grand here these days. The farm is sufficiently developed. Most of the twelve acres are being well utilized, although I have great plans for making areas more productive. More than enough food is produced each year and preserved to keep the Cookhouse stocked year-round. Enough of the fruit trees have matured to produce a serious volume and variety of fruit throughout the season.

On my morning walks around the perimeter I often wonder what this farm will be like in one hundred years. The image that always comes to mind is a series of photographs in Michael Ableman's book *On Good Land: The Autobiography of an Urban Farm*. The book is the story of Fairview Gardens, a farm in southern California that pushes on despite being surrounded by ever-encroaching suburbs. I like to imagine a contemporary aerial photograph of Kurtwood Farms being compared to a photograph decades in the future.

Hugh Fearnley-Whittingstall, in the introduction to his seminal book *The River Cottage Cookbook*, discusses a continuum of self-sufficiency. On one end of the spectrum is eating entirely from the commercial food production system. On the other extreme of the scale is total self-sufficiency from the land. For myself, I strive to inch down the scale toward a total abandonment of produced industrial foodstuffs. Two

decades ago, I started with a bag of apples and plums I
picked from the fruit trees at the property that at the time
of that harvest was not yet mine. I essentially stole that fruit
from the people that I would soon buy my land from. I took
the fruit back to my apartment in downtown Seattle and
relished it. The plums were as big as bulls' balls, filled with
sweet juice, ready to burst. The apples were russeted, crisp,
juicy and unlike those that I was accustomed to from my
local supermarket. That paper bag with twenty pounds of
fruit was my first harvest here at Kurtwood Farms. The next
year the bounty was hardly a bounty: a few more apples,
bucketsful of the blackberries that ran rampant over this
land, a few weeds in the flowers that I cut, thinking them of
great beauty.

It would be more than a few years before I could make a
meal entirely from this soil. Only in the past half decade could
I leave the supermarket behind, except for that short list of
staples I never expect to provide for myself. I am reminded of
a recent conversation I had over dinner with a math professor
here on the island. Thomas described the uses of calculus and
its basic concept. She used the example of going half the distance from A to B, then halving the remainder and traveling
that distance, then going half of that distance and so on. The
general wisdom is that you will never reach point B; there will
always be the remaining infinitely small half remaining. This
is known as one of Zeno's paradoxes. With calculus that total
distance can be calculated. We can achieve point B, if only in
a theoretical sense.

What makes this calculus problem all the more interesting
is that with each halving of the remaining distance toward
self-sufficiency, the degree of difficulty increases. The first big
half is fairly straightforward. Most of us can grow tomatoes,
potatoes, carrots and peas. The second half of a half is a bit

more involved: year-round vegetables, beef cows, pigs, dairy products. The third half of a half of a half is where it gets challenging: grains ample to make it through the year, for example. As we approach that imagined terminus, increasing effort must be exerted.

It matters how we define the chase to the end of the spectrum: Is animal feed included? Do I need to grow all my own grain for the chickens? Toothpaste—is that a foodstuff or is that outside of the whole project? Is being off of the electrical grid essential or is that just a silly idea?

There have been a glut of books and blogs recently that make this challenge into a game. A "one-hundred-mile diet" is one premise: you limit your food purchases to those things that are produced or grown within one hundred miles of your locale. I find it all rather silly. The point isn't to find that final sigma that signals that you are at the finishing line, but rather to head down that path.

I have run into the odd locavores who smugly announce to me that they are producing their own salt, and shouldn't I join them in this endeavor. My response, generally in a polite fashion, is to let them know that if they want to row out into the bay and dredge up five-gallon buckets of seawater, bring them back to shore and boil them down to capture a bit of questionable-quality sea salt, that they are most welcome to. I am quite content with my bright red box of kosher salt, thank you. I could apply some cost-benefit analysis here, but it is simply a matter that I find uninteresting. Kosher salt from the supermarket is of high quality, low price and appears to be rather pure. Heavy cream from the dairy case at the store does not pass my same gut-level test. It is worth it to me to drag my body out of bed each day to milk my often unappreciative cows in order to score some lovely cream. Boiling seawater just doesn't have the same return.

I have another continuum, another trek that I am moving forward through. In addition to pursuing the best food, the most locally grown food, I also want to create a place, a thriving family, a real community. Whether I knew it or not at the outset, I sought to create a family here for myself. Not a family in the *Leave It to Beaver* sense, but along more abstract lines. Maybe it is just noise I am seeking: the din of kids running around playing with the dogs, the sounds of friends eating and drinking at the long fir table in the farm kitchen, the sounds of workmen coming and going, their loud trucks and clunky machines filling the air. This farm has become a community of sorts. It is a place where parents can bring their kids to see the young calves, the baby lambs, the huge pigs. It is the place for city chefs to butcher hogs, slaughter calves, press apples for cider.

Over the years my impressions of fruits, vegetables and herbs have altered little. Certainly carrots fresh from the soil have more carrotness to them than those picked days or weeks prior and shipped across the country. I enjoy my carrots more than commercial carrots; mine are better carrots. I haven't changed my intrinsic ideas of carrots, however. Carrots are essentially the same as the first one I ate, some forty-plus years ago.

I cannot say the same for meat. The pork, the beef, the lamb that are raised, slaughtered, butchered and eaten here are of superior quality in my opinion to any other. I am biased, of course, but they are excellent. I can control how the animals are born, how they are fed and raised and how they are slaughtered. The end result is a superior product. Meat is no longer simply a fine product on a plate, the steak at the end of a long work week, the bacon next to the fried eggs on Sunday morning, the lamb on the spit at the summer party. All meat is the result of a life. An animal is born, lives its days and is slaughtered, completely for our nourishment.

This is a sea change from picking up that flat Styrofoam tray in the supermarket: the small piece of meat lying on the foam pad, covered with plastic food film, a sticker affixed. That meat has no context. There is no animal there, no life. That small sticker may have a cartoonish reference to a farm that exists in our collective consciousness, but it doesn't refer to an animal itself or to the farm where that animal was raised.

My great education over the past two decades is just that: meat comes from animals; not from the abstraction of animals, but rather from actual animals. I do not mean to imply that having a hamburger off of the grill in the heat of a summer day should be morose, tearful or sentimental. Rather, that it should be enjoyed, savored and respected.

I have spent a great part of my years creating and improving this spot of earth and expect to continue on for many more years. It is primarily a selfish and solitary act. I do, however, hope for similar like-minded projects to pop up around the country. I want there to be more small farms, more ways to connect to our food, more links to our cultural past of food raising, preparation and preservation.

I wouldn't recommend that every household spend their Saturday afternoons churning butter—it's time-consuming, tedious and inefficient. Televisions can and should be produced in large factories where it is most efficient to produce them. We can live without TV. Food is different; it is special and unique. A centralized food production system is dangerous and foolhardy. Relying on a distant company to perform an essential skill is problematic. We all need to eat every day. Someone needs to know how to slaughter the pig.

The state of food, however, should not be clouded by gloom

and doom. It is the great joy of eating that makes me get to work on those less-than-sunny mornings. It is how I mark time. I remember a birthday party for the pork roast and tomato pizzas more than the weather or the time of year; the barn-warming was a lovely evening but I can still taste the grilled leg of lamb and the fresh figs; and steak night was all about the large grilled rib eye steaks courtesy of the steer Bruno, as well as the baked potatoes with butter, chives and bacon. Food is what brings us together.

I like cooking from the land. I look at food differently now, I prepare a meal differently. Previously, cooking was assembling ingredients to replicate a specific dish. The recipes for cassoulet, that Thai curry soup, those potato gnocchis came from this restaurant or that one, from a trip abroad or even from the odd mention in a movie. Certainly I could and would often change an ingredient here or there, but essentially the goal was to reproduce a standard meal already canonized in numerous cookbooks. Thai curry with shrimps, coconut milk, basil and kaffir lime was perfectly appropriate and delicious on a chilly snowy evening in January.

Feeding my guests and myself strictly from this land has changed that mind-set. The meals here must reflect this climate, this region and this culture; they cannot be borrowed from elsewhere and cannot defy the seasons. The cheese that is made at this dairy is of this time and place exclusively. Sure, it may resemble the cuisine of Normandy, for example, but the climate there is similar and presumably the larder stocked with like products. This is not to say that there is only one single interpretation of this spot on the earth. Folks at the neighboring farm down the valley could create an entirely different farm, one without Jersey cows, rows of cider apple trees and a garden of Belgian endive, Chiogga beets, green beans and leafy lettuces. I can imagine neighbors arriving here from Laos, Senegal or Mexico to grow and cook a totally distinct cuisine, all thanks to the same soil and climate.

This has been a lovely journey, pursuing my goals and heading toward self-sufficiency. Except in the abstraction of calculus, I know I will never reach it and I have little desire to do so. The animals are content in the field, the gardens lush with vegetables, the orchards ever more prolific and most importantly the table, the center of this farm, is filled with food and family.

Acknowledgments

When I started this book project, I was a complete novice, with little or no writing experience. Despite this inexperience, one person encouraged me to write a book proposal and then presented that proposal on my behalf. Without Hsiao-Ching Chou, I never would have written this book. She became my de facto agent on a moment's notice and kept me sane during the early days of my attempting to write a manuscript far more involved than anything I had ever written. I owe her a great debt of gratitude. I would also like to thank my editor at W. W. Norton, Maria Guarnaschelli, both for agreeing to take me on based on Hsiao-Ching Chou's recommendation and then for editing a difficult manuscript, helping me to see the story when I could not. Any other editor would have released this book in a far more immature state. Also at W. W. Norton, Melanie Tortoroli and Aaron Lammer gave my manuscript the individual attention it needed, to make it readable and cohesive. I am most thankful.

Here at the farm, I would like to thank Matt Lawrence both for being a part of this farming enterprise in its early days and for reading my very rough drafts and providing insight on the book's agricultural accuracy. His encouragement along the way was essential. Without Jorge Garnica, I never could have completed this book. Throughout the winter months, as I sat in the warm, dry kitchen, writing, pacing and talking out my ideas, Jorge would attend to the cows, the sheep and the pigs, keeping the farm running when my attention was kept more on my laptop than in the barnyard. I thank you, as do the beasts of Kurtwood Farms.

Glossary

Acre—43,560 square feet of land.

Artificial insemination (AI)—To breed an animal with mechanical means; generally to inject a cow with frozen semen from a remote bull.

Bacteria—Small one-celled microorganisms, some beneficial, some benign and some pathogenic.

Bee frame—The wooden rack that holds the bee foundation; nine inches by eighteen inches.

Bee hive—The wooden structure that contains the bee colony.

Bell scraper—A small hand tool consisting of a half dome, sharpened on the leading edge for scraping the hair from a slaughtered pig.

Bloat—The condition when the stomach of a ruminant is unable to process new grass, resulting in extreme fermentation and the production of gas trapped in the stomach.

Boar—A male pig, used for stud.

Brine—Heavily salinated water. Used to season hard cheeses and meat products such as hams by immersion.

Brooder coop—A small box for baby chicks in their first few weeks, designed to protect the chicks from predators and cold drafts.

Casein protein—The primary protein present in milk. The addition of rennet in milk precipitates the casein proteins, creating curds that will become cheese.

Caul fat—Thin gossamer fat that surrounds the internal organs of a pig, cow or lamb.

Charcuterie—The processing of products (generally pork) for later consumption. Standard final products include: hams, bacon, sausages and pâtés. Also the French term for the store where those items are sold.

Chicken vent—The anterior hole of a chicken where the eggs exit.

Chinoise—A fine sieve used to strain liquids—named after the shape it resembles—a Chinese hat.

Coliform—Bacteria present in the intestines of animals; not necessarily pathogenic, although many are. Their presence is indicative of poor hygiene in food products.

Colostrum—The first milk product that a mammal produces to feed her offspring. Thicker and richer than the eventual milk; full of nutrients needed for the baby's first days.

Community-supported agriculture (CSA)—A sales program in which small, primarily vegetable farms pre-sell an allotment of their produce for weekly pick up to their customers.

Cornish X—The standard chicken breed used for meat birds.

Crème fraîche—Fresh cream, traditionally the cream that cultures naturally with flora present from raw milk.

Curds—The solids in milk that are separated from the whey of milk to produce cheese.

Drone bee—The male bee. Except for the role of inseminating a bee that will become the new queen, the drone has no role in the hive.

Ewe—A female sheep.

Foundation—The flat sheets, generally made of beeswax, that form the basis of a beehive. Commercially indented with the outline of the hexagonal shape that the bees will transform into honeycomb.

Freemartin—The female offspring of a cow who was born with a twin sibling. Contains both characteristics of male and female. Generally unable to be bred.

Gambrel—A metal bar, approximately fourteen inches across, that holds the rear tendons of an animal when the animal is hung for gutting.

Guanciale—The jowls of a hog, cured in salt, air dried and aged.

Grade "A" license—The federal license that confers the right to sell fluid milk for human consumption; includes both pasteurized and raw milk.

Hay—Feed for animals. Grass cut and air-dried and bound into bales for feeding out of season, different than straw.

When I am feeling like I have learned little over these many years of becoming a farmer I look at the tall stack of bales of hay stored in the hay room of the barn and realize that I have made great strides. When I got those first sheep years ago and brought them back to the farm, I needed to feed them and went to a local feed store in search of food. What I wanted was *hay*, but as *straw* was cheaper, I asked for a bale of straw. I had no idea what either one was. The sheep were not happy with my mischoice.

In popular culture, the two words are interchangeable. A bale is used as a prop for a school play, or propped up by the front door for a Halloween theme, or possibly laid out for seating at that hoedown party.

Although both hay and straw are packaged in the form of a bale, and both have something to do with agriculture, they are vastly different. Hay is cut grass. It is food. The grass is cut and dried in the field and then meticulously harvested to capture the proteins in the grass that are easily lost if mishandled. Well-made hay is green, bright-smelling and full of nutrition. Poor-quality hay is dull brown, moldy and of no nutritional value whatsoever.

Straw is also baled, but is the by-product of grain production. When a field of rye or barley or wheat is harvested, the grain is removed. The tall stalks remain in the field. The stalks are cut and the baler is run through the field to pick up those stalks and bale them. Straw bales are lightweight, a collection of brittle stems, golden brown. They have absolutely no nutritional value. We buy straw bales now for bedding. It is spread out over the floor of the barn for the cows to sleep on, to soak up the urine. When the barn is scraped clean of the cows' manure, the straw is mixed in, creating an ideal base for the composting of the manure. The straw lightens the manure, adds the carbon necessary for the compost to break down and brings air into the manure pile.

It is remarkable for me to think there was a time when I used these two words interchangeably.

Heifer—A female cow, before she has had her first calf. Like the mistakes I made with hay and straw, *heifer* also proved to be a difficult term for me to master. Before I saw it written, I heard the term. Unfortunately, the word *Hereford* sounds very similar. A Hereford is also a cow, but is a breed of a cow, specifically a meat cow and of either gender.

Holsteins—The primary breed of milking cow in America. Large, black and white, heavy producers, low in butterfat.

Homogenize—To break up the fat in milk by forcing the milk through very small holes. The result is milk that does not separate into cream and milk.

Honey extractor—A centrifuge that spins the frames of beeswax containing honey. The honey is expelled by the centrifugal force, hits the sides of the extractor and accumulates on the bottom, where it is collected.

Hoop house—Large, temporary, portable greenhouses made of aluminum or PVC and covered in plastic sheeting.

IM; intramuscular—The method of giving an injection into the muscles of an animal.

Inflations—Flexible rubber tubes that slip over the teats of a cow or goat. Together with the vacuum pump and pulsator, the inflations open and close, simulating the motion of a suckling calf on the mother's teat.

IV; intravenous—The administration of medicine directly into the vein of an animal.

Jerseys—Breed of milking cow known for their lower milk volume and higher butterfat content. Curious, gentle, generally fawn-colored and smaller than Holsteins.

Kosher salt—Salt used to *kosher*, or preserve, meats. Does not refer to a blessing by a rabbi.

Lactation—The period when a mammal produces milk.

Lactobacillus bulgaricus—The culture generally used to thicken buttermilk, to create Hungarian buttermilk.

Legumes—A type of plant that produces pods, including alfalfa, favas, peas, and lupines with the ability to fix nitrogen from the air; part of pastures.

Loafing shed—A separate building or a part of a barn where the cows rest after milking and after eating.

Louis Pasteur—The Frenchman who discovered the process of heating wine to kill harmful bacteria; the process was later used to make milk safe to drink.

Mastitis—An infection of the udder of a cow, primarily due to dirty milking conditions, which results in high somatic cell counts and poor-quality milk; difficult to eradicate even with the use of antibiotics.

Milk can—The vessel of a small portable milking system where the milk accumulates.

Milk fever—Hypocalcaemia, the disease of dairy cows in which their inability to produce calcium immediately after calving results in an immediate collapse of the animal.

Milk room—The area of a dairy where the milk is cooled and stored, and where the milking equipment is stored and cleaned.

Milking parlor—The part of a dairy where the cows are milked.

Offal—The organ meats utilized for culinary uses. Includes kidneys, hearts, livers, spleens.

Package bees—Boxes of bees, generally three or four pounds in weight, that are collected at a large apiary and shipped to small beekeepers to start a new bee colony; the boxes contain hundreds of worker bees and one queen bee.

Paddocks—Pastures enclosed by fences and gates to house animals. Generally smaller than open pastures and used to contain animals for a specific purpose or time.

Pasteurization—The process of heating for a specified time to a specified temperature with the intent of killing all bacteria present.

Pasteurized Milk Ordinance (PMO)—The federal legislation that governs all dairies.

Pathogen—A bacterium that harms the human body rather than either assisting or remaining neutral.

Pig tape—A small paper ribbon used to gauge the approximate weight of a pig by measuring the distance around the pig's chest.

Pink salt—Salt cure that contains a small percentage of nitrites, to aid in the curing of meats; not naturally pink, but rather it is dyed pink to distinguish it from common salt.

Propolis—The sticky substance made by bees to glue their hives together.

Pulsator—The part of a milking system that interrupts the vacuum surge during the milking process, creating an on-and-off pulse on the teats of the cow.

Queen bee—The matriarch of a beehive; the female leader that lays all of the eggs for the continuation of the colony.

Raw milk—Milk that has not been pasteurized, that has never been heated to kill any bacteria.

Rennet—The substance that causes milk to break into curds and whey; derived from the stomach of a day-old calf.

Rumen—The first stomach of a cow, followed by the reticulum, the omasum and the abomasum.

Ruminants—Those mammals that have multiple stomachs and that chew their cud; primarily cows, goats and sheep.

Somatic cell count (SCC)—The laboratory count of the leukocytes present in milk in order to give an indication of the relative health of the cow's udder and therefore the milk as well.

Sow—A female pig after she has had her first litter of piglets.

Stanchion—An apparatus, generally of strong metal, that holds a cow in place during milking by closing loosely around the neck of the cow, although tight enough to not allow the cow to pull her head through.

Staphylococcus aureus—Bacterium that causes essentially incurable mastitis in cows.

Steptococcus thermophilus—A benign organism that is generally used to culture milk to produce yogurt.

Stray voltage—An errant electrical charge, imperceptible to humans, that is perceptible to animals, especially cows and pigs.

Sub Q—Abbreviation of *subcutaneous*, meaning below the skin; to inject medication below the skin of an animal.

Suckling pig—A small baby pig that is still nursing.

Sustainability—For a system to be in balance of its needs and its ability to replenish.

Swill dairies; slop dairies—Early milk-producing factories connected with whiskey distillers, which fed the cows the waste from the distilling process.

Tamis—A round sieve or strainer, made of a round wooden band and a fine mesh base of brass or stainless steel.

Three-point hitch—The mechanism on the rear of a tractor that allows implements to be raised and lowered by hydraulics. An important tractor innovation from 1949 that moved tractors from pulling implements in the same way as a draft horse had, to a modern farm tool. The three points are in the shape of a triangle. The two lower points are the hydraulic lifts; the third point, the upper middle point, is a stabilizing bar.

Vinegar mother—A thick, jelly-like substance that transforms alcohol to acid, creating vinegar from wine, hard cider, or other fermented product. The mother is introduced into the wine, sinking to the bottom and remaining there as it slowly replaces the alcohol with acid over many weeks. The container of wine, with the mother introduced, is intentionally left with the lid slightly ajar, allowing oxygen to help feed the mother. The result is the vinegar—tart yet no longer alcoholic. The mother can be removed when the process is complete or continue to reside in the newly created vinegar. Although the continued presence of the mother will leave the vinegar cloudy, it does no harm to the taste of the vinegar. The mother is generally removed from the vinegar, part to be saved for the next batch and part passed on to others who want to create their own vinegar. The primary agent in the vinegar mother is acetobacter, bacteria that have the ability to colonize wine and change the ethanol in the wine to acetic acid. Although these bacteria are ubiquitous in the atmosphere and able to affect any wine left open to the air, it is only with a cultured, controlled mother that a high-quality vinegar can be created. Wine is kept sealed from the air at all times to prevent the accidental and ruinous colonization of wild, airborne acetobacter.

Weaner pig—A small baby pig that is no longer nursing. Generally eight weeks old. Also known as a feeder pig.

Whey—The thin, liquid by-product of cheese making. When the curds are removed from milk during cheese making, the whey remains. Generally fed to pigs or used to make ricotta.

Worker bees—The small female members of a beehive.

The Farm Bookshelf

Although I often refer to many books when confronted with a new challenge or simply looking for new ideas for the farm, these are the books that get the most use. They are all splattered with milk, dog-eared, their spines broken from use. All good reads.

All Flesh Is Grass—Gene Logsdon, Swallow Press, 2004

The Contrary Farmer—Gene Logsdon, Chelsea Green, 1994
   Gene Logsdon has written many books over his career; these two are my favorites. Both are series of essays that address the life of a small farmer in America today. Logsdon's obvious familiarity with the subject and his great love of farming and his own Ohio farm are what make his books so pleasurable, inspiring and educational.

Charcuterie—Michael Ruhlman and Brian Polcyn, W. W. Norton & Company, 2005
   Ruhlman and Polcyn have created a book explaining the preservation of meats for everyman in a simple and accessible manner while at the same time maintaining a depth of understanding of the processes. This is the book I grab when I need a quick refreshing on the making of bacon, the stuffing of sausage, the curing of salami.

Cooking by Hand—Paul Bertolli, Clarkson Potter, 2003
   I distinctly remember the day when I found Bertolli's book on the shelf at my local bookstore. After thumbing through it for a few minutes, I walked over to the owner of the bookstore and informed him that this book is *important*. After reading and rereading this textbook, I continue to value its importance. Bertolli's essay to his young son on balsamic vinegar makes me sad and joyful every time I read it. Although Bertolli's style of cooking is far more exacting than mine, I head to *Cooking by Hand* first when tackling a new charcuterie project, and

only after trying his method will I begin my much more rustic approach. The gold standard for pork cookery.

Country Life—Paul Heiney, DK Publishing, 1998

A beautiful book filled with photographs and that on first look appears to be a simple, pedestrian guide to small farming. In fact, it is chock-full of information on a myriad of agricultural practices. On dreary, wet winter days, I turn to *Country Life* for inspiration. Although I doubt I will ever cut grains in the field with horse-drawn implements, reading this book makes me think that I could.

First Lessons in Beekeeping—C. P. Dadant, *American Bee Journal*, 1917

Reprinted often for close to a hundred years, a true classic. Beekeeping has changed little over the century and this little volume has informed generations of beekeeping. Simple, straightforward and yet also remarkably complete, it is the only bee book I use.

Growing Vegetables West of the Cascades—Steve Solomon, Sasquatch Books, 2000

Although specifically written for the Pacific Northwest region, Solomon's work is certainly useful for many parts of the country. Detailed instructions on growing vegetables both in small backyard gardens and equally applicable for larger market growers.

Home Cheese Making—Ricki Carroll, Storey Publishing, 2002

I love this quirky book with its how-to spirit and ease of instruction. The message is certainly that cheese making is for everyman. Limited to home cheese making, but the most accessible book available. When I want to set up a trial for a new cheese, these are the recipes I start with.

Lean Years, Happy Years—Angelo Pellegrini, Madrona Publishers, 1983

The Unprejudiced Palate—Angelo Pellegrini, North Point Press, 1984

Angelo Pellegrini came to this country as a small boy from Italy, originally settling on the Washington coast and eventually becoming a professor at the University of Washington, living in a neighborhood a few blocks from my childhood home. Simply the idea that the author lived near me was enough for me to pick up these books to investigate them. Many cookbooks and food essays are written every year, but for a joyful, passionate treatise on life, and not just a culinary life, no author surpasses Pellegrini. I must admit that I read about cardoons in his books for more than thirty years before I actually planted one in my garden. Better late than never. He knew what he was talking about.

Living the Good Life—Helen and Scott Nearing, Schocken Books, 1954

The classic story of the city dwellers who leave the city in search of a better, fuller life in the country. In this case the Nearings left as socialist economists, headed to Maine to begin a new life. They left a legacy of books, writings and farms that have inspired more than one generation of young farmers, including myself.

Look to the Land—Lord Northbourne, Sophia Perennis, 1940, 2003

I found this reprint of a classic agricultural text almost by accident. I have rarely seen it quoted in the literature and yet I found it to be an amazing treatise on the challenges of farms. Although written seventy years ago in England, it is incredibly timely. Reading it, I am both astounded that our problems are not unique to our era and at the same time also saddened that we have not solved these problems in the past seven decades.

On Food and Cooking—Harold McGee, Charles Scribner's Sons, 1984

The go-to book for all questions culinary. For years I have wondered about the specifics of foods and cookery, only to have all my questions answered by McGee's tome.

On Good Land: The Autobiography of an Urban Farm—Michael Ableman, Chronicle Books, 1998

Ableman, now a farmer on Salt Spring Island, wrote this great story about a farm in southern California. I enjoy the story, but even more so, I love looking at the satellite photos of the farm over the four decades of its existence as the suburbs catch up to the rural community, his farm the last one standing. The most visible proof I have of the encroachment of development on farmland.

Salad Bar Beef—Joel Salatin, Polyface, Inc, 1995

Salatin is the master of grass-based animal farming. He has written many books on the subject, and *Salad Bar Beef* is my favorite. His folksy writing draws me in, makes me think that I too can raise cows successfully. A thorough and complete treatise on rotational grazing completes this book.

Simple French Food—Richard Olney, Macmillan, 1974

Olney inspired me with this book in a few ways. Specifically his treatise on making vinegar propelled me to now have four casks filled with the stuff in my own kitchen. But in a broader sense, there is a joie de vivre that is expressed in his written word. I get the feeling that he loves food, loves to cook and to entertain his guests. The arrogance that trickles out every so often only adds to his intrigue for me.

The Botany of Desire—Michael Pollan, Random House, 2002
The Omnivore's Dilemma—Michael Pollan, Penguin Books, 2006

All of Pollan's books are excellent; these two, however, are my favorites. Pollan has that unique ability to describe in simple terms situations that make us all, including myself, stop and say, "Why didn't I think of that? That is so simple—now I will look at things in a new way. . . ." *The Botany of Desire* made me look at plants completely differently. To me plants now have an innate intelligence to them. *The Omnivore's Dilemma* did the same for me in reference to animals. I look at animals and farming and eating with a fresh approach since reading this book.

Chez Panisse Menu Cookbook—Alice Waters, Random House, 1982

Although the Waters's recipes are valuable, I cherish this book simply for the opening five-page essay entitled "What I Believe About Cooking." I have reread this passage many times, finding inspiration for cooking and serving guests. Raising animals, making cheese and growing vegetables are my present goals, yet I need to be sure never to forget that the goal is not simply a beautiful lamb, but rather a leg of lamb, roasted, served and eaten for the enjoyment of the guests. Waters bridges this continuum well in this timeless essay.

The Encyclopedia of Country Living—Carla Emery, Sasquatch Books, 1994

This voluminous paperback, a compendium of rural life, is indispensable. Although many books address the same topics and often in more depth, the encyclopedic nature of this book is invaluable. I also enjoy Emery's style. She obviously did not raise every animal, grow every plant she talks about here—she quotes liberally from others, bringing in many views on a subject.

The Family Cow—Dirk van Loon, Garden Way Publishing, 1976

The classic writing on keeping a cow for personal use. The first book I turned to when I had no idea what to do with my bovine. Van Loom has presented owning a family cow with such a calmness that reading his book makes me think that keeping a cow is surmountable, and a joy. And it often is.

The River Cottage Cookbook—Hugh Fearnley-Whittingstall, Harper-Collins, 2001

I love this book. I want to live at the River Cottage. I want to jump into the pictures, eat dinner with Hugh and sop up the sauce in the bottom of the pan with that crusty bread. *The River Cottage Cookbook* has inspired many, including myself, to look around for our local foods: underfoot, in our neighborhoods and in our hedgerows. I don't have any hedgerows, not really sure what they are, but I want some. Cheers to Hugh.

The Untold Story of Milk—Ron Schmid, ND, New Trends Publishing, 2003

Although Schmid certainly has a perspective of promoting the virtues of raw milk in this book, the sheer volume of research he has done makes this a necessary read. I only wish that those in public health could see the value in raw milk as much as Schmid does.

The Whole Beast: Nose to Tail Eating, Fergus Henderson, Ecco, 2004.

Fergus Henderson has given offal the respect it deserves. He took the least-loved parts of animals—kidneys, spleens, livers, brains—and crafted great recipes to utilize them to their best potential. He also has a style, both to his writing and his London restaurant St. John, that I love: clean, crisp and confident with a touch of humor.

Index

About the Author

Kurt Timmermeister is the owner of Kurtwood Farms, a thirteen-acre farm located on Vashon Island, one of the rural islands adjacent to Seattle. He studied international affairs at the American College in Paris, where he discovered his love of food and restaurants far surpassed his affinity for government work. He returned to Seattle to begin a career in food service and opened his own café called Café Septieme at the age of twenty-four. For eighteen years he ran a series of ever-larger Café Septiemes while at the same time beginning his education in small-scale farming. In 1991 he moved to Vashon Island, buying land that would eventually become Kurtwood Farms, and sold his restaurants. Kurtwood Farms is now home to a small herd of Jersey cows; a motley crew of sheep; happy free rooting pigs; an ever-changing flock of chickens, geese, and ducks; and his two dogs, Byron and Daisy.